COOK
WHAT
YOU
HAVE

MILK STREET

COOK WHAT YOU HAVE

Make a Meal Out of Almost Anything

CHRISTOPHER KIMBALL

WRITING AND EDITING BY

J. M. Hirsch, Michelle Locke and Dawn Yanagihara

RECIPES BY

Wes Martin, Diane Unger, Bianca Borges, Matthew Card
and the Cooks at Milk Street

ART DIRECTION BY

Jennifer Baldino Cox and Ali Zeigler

PHOTOGRAPHY BY   STYLING BY

Connie Miller   Christine Tobin

VORACIOUS

LITTLE, BROWN AND COMPANY
NEW YORK BOSTON LONDON

Little, Brown and Company
Hachette Book Group
1290 Avenue of the Americas, New York, NY 10104
littlebrown.com

First edition: October 2022

Voracious is an imprint of Little, Brown and Company, a division of Hachette Book Group, Inc.

The Voracious name and logo are trademarks of Hachette Book Group, Inc.

The publisher is not responsible for websites (or their content) that are not owned by the publisher.

The Hachette Speakers Bureau provides a wide range of authors for speaking events. To find out more, go to hachette-speakersbureau.com or call (866) 376-6591.

Photography Credits: Connie Miller of CB Creatives
Prop styling by Ali Zeigler
Author photograph by Channing Johnson
Illustrations by Joel Holland

ISBN 9780316387569
LCCN 2021952884
10 9 8 7 6 5 4 3 2 1

IM

Print book interior design by Gary Tooth / Empire Design Studio

Contents

Introduction

For thousands of years, we have cooked what we have. The ingredients on hand always drove the decision of what to make, whether that was a haunch of venison, a bowl of chickpeas or a tangle of wild greens. The notion of eating what we want—selecting from a menu of desires, if you will—rather than what is available, is relatively new.

This is how any good cook thinks about preparing dinner: Cook what is handy instead of starting with a shopping list that adds expense and effort. It's not just a better way to cook, it also is more economical and makes meal planning easier, maybe even unnecessary.

And it's not just an exercise in the practical. It also is a way to teach people how to think about cooking so that one starts to behave like a real cook who can make something delicious from whatever is available, rather than simply follow a recipe.

A humble can of chickpeas, for example. It can be the start of something special, including the obvious hummus, or it can be transformed into something more adventurous, such as a chickpea and carrot curry, a garlicky chickpea soup, or smashed and charred chickpeas with lemons and scallions.

A basic can of tomatoes can become a sweet-and-savory tomato and rice soup, chilaquiles rojos, or an Indian-style tomato-ginger soup. Eggs and leftover vegetables can become frittatas or omelets, of course, but that's just the start. They also can be cheesy migas, the Turkish spinach-and-egg dish known as ispanakli yumurta, or a Spanish tortilla with potato chips.

With practice, a peek in the cupboard or refrigerator becomes the starting point for a meal. A trip to the farmers market or supermarket can be a source of inspiration rather than an exercise in following a checklist.

Our "on hand" pantry includes the obvious: dried beans, grains, root vegetables, canned goods such as tomatoes and tuna, pasta, eggs, bread, etc. And we dip into the freezer—now a mainstay of the modern pantry—where we find chicken, ground beef, shrimp and vegetables. We even assembled a reliable list of cupboard confections easily created from baking items everyone has.

Freed from a recipe, we start to connect with our ingredients and develop the creativity and intuition that allow us to improvise based on the season and food in front of us. And that's when cooking becomes an adventure, because you never know what tomorrow may bring.

Have This?
TRY THAT!

CHICKEN & EGGS

Chicken

Pearl Couscous "Risotto" with Chicken and Spinach / 61

Pasta with Chicken, Green Beans and Harissa / 63

Vietnamese Rice Soup with Chicken (Cháo Gà) / 70

Garlic Fried Rice with Chicken / 71

Greek Egg-Lemon Soup (Avgolemono) / 109

Plov with Chicken / 190

Chicken and Chickpea Tagine / 191

Red Stew with Chicken / 193

Stir-Fried Hoisin Chicken and Bell Peppers / 194

Chicken Braised with Sweet Peppers and Tomatoes / 195

Chicken Paprikash / 196

Bulgur and Chicken Salad with Pomegranate Molasses / 198

Chicken and Potato Traybake with Garlic, Lemon and Parsley / 199

Cabbage and Chicken Salad with Gochujang and Sesame / 200

Miso-Garlic Slashed Chicken / 201

Chicken with Apples and Cider Vinegar Sauce / 202

Tandoori-Inspired Chicken Kebabs / 203

Chicken and Tortilla Soup / 291

Eggs

Shakshuka / 26

Deviled Eggs with Tuna, Olives and Capers / 47

Roman-Style Egg Drop Soup / 98

Greek Egg-Lemon Soup (Avgolemono) / 109

Eggs Fried in Parmesan Breadcrumbs with Wilted Spinach / 162

Cheesy Tex-Mex Migas / 163

Spanish Tortilla with Potato Chips / 164

Chinese Stir-Fried Eggs with Tomatoes / 65

Egg Salad with Harissa, Olives and Almonds / 166

Chinese-Style Vegetable Omelets / 168

Oven-Baked Eggs in a Hole with Toasted Parmesan / 170

Turkish-Style Eggs and Spinach / 171

Pinto Beans with Sausage, Kale and Eggs / 212

Vietnamese Pork and Scallion Omelet / 218

Spinach, Ham and Cheddar Strata / 229

Frittata with Toasted Bread, Cheese and Caramelized Onions / 283

Bread, Bacon and Tomato Hash / 284

GROUND MEAT & SAUSAGE

Ground Beef

Harissa-Spiced Beef with Couscous and Scallions / 207

Weeknight Lahmajoun / 210

Lebanese-Style Beef and Spinach Stew / 215

Eight-Ingredient Beef and Bean Chili / 217

Syrian-Style Meatball Soup with Rice and Tomatoes / 219

Turkish-Inspired Beef Wraps with Tomato-Onion Salad / 289

Ground Pork

Spicy Pork and Oyster Sauce Noodles / 213

Vietnamese Pork and Scallion Omelet / 218

Sausage

Braised Sausages and Lentils
with Parsley-Caper Relish / 93

Portuguese-Style Soup with
Potatoes, Kale and Sausage / 129

Cabbage, Apples and Kielbasa / 145

Tomato and Sausage Ragù
over Polenta / 206

Risotto with Sausage and
Sun-Dried Tomatoes / 208

Italian Sausages with Grapes
and Wine Vinegar / 209

Pinto Beans with Sausage, Kale
and Eggs / 212

Sausage, Potato and Sweet
Pepper Traybake / 214

FISH & SHELLFISH

Fish

Fish Baked with Tomatoes,
Capers and White Wine / 254

Miso-Glazed Broiled Salmon / 256

Cod and Chickpeas in Tomato-
Rosemary Sauce / 257

Salmon with Matbucha / 258

Salmon in Coconut-Curry
Sauce / 260

Greek-Inspired Fish Soup with
Rice and Lemon / 261

Oven-Fried Fish Sticks / 262

Seared Cod with Peruvian-Style
Olive Sauce / 264

Sesame-Crusted Salmon with
Black Pepper and Lime Sauce / 266

Iraqi-Inspired Broiled Salmon with
Tomatoes and Onion / 267

Salmon and Kimchi Burgers / 269

Shrimp

Curried Fried Rice with Shrimp
and Pineapple / 83

Spanish-Style Shrimp with
Garlic and Olive Oil / 240

Stir-Fried Chili Shrimp / 241

Tuscan-Style Shrimp with
White Beans / 242

Veracruz-Style Rice and Shrimp / 243

Shrimp Fra Diavolo / 245

Broiled Shrimp with Garlic, Lemon
and Herbs / 246

Vietnamese-Style Hot and Sour Soup
with Shrimp / 248

Thai Stir-Fried Shrimp with Garlic
and Black Pepper / 249

Shrimp and Cheese Tacos
(Tacos Gobernador) / 251

Canned Tuna

Portuguese-Style Tuna with
Chickpeas / 38

Potato Salad with Capers, Olives
and Olive Oil Tuna / 39

Pan-Fried Tuna Cakes with
Yogurt-Caper Sauce / 41

Spaghetti with Tuna and
Mushrooms / 42

Tuna Gochujang Noodles / 43

Harissa-Spiced Tuna Tartines / 45

Tuna Tostadas with Chipotle,
Corn and Quick-Pickled Onion / 46

Deviled Eggs with Tuna, Olives
and Capers / 47

TOFU

Kale and Miso Soup with
Tofu and Ginger / 155

Tofu and Sweet Pepper Scramble
with Smoked Paprika / 174

Tofu and Kimchi Soup / 175

Salt and Pepper Tofu / 177

Stir-Fried Tofu and Ginger
Green Beans / 178

Spicy Seared Tofu with
Sweet Pepper / 180

Jamaican-Style Tofu Curry / 181

Vietnamese-Style Tofu with
Gingery Tomato Sauce / 182

Stir-Fried Cumin Tofu / 185

Tofu Katsu / 187

PASTA & POLENTA

Short pasta

Pasta e Fagioli / 21

One-Pot Pasta all'Arrabbiata / 33

Pasta with Roasted Tomato and Anchovy Sauce / 35

Pasta with Fennel, Green Olive and Pistachio Pesto / 53

Pasta with Parsley, Walnut and Caper Pesto / 55

Pasta with Pesto Rosso / 56

Farfalle with Cabbage, Walnuts and Parmesan / 58

Pasta with Chicken, Green Beans and Harissa / 63

Roman-Style Egg Drop Soup / 98

Pasta e Ceci / 100

Potato and Pasta Soup / 139

Orecchiette with Broccolini / 143

Pasta with Kale Pesto and Sun-Dried Tomatoes / 150

Pasta with Cauliflower, Olives and Sun-Dried Tomatoes / 156

Rigatoni Carbonara with Peas / 231

Long pasta

Pasta al Pomodoro / 29

Spaghetti with Tuna and Mushrooms / 42

Tuna Gochujang Noodles / 43

Hoisin-Ginger Noodles / 52

Spaghetti with Garlic, Oil and Lemon-Parmesan Breadcrumbs / 57

Garlicky Peanut Noodles / 59

Egg Noodles with Cabbage, Bacon and Sour Cream / 62

Spaghetti with Lemon Pesto / 65

Pasta with Tomato, Onion and Butter / 66

Mexican Noodle Soup with Fire-Roasted Tomatoes / 99

Stir-Fried Broccoli and Noodles / 146

Spicy Pork and Oyster Sauce Noodles / 213

Spaghetti with Broccoli-Miso Sauce and Toasted Walnuts / 226

Fettuccine with Corn, Tomatoes and Bacon / 228

Couscous

Couscous Cakes with Harissa and Olives / 54

Toasted Pearl Couscous with Sweet Potato and Cranberries / 60

Pearl Couscous "Risotto" with Chicken and Spinach / 61

Harissa-Spiced Beef with Couscous and Scallions / 207

Polenta

Tomato and Sausage Ragù over Polenta / 206

BEANS

Black beans

Black Bean–Bell Pepper Salad with Coconut and Lime / 5

Cuban-Style Black Beans and Rice / 7

Spicy Black Bean and Coconut Soup / 8

Quinoa and Black Bean Burgers / 75

Refried Bean and Cheese Tostadas / 294

Enfrijoladas / 295

Kidney beans

Bacon and Red Wine–Braised Kidney Beans / 4

Kidney Bean and Rice Salad with Bacon and Cider Vinegar / 9

Spicy Kidney Bean and Sweet Potato Soup / 117

Barley, Bean and Butternut Stew / 119

Pinto beans

Pinto Beans with Bacon and Chipotle / 12

Egyptian-Style Pinto Beans / 17

Creamy Pinto Bean and Tomato Soup / 102

Pinto Beans with Sausage, Kale and Eggs / 212

Eight-Ingredient Beef and Bean Chili / 217

Chilean-Style Bean, Butternut and Corn Stew / 233

White beans

White Bean Soup with Potatoes and Greens / 11

Fried White Beans with Bacon, Garlic and Spinach / 15

Turkish White Bean Salad / 16

White Beans and Tomatoes with Anchovies and Vinegar / 20

Pasta e Fagioli / 21

Greens and Beans with Pecorino Crostini / 159

Tuscan-Style Shrimp with White Beans / 242

White Bean Bruschette with Lemon, Parsley and Caper Relish / 278

LENTILS & CHICKPEAS

Chickpeas

Chickpea and Garlic Soup with Cumin-Spiced Butter / 6

Chickpea and Carrot Curry / 10

Smashed Chickpeas with Lemon and Scallions / 14

Quick Creamy Hummus / 18

Portuguese-Style Tuna with Chickpeas / 38

Pasta e Ceci / 100

Roasted Broccolini and Chickpea Salad with Tahini-Lemon Dressing / 151

Chicken and Chickpea Tagine / 191

Cod and Chickpeas in Tomato-Rosemary Sauce / 257

Lentils

Rice and Lentils with Onion Tarka / 88

Lentil Salad with Tahini, Almonds and Pomegranate Molasses / 89

Red Lentil and Coconut Dal with Ginger-Garlic Tarka / 90

Spanish-Style Lentil Stew with Garlic and Smoked Paprika / 92

Braised Sausages and Lentils with Parsley-Caper Relish / 93

Umbrian-Style Lentil Soup / 94

GRAINS

Bulgur

Toasted Bulgur with Walnuts and Pickled Grapes / 72

Baked Kibbeh with Sweet Potato / 115

Bulgur and Winter Squash Pilaf / 125

Bulgur and Chicken Salad with Pomegranate Molasses / 198

Barley

Persian-Style Barley and Carrot Soup / 84

Barley, Bean and Butternut Stew / 119

Farro

Two-Cheese Baked Farro with Kale and Tomatoes / 73

Toasted Farro and Apple Salad with Mustard Vinaigrette / 78

Farro Soup with Celery and Parmesan / 80

Stir-Fried Grains with Charred Cabbage and Tomatoes / 85

QUINOA

Quinoa and Black Bean Burgers / 75

Quinoa Salad with Oranges, Olives and Arugula / 76

Quinoa Chaufa with Mixed Vegetables / 82

Sweet Potato and Quinoa Stew / 120

Rice

Cuban-Style Black Beans and Rice / 7

Kidney Bean and Rice Salad with Bacon and Cider Vinegar / 9

Tomato-Rice Soup with Caramelized Onion / 28

Vietnamese Rice Soup with Chicken (Cháo Gà) / 70

Garlic Fried Rice with Chicken / 71

Greek-Style Spinach and Tomato Rice / 79

Curried Fried Rice with Shrimp and Pineapple / 83

Rice and Lentils with Onion Tarka / 88

Curried Rice and Vegetable Soup / 101

Greek Egg-Lemon Soup (Avgolemono) / 109

Sweet Potato Brown Rice with Soy and Scallions / 124

Plov with Chicken / 190

Risotto with Sausage and Sun-Dried Tomatoes / 208

Syrian-Style Meatball Soup with Rice and Tomatoes / 219

Japanese-Style Rice with Corn, Butter and Soy Sauce / 224

Lemon and Green Pea Risotto / 225

Baked Butternut Squash Risotto / 235

Fried Rice with Peas, Corn and Bacon / 237

Veracruz-Style Rice and Shrimp / 243

Greek-Inspired Fish Soup with Rice and Lemon / 261

GREENS

Arugula

Toasted Pearl Couscous with Sweet Potato and Cranberries / 60

Quinoa Salad with Oranges, Olives and Arugula / 76

Seared Cod with Peruvian-Style Olive Sauce / 264

Panzanella with Roasted Tomatoes and Olives / 274

Kale

White Bean Soup with Potatoes and Greens / 11

Two-Cheese Baked Farro with Kale and Tomatoes / 73

Portuguese-Style Soup with Potatoes, Kale and Sausage / 129

Kale and Cheddar Melts with Caramelized Onion / 148

Pasta with Kale Pesto and Sun-Dried Tomatoes / 150

Greek-Style Braised Greens with Tomatoes and Paprika / 153

Kale and Miso Soup with Tofu and Ginger / 155

Greens and Beans with Pecorino Crostini / 159

Pinto Beans with Sausage, Kale and Eggs / 212

Cabbage

Farfalle with Cabbage, Walnuts and Parmesan / 58

Egg Noodles with Cabbage, Bacon and Sour Cream / 62

Stir-Fried Grains with Charred Cabbage and Tomatoes / 85

Romanian-Style Cabbage and Potato Soup with Bacon and Paprika / 105

Cabbage, Apples and Kielbasa / 145

Chinese-Style Vegetable Omelets / 168

Cabbage and Chicken Salad with Gochujang and Sesame / 200

Spinach

Fried White Beans with Bacon, Garlic and Spinach / 15

Pearl Couscous "Risotto" with Chicken and Spinach / 61

Greek-Style Spinach and Tomato Rice / 79

Roman-Style Egg Drop Soup / 98

Pasta e Ceci / 100

Eggs Fried in Parmesan Breadcrumbs with Wilted Spinach / 162

Turkish-Style Eggs and Spinach / 171

Lebanese-Style Beef and Spinach
Stew / 215

Spinach, Ham and Cheddar
Strata / 229

Turmeric-Spiced Spinach and
Potatoes / 234

Bread and Tomato Soup with
Spinach and Parmesan / 276

TOMATOES

Canned tomatoes

Pinto Beans with Bacon and
Chipotle / 12

Pasta e Fagioli / 21

Indian-Style Tomato-Ginger Soup / 24

Double-Tomato Soup with Cilantro,
Lime and Fried Garlic / 25

Shakshuka / 26

Cream-Free Tomato Bisque
with Parmesan Croutons / 27

Tomato-Rice Soup with
Caramelized Onion / 28

Pasta al Pomodoro / 29

Tomato-Mushroom Curry / 30

Chilaquiles Rojos / 32

One-Pot Pasta all'Arrabbiata / 33

Pasta with Roasted Tomato and
Anchovy Sauce / 35

Spaghetti with Tuna and
Mushrooms / 42

Two-Cheese Baked Farro with
Kale and Tomatoes / 73

Spanish-Style Lentil Stew with
Garlic and Smoked Paprika / 92

Mexican Noodle Soup with
Fire-Roasted Tomatoes / 99

Pasta e Ceci / 100

Curried Rice and Vegetable
Soup / 101

Creamy Pinto Bean and
Tomato Soup / 102

Sweet Potato and Quinoa Stew / 120

Greek-Style Braised Greens with
Tomatoes and Paprika / 153

Red Stew with Chicken / 193

Chicken Braised with Sweet Peppers
and Tomatoes / 195

Tomato and Sausage Ragù
over Polenta / 206

Eight-Ingredient Beef and
Bean Chili / 217

Syrian-Style Meatball Soup
with Rice and Tomatoes / 219

Chilean-Style Bean, Butternut
and Corn Stew / 233

Shrimp Fra Diavolo / 245

Cod and Chickpeas in Tomato-
Rosemary Sauce / 257

Salmon with Matbucha / 258

Bread and Tomato Soup with
Spinach and Parmesan / 276

Chicken and Tortilla Soup / 291

Fresh tomatoes

Turkish White Bean Salad / 16

White Beans and Tomatoes
with Anchovies and Vinegar / 20

Stir-Fried Grains with Charred
Cabbage and Tomatoes / 85

Cheesy Tex-Mex Migas / 163

Chinese Stir-Fried Eggs with
Tomatoes / 165

Vietnamese-Style Tofu with
Gingery Tomato Sauce / 182

Fettuccine with Corn,
Tomatoes and Bacon / 228

Vietnamese-Style Hot and
Sour Soup with Shrimp / 248

Fish Baked with Tomatoes,
Capers and White Wine / 254

Salmon in Coconut-Curry
Sauce / 260

Seared Cod with Peruvian-Style
Olive Sauce / 264

Iraqi-Inspired Broiled Salmon with
Tomatoes and Onion / 267

Panzanella with Roasted Tomatoes
and Olives / 274

Bread, Bacon and Tomato
Hash / 284

Turkish-Inspired Beef Wraps
with Tomato-Onion Salad / 289

Pizzadilla with Tomatoes and
Olives / 290

BROCCOLI & BROCCOLINI

Quinoa Chaufa with
Mixed Vegetables / 82

Orecchiette with Broccolini / 143

Stir-Fried Broccoli and Noodles / 146

Roasted Broccolini and Chickpea
Salad with Tahini-Lemon Dressing / 151

Spaghetti with Broccoli-Miso
Sauce and Toasted Walnuts / 226

Curried Broccoli and
Cilantro Soup / 230

CAULIFLOWER

Creamy, Garlicky Cauliflower
and Cheddar Soup / 144

Pasta with Cauliflower, Olives
and Sun-Dried Tomatoes / 156

Braised Cauliflower with Garlic,
Bacon and Scallions / 157

FROZEN CORN

Tuna Tostadas with Chipotle, Corn
and Quick-Pickled Onion / 46

Japanese-Style Rice with Corn,
Butter and Soy Sauce / 224

Fettuccine with Corn,
Tomatoes and Bacon / 228

Chilean-Style Bean, Butternut
and Corn Stew / 233

Corn and Coconut Soup with
Ginger and Scallions / 236

Fried Rice with Peas, Corn
and Bacon / 237

FROZEN PEAS

Lemon and Green Pea Risotto / 225

Rigatoni Carbonara with Peas / 231

Fried Rice with Peas, Corn
and Bacon / 237

GREEN BEANS

Pasta with Chicken, Green
Beans and Harissa / 63

Stir-Fried Tofu with Ginger
Green Beans / 178

MUSHROOMS

Tomato-Mushroom Curry / 30

Spaghetti with Tuna and
Mushrooms / 42

Miso, Shiitake Mushroom
and Kimchi Soup / 106

POTATOES

Potatoes

White Bean Soup with
Potatoes and Greens / 11

Potato Salad with Capers,
Olives and Olive Oil Tuna / 39

Romanian-Style Cabbage and Potato
Soup with Bacon and Paprika / 105

Portuguese-Style Soup with
Potatoes, Kale and Sausage / 129

Cairo-Style Potatoes with Cumin,
Coriander and Cilantro / 130

Wine-Braised Potatoes with
Garlic and Bay / 131

Potato Soup with Almonds,
Garlic and Lemon / 132

Smashed Potatoes with Red
Chimichurri / 135

Potatoes Boulangère / 136

Butter-Browned Potatoes with
Onion and Mustard / 137

Turmeric Potatoes with
Cumin Seeds and Ginger / 138

Potato and Pasta Soup / 139

Chicken and Potato Traybake with
Garlic, Lemon and Parsley / 199

Sausage, Potato and Sweet
Pepper Traybake / 214

Turmeric-Spiced Spinach and
Potatoes / 234

Corn and Coconut Soup with
Ginger and Scallions / 236

Oven-Fried Potato and
Cheese Tacos Dorados / 292

Instant Potato Flakes

Gnocchi in an Instant / 128

Sweet Potatoes

Toasted Pearl Couscous with
Sweet Potato and Cranberries / 60

Curried Rice and Vegetable
Soup / 101

Baked Kibbeh with Sweet
Potato / 115

Spicy Kidney Bean and Sweet
Potato Soup / 117

Sweet Potato and Quinoa Stew / 120

Sweet Potatoes with Coriander,
Orange and Olives / 121

Sweet Potato Brown Rice
with Soy and Scallions / 124

WINTER SQUASH

Afghan-Style Braised Butternut
Squash / 116

Barley, Bean and
Butternut Stew / 119

Agrodolce Acorn Squash / 123

Bulgur and Winter Squash
Pilaf / 125

Chilean-Style Bean, Butternut
and Corn Stew / 233

Baked Butternut Squash
Risotto / 235

BREAD & TORTILLAS

Bread

Cream-Free Tomato Bisque with
Parmesan Croutons / 27

Harissa-Spiced Tuna Tartines / 45

Spanish Garlic and Bread Soup / 104

Kale and Cheddar Melts with
Caramelized Onion / 148

Greens and Beans with Pecorino
Crostini / 159

Oven-Baked Eggs in a Hole with
Toasted Parmesan / 170

Weeknight Lahmajoun / 210

Spinach, Ham and
Cheddar Strata / 229

Panzanella with Roasted
Tomatoes and Olives / 274

Bread and Tomato Soup
with Spinach and Parmesan / 276

Kimchi Grilled Cheese with Ham / 277

White Bean Bruschette with
Lemon, Parsley and Caper
Relish / 278

Cheddar, Roasted Onion
and Apple Tartines / 280

Frittata with Toasted Bread, Cheese
and Caramelized Onions / 283

Bread, Bacon and Tomato Hash / 284

Tortillas

Tuna Tostadas with Chipotle, Corn
and Quick-Pickled Onion / 46

Shrimp and Cheese Tacos
(Tacos Gobernador) / 251

Turkish-Inspired Beef Wraps with
Tomato-Onion Salad / 289

Pizzadilla with Tomatoes
and Olives / 290

Chicken and Tortilla Soup / 291

Oven-Fried Potato and
Cheese Tacos Dorados / 292

Ham and Cheese Quesadillas
with Pickled Jalapeños / 293

Refried Bean and Cheese
Tostadas / 294

Enfrijoladas / 295

CHIPS

Potato Chips

Spanish Tortilla with
Potato Chips / 164

Tortilla Chips

Chilaquiles Rojos / 32

Cheesy Tex-Mex Migas / 163

Milk Street
MUST-HAVES

At Milk Street, our basic pantry staples are similar to those of most home cooks. We always keep canned tomatoes, beans and tuna on our shelves, along with a variety of grains, noodles and broth. We also make sure to have go-to spices and seasonings that are one-stop shopping for big flavor, fast, such as chili and curry powders. And, of course, we always have hot sauce, vinegars and a few dried herbs, as well as potatoes and alliums stored somewhere cool and dark. In the refrigerator, we have relatively sturdy dairy products, such as yogurt and cheese, and in the freezer we keep the basic meats and vegetables.

But while those pantry staples are an excellent place to start for getting supper on the table without a fuss, sometimes even those heroes need a little help. We get that by way of what we consider our high-impact must-haves, bold ingredients that effortlessly deliver tons of flavor and texture.

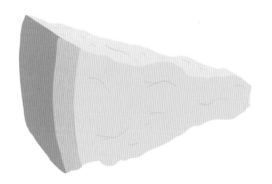

HERE ARE OUR TOP 25 MUST-HAVES AND WHY WE LOVE THEM.

ANCHOVIES PACKED IN OIL

These tiny, salt-cured and oil-packed fish are intensely savory and lend depth to sauces, pastas, braises and dressings. Look for large, meaty fillets from Spain, Portugal and Italy. Jarred anchovies tend to be fuller flavored and easier to store once opened than flat-packed cans. We don't recommend anchovy paste; it can be too salty.

BACON

Bacon adds sweet smoky depth to all types of dishes. It stores well in the freezer, and can be cooked without defrosting, so we always keep it on hand for quick meals. In some instances, we'll render the fat and crisp the bacon, then remove that to serve as a crispy garnish. Save the rendered fat for flavoring beans and potatoes, or adding to fried rice or noodles for its trademark smokiness and lush texture.

CAPERS

The cured buds of the caper plant (Capparis spinosa), which grows throughout the Mediterranean, capers are piquant and herbal and can add a pop of flavor to pastas, sauces, relishes and more. The most common variety is bottled in brine, though capers also are packed in coarse salt (these taste stronger and should be rinsed before use). Refrigerate once opened.

CANNED CHIPOTLES IN ADOBO

Chipotle chilies are smoked jalapeño chilies that have been rehydrated and packed in a garlicky, vinegary tomato sauce (which also can be used to flavor dishes). Chop chipotles to add to bean dishes, salsa, marinades, dips, sandwiches and quesadillas. Once opened, they should be transferred to an airtight container and refrigerated.

FISH SAUCE

Deep, funky and pungent, fish sauce packs an umami punch. Used throughout Southeast Asia (and Italy, too, since Roman times, though they call it garum), it can star in quick dipping sauces and stir-fries, or fade into the background in stews. Brands vary in flavor; we prefer the crisp, complex flavor of Red Boat brand.

FRESH GINGER ROOT

Ginger adds bright, zippy flavor and is essential to many Asian and Indian dishes. It's best fresh; we typically peel and grate it to a coarse paste, but when we want ginger to have more presence in a dish, we might thinly slice it or cut it into matchsticks. Cooking mellows the spiciness of fresh ginger. Store ginger in a zip-close bag in the refrigerator; it will keep for a few weeks. For longer storage, keep it in the freezer.

GOCHUJANG (KOREAN RED CHILI PASTE)

Savory, spicy and subtly sweet, gochujang is an elemental building block in Korean cooking. It's made from fermented rice, chili powder, a sweetener and

sometimes flavorings, like garlic. Thick and sticky, it can be blended into sauces or marinades, stirred into soups, and blended with rice vinegar, sugar (or honey), sesame oil and grated garlic for an all-purpose dipping sauce. It's prepared in varying heat levels; we suggest starting with mild.

HARISSA PASTE

This North African fiery pepper-based spread is flavored with caraway, cumin, coriander and garlic. Flavors—and heat levels—vary by brand; start with a little and build up as desired. Stir into tomato sauces to flavor pasta and couscous (or cook eggs for shakshuka), blend with butter to melt over grilled meat or vegetables, or squirt into yogurt and flavor with cilantro for a dipping sauce.

HOISIN SAUCE

Hoisin is a thick, sticky sauce made from fermented soybean paste, wheat flour, garlic and sometimes other seasonings, like five-spice powder or sesame. Salty-sweet, earthy and deep, it can be used straight as a dipping sauce, blended into marinades and sauces, or brushed onto grilled or roasted meats instead of barbecue sauce. Brands vary in consistency and flavor; we like Tan Tan Vietnamese hoisin sauce.

JARRED ROASTED PEPPERS

Sweet tasting and supple textured, roasted peppers are welcome additions to everything from soups, stews and pasta sauces to omelets or frittatas, quesadillas and grilled cheese sandwiches. We favor widely available Spanish piquillo peppers, which are medium-sized and sweet, or long and slender Greek Florina peppers.

KIMCHI

Kimchi is a Korean relish of vegetables fermented with chilies, garlic, ginger, scallions and typically something fishy for depth. The most common varieties include Napa cabbage or a mix of cabbage, carrot and daikon, and it can be found in the refrigerator case of most supermarkets. It can be served raw as a salad or condiment alongside grilled meats, folded into fried rice, noodles, soups and stews, or pureed to a thick paste to serve as a dipping sauce or smear inside a grilled cheese sandwich or quesadilla.

MIRIN

Mirin is a Japanese sweet rice wine that is essential to Japanese sauces, glazes and soups. It comes in two styles: aji-mirin, with added sweetener, and hon-mirin, without added sweetener. The latter typically is better quality and we recommend it, though it can be harder to find in supermarkets because of its alcohol content.

MISO

Miso is a fermented paste typically prepared from soybeans, steamed rice or barley, salt and koji culture. There are dozens of varieties and regional specialities; we usually recommend mellow white, or shiro, miso or bold, bittersweet red miso. Most taste sweet, intensely savory and earthy. Beyond classic use in soups, stews and braises, we also blend miso with an equal amount of butter and a splash of lemon juice to melt over sauteed vegetables, blanched greens and roasted sweet potatoes. We also mix a spoonful into caramel sauce, chocolate pudding or peanut butter cookies.

OIL-PACKED SUN-DRIED TOMATOES

Flavor-packed sun-dried tomatoes are available dried or rehydrated and packed in flavored oil. We prefer the convenience, flavor and texture of the latter. Beyond their sweet, tart and tangy flavor, sun-dried tomatoes have an appealing chewiness that punctuates pilafs and pastas, or bean, tuna or egg salads. If the oil the tomatoes are packed in isn't overly flavored with dried herbs, it can be used for cooking and to flavor vinaigrettes.

OLIVES

Salty, sweet, firm and chewy, olives add contrasting flavor and texture. Green olives are immature and, depending on variety, can taste fruity, nutty, grassy and a little sweet. Black olives are harvested when ripe and have a more aggressive flavor. Salt-cured olives have a chewier, drier texture. Add them toward the end of cooking to prevent them from turning the dish bitter. We finely chop them to add to lemony dressings for salads, chicken and fish, or puree with herbs, olive oil and garlic to smear on pizzas or flatbreads and mix into omelets with goat cheese. Brine-cured olives should be refrigerated in their brine and will store for up to a month.

OYSTER SAUCE

Caramel colored, sweet and subtly fishy, oyster sauce is a common seasoning in Chinese and regional Thai cooking because of its sweet, briny, umami-rich flavor. It can be used on its own to season stir-fries or fried rice, or be blended into more complex sauces. Flavors vary wildly in oyster sauces and we recommend spending a little more to get a bottle that actually tastes of oysters. Our favorite brand, Megachef, is made in Thailand from smoked oysters, brown sugar and salt, not oyster extracts.

PANKO BREADCRUMBS

A staple of Japanese cooking and now common in most supermarkets, panko breadcrumbs are flaky, crisp breadcrumbs prepared from crustless white bread. It's lightly sweet, wheaty flavor makes panko ideal for breaded coatings. It also can be softened into panades for moistening meatballs. Panko can be sauteed in olive oil or butter—if you like, add chilies, grated garlic or herbs—to toss as a crunchy topping for vegetables or pasta dishes.

PARMESAN OR PECORINO ROMANO CHEESE

Parmesan cheese is an aged, umami-rich cow's milk cheese produced in the Parma region of Italy. Pecorino Romano is a sharp, pungent sheep's milk cheese originally made in the regions around Rome. We use both to top pasta, enrich sauces and season meatballs. There's no substitute, so buy quality, imported cheese. Both keep well if wrapped in kitchen parchment, then an air-tight container or zip-close bag.

PICKLED JALAPEÑOS

Pickled jalapeños add spicy, piquant pops of flavor. We chop them to stir into beans and grains, and blend them into dressings for salads or roasted vegetables. Don't forget the brine: a splash can balance rich braises, accent soups and stews, or loosen up refried beans.

POMEGRANATE MOLASSES

Deeply sweet and sour, pomegranate molasses is boiled-down and concentrated pomegranate juice. It's used throughout Levantine cooking to add tang to sauces and dressings and to glaze grilled meats. A drizzle can cut through rich braised meats, starchy grains or legumes. We prefer unsweetened brands of pomegranate molasses (no added sugar).

SESAME SEEDS

Sesame seeds provide a pop of earthy nuttiness and bittersweet crunch. Toasting intensifies and sweetens their flavor. We toss them with fried noodles and fried rice, stir-fried vegetables or chicken, and sprinkle them over flatbreads. Store in the freezer in an air-tight container to maintain freshness.

TAHINI

Tahini is a creamy, bittersweet paste made from ground sesame seeds. We use it to enrich sauces and dips, as a coating on roasted vegetables, or as a finishing drizzle that adds rich flavor. Also try it stirred it into your morning yogurt topped with fruit and granola. We like Soom brand tahini. Always be sure to stir before use to re-emulsify the oil and solids.

TOASTED SESAME OIL

Rich and earthy, toasted sesame oil isn't for cooking; it's a finishing oil, so consider it a condiment. Try it drizzled over roasted chicken or fish and noodles and stir-fried vegetables. We also like to blend it into dressings and sauces. Combined with lemon or lime juice, it's all the sauce some dishes need. Buy good quality and store in the refrigerator once open.

TOMATO PASTE

Thick, concentrated tomato paste provides a fruity, sweet and rich flavor to boost soups, stews and sauces. We often brown tomato paste when building sauces, caramelizing its natural sugars to deepen its flavor.

UNSEASONED RICE VINEGAR

Rice vinegar is a mild-tasting vinegar used liberally in Japanese cooking for dressings, pickles and adding bright balance to rich dishes. It pairs well with lighter vegetables, greens and proteins, such as chicken and fish. Be sure to purchase unseasoned rice vinegar for the crispest, most neutral flavor (seasoned rice vinegar contains both sweetener and salt).

Canned
GOODS

Not So Basic
BEANS

Bacon and Red Wine–Braised Kidney Beans / 4

Black Bean–Bell Pepper Salad with Coconut and Lime / 5

Chickpea and Garlic Soup with Cumin-Spiced Butter / 6

Cuban-Style Black Beans and Rice / 7

Spicy Black Bean and Coconut Soup / 8

Kidney Bean and Rice Salad with Bacon and Cider Vinegar / 9

Chickpea and Carrot Curry / 10

White Bean Soup with Potatoes and Greens / 11

Pinto Beans with Bacon and Chipotle / 12

Smashed Chickpeas with Lemon and Scallions / 14

Fried White Beans with Bacon, Garlic and Spinach / 15

Turkish White Bean Salad / 16

Egyptian-Style Pinto Beans / 17

Quick Creamy Hummus / 18

White Beans and Tomatoes with Anchovies and Vinegar / 20

Pasta e Fagioli / 21

Bacon and Red Wine–Braised Kidney Beans

45 minutes (15 minutes active) / Servings: 4

The rustic French dish called haricots rouges à la vigneronne, or winemaker's red beans, boasts rich, bold, beef bourguignon-like flavors. Our version, made with canned kidney beans, is quick and easy. Carrots and onion add sweetness to balance the tannins of the red wine, while bacon contributes a smoky, long-cooked flavor. This is the perfect accompaniment to roasted pork or chicken. Or make it the center of a meal with a bright arugula salad and crusty bread alongside.

4 ounces bacon, chopped

2 medium carrots, peeled, halved lengthwise and thinly sliced

1 medium yellow onion, finely chopped

Two 15½-ounce cans red kidney beans, rinsed and drained

1 cup dry red wine

1 cup lightly packed fresh flat-leaf parsley, chopped

Kosher salt and ground black pepper

In a large saucepan over medium-high, cook the bacon, stirring, until browned and crisp, 5 to 8 minutes. Using a slotted spoon, transfer to a plate; set aside.

To the fat in the pot, add the carrots and onion. Cook over medium-high, stirring occasionally, until the vegetables are lightly browned, about 7 minutes. Add the beans, wine and 1 cup water; bring to a simmer, scraping up any browned bits. Cook, uncovered and stirring occasionally, until just a little liquid remains and the beans begin to split, 10 to 15 minutes.

Off heat, stir in the parsley and half the bacon, then taste and season with salt and pepper. Serve sprinkled with the remaining bacon.

4

Black Bean–Bell Pepper Salad with Coconut and Lime

20 minutes / Servings: 4

This simple Caribbean-inspired black bean salad has a spicy-sweet brightness to match its festive appearance. Heating the beans so they're piping hot when dressed helps them absorb seasonings as they cool so each forkful is flavorful. For ease, we use the microwave to heat the beans. If you happen to have fresh mango or pineapple on hand, dice some and toss it into the salad just before serving. This is a perfect side to grilled seafood, pork or chicken.

Two 15½-ounce cans black beans, rinsed and drained

Kosher salt and ground black pepper

2 tablespoons extra-virgin olive oil

1 teaspoon grated lime zest, plus ¼ cup lime juice

½ medium red onion, finely chopped

1 jalapeño chili, stemmed, seeded and finely chopped

1 medium orange bell pepper OR red bell pepper, stemmed, seeded and finely chopped

½ cup unsweetened wide-flake coconut

In a large microwave-safe bowl, toss the beans with ½ teaspoon salt. Cover and microwave on high until hot, 1½ to 2 minutes, stirring once about halfway through.

To **the hot beans** add the oil and lime zest and juice; toss to combine. While the beans are still warm, stir in the onion, jalapeño, bell pepper and coconut. Cool to room temperature, then taste and season with salt and pepper.

Chickpea and Garlic Soup with Cumin-Spiced Butter

1 hour (25 minutes active) / Servings: 4

This recipe transforms canned chickpeas into an elegant soup. Cumin, cayenne and garlic add a bold kick to complement the chickpeas' earthiness, while carrots and onion add sweetness. Before draining the chickpeas, be sure to reserve 1 cup of the liquid for simmering with the soup ingredients. The liquid lends body to the soup, for a creamy, velvety consistency. If you own an immersion blender, you can use it to puree the soup directly in the saucepan; the texture won't be perfectly smooth, but the flavors still will be great.

5 tablespoons salted butter, cut into 1-tablespoon pieces, divided

1 medium yellow onion, chopped

2 medium carrots, peeled and chopped

Kosher salt and ground black pepper

3 teaspoons cumin seeds, divided

¼ teaspoon cayenne pepper **OR** red pepper flakes, plus another ¼ teaspoon (optional)

Two 15½-ounce cans chickpeas, 1 cup liquid reserved, rinsed and drained

1 head garlic, outer papery skins removed, top third cut off and discarded

1 teaspoon white **OR** black sesame seeds

In a large saucepan over medium-high, melt 2 tablespoons butter. Add the onion, carrots and ½ teaspoon salt; cook, stirring occasionally, until the vegetables are lightly browned, 4 to 6 minutes. Add 1 teaspoon cumin seeds, ¼ teaspoon cayenne and ¼ teaspoon black pepper; cook, stirring, until fragrant, about 2 minutes. Add the chickpeas and the 1 cup reserved liquid, the garlic, 4 cups water and ¼ teaspoon salt. Bring to a boil over medium-high, then reduce to medium-low, cover and cook, stirring occasionally, until the garlic is soft when the head is squeezed with tongs, 30 to 35 minutes.

Remove the pot from the heat. Squeeze the garlic cloves from the head into the chickpea mixture; discard the empty skins. Let the chickpea mixture cool for about 5 minutes.

Meanwhile, in a small saucepan over medium-high, melt the remaining 3 tablespoons butter. Add the remaining 2 teaspoons cumin seeds and cook, stirring, until fragrant and the butter has stopped foaming, 1 to 1½ minutes. Add the sesame seeds and another ¼ teaspoon cayenne (if using); cook, stirring, until the sesame seeds are toasted and fragrant, about 1½ minutes. Remove from the heat and set aside, covered.

Using a blender and working in batches so the jar is never more than half full, puree the chickpea mixture until smooth. Return the soup to the pan and cook over medium-low, stirring often, until warmed through, 2 to 5 minutes. (Alternatively, use an immersion blender to puree the soup directly in the saucepan.) Taste and season with salt and black pepper. Serve drizzled with the butter mixture.

Optional garnish: Lemon wedges **OR** chopped fresh cilantro **OR** both

Cuban-Style Black Beans and Rice

45 minutes / Servings: 4 to 6

This is a classic Cuban combination of black beans and rice that uses sautéed onion, green bell pepper and garlic as foundational flavors. The beans usually are cooked from dried, but with canned black beans, the dish is a breeze to prepare and can be thrown together at a moment's notice. Some versions are made with pork—and indeed, smoky, salty bacon is a delicious addition. If you wish to include bacon, begin by cooking 4 ounces, chopped, in the saucepan over medium-high until crisp, 6 to 7 minutes; add the onion and bell pepper to the bacon and its rendered fat, omitting the oil, then proceed with the recipe.

3 tablespoons grapeseed or other neutral oil

1 medium yellow onion, chopped

1 medium green bell pepper, stemmed, seeded and chopped

Kosher salt and ground black pepper

4 medium garlic cloves, chopped

1 teaspoon ground cumin

¾ teaspoon dried oregano OR 2 bay leaves OR both

1 cup long-grain white rice, rinsed and drained

1½ cups low-sodium chicken broth

Two 15½-ounce cans black beans, rinsed and drained

In a large saucepan over medium-high, heat the oil until shimmering. Add the onion, bell pepper and ¼ teaspoon salt, then cook, stirring occasionally, until softened, 7 to 9 minutes. Add the garlic, cumin and oregano; cook, stirring, until fragrant, about 1 minute. Stir in the rice, then add the broth, beans and ¼ teaspoon pepper. Bring to a simmer, then cover, reduce to low and cook until the rice has absorbed the liquid, 20 to 25 minutes.

Remove the pot from the heat. Let stand, covered, for 10 minutes. Fluff the mixture with a fork, then remove and discard the bay. Taste and season with salt and pepper.

Spicy Black Bean and Coconut Soup

50 minutes / Servings: 4 to 6

Nigerian frejon, a smooth puree of beans and coconut milk, inspired this rich, flavorful soup that happens to be vegetarian (even vegan). We blend only a portion of the bean mixture so the soup is lightly thickened, not a heavy puree, with lots of texture from creamy whole beans. If you have coconut oil in the pantry, use it in place of the neutral oil—it will add extra coconut flavor and aroma.

2 tablespoons grapeseed or other neutral oil (see headnote), divided

½ medium red onion, finely chopped, plus more to serve

3 medium garlic cloves, chopped

14½-ounce can coconut milk

2 jalapeño chilies, stemmed, halved and seeded

¼ teaspoon ground allspice

½ teaspoon dried thyme OR 1 teaspoon minced fresh thyme

Kosher salt

Four 15½-ounce cans black beans, rinsed and drained

1½ tablespoons lime juice, plus lime wedges to serve

In a large pot over medium-high, heat 2 tablespoons oil until shimmering. Add the onion and cook, stirring occasionally, until translucent, 5 to 7 minutes. Add the garlic and cook, stirring, until fragrant, about 1 minute. Add 2½ cups water, the coconut milk, jalapeños, allspice, thyme and ¾ teaspoon salt, then bring to a simmer. Add the beans and simmer, uncovered and stirring occasionally, for 20 minutes.

Remove the pot from the heat and cool for 10 minutes. Transfer 3 cups of the bean mixture to a blender along with the jalapeños and puree until smooth. Return the puree to the pot and bring to a simmer over medium.

Off heat, stir in the lime juice, then taste and season with salt. Ladle into bowls and garnish with chopped onion; serve with lime wedges.

Optional garnish: Chopped plum tomatoes

Kidney Bean and Rice Salad with Bacon and Cider Vinegar

25 minutes / Servings: 4 to 6

Red beans and rice, a Louisiana classic, inspired this salad. Smoky bacon, fruity cider vinegar and an entire bunch of scallions add loads of flavor, while red bell pepper and celery bring sweetness and crunch. Straight from the can, beans are bland, but heating them with seasonings ensures tastiness on the inside as well as on the outside because as the beans cool, they soak up lots of flavor. Serve the salad at room temperature.

4 ounces bacon, chopped

1 tablespoon extra-virgin olive oil

1 bunch scallions, thinly sliced on the diagonal, whites and greens reserved separately

⅓ cup cider vinegar

Kosher salt and ground black pepper

Two 15½-ounce cans kidney beans, rinsed and drained

2 cups cooked white rice

2 medium celery stalks, thinly sliced

1 medium red bell pepper, stemmed, seeded and chopped

In a 12-inch skillet over medium-high, cook the bacon, stirring occasionally, until browned and crisp, 5 to 6 minutes. Using a slotted spoon, transfer the bacon to a paper towel–lined plate; set aside. Pour off and discard all but 2 tablespoons of the fat from the skillet.

Return the skillet to medium-high, add the oil, scallion whites, vinegar and ½ teaspoon each salt and pepper. Bring to a simmer, scraping up any browned bits. Add the beans and cook, uncovered and stirring occasionally, until heated through, 3 to 5 minutes.

Transfer the bean mixture to a medium bowl. Add the rice, celery, bell pepper, scallion greens and bacon; toss to combine. Taste and season with salt and pepper. Serve at room temperature.

Chickpea and Carrot Curry

45 minutes / Servings: 4 to 6

In our spin on the Indian chickpea and potato curry known as chana masala aloo, we swap carrots for the usual potatoes. If you'd rather stick to tradition, feel free to use potatoes instead—or try a combination of the two. Garam masala, a warming Indian spice blend that packs a big flavor punch, is the primary flavoring. The mix typically includes cinnamon, cardamom, cloves, cumin, coriander, nutmeg, peppercorns and cloves. Garam masala is widely available in supermarkets; we always keep a jar in the pantry. Serve warmed flatbread or basmati rice alongside.

2 tablespoons grapeseed or other neutral oil

1 medium red onion, finely chopped

3 medium garlic cloves, minced

1 tablespoon finely grated fresh ginger

1 tablespoon garam masala

½ teaspoon ground cumin OR ¾ teaspoon cumin seeds

Kosher salt and ground black pepper

¼ cup tomato paste

3 medium carrots, peeled and cut into ½-inch rounds OR 8 ounces Yukon Gold potatoes, peeled and cut into ½-inch chunks OR a combination

Two 15½-ounce cans chickpeas, rinsed and drained

In a 12-inch skillet over medium, heat the oil until shimmering. Add half of the onion and cook, stirring occasionally, until starting to brown, 4 to 6 minutes. Add the garlic, ginger, garam masala, cumin, 1 teaspoon salt and ½ teaspoon pepper, then cook, stirring, until fragrant, about 30 seconds. Add the tomato paste and cook, stirring, until it slightly sticks to the pan, about 1 minute.

Add 2 cups water and bring to a simmer over medium-high, scraping up any browned bits. Stir in the carrots and chickpeas. Bring to a simmer over medium-high. Cover partially, reduce to medium-low and simmer, stirring occasionally, until the carrots are tender, 25 to 30 minutes.

Off heat, taste and season with salt and pepper. Serve garnished with the remaining onion.

Optional garnish: Chopped fresh cilantro **OR** thinly sliced jalapeño chilies **OR** plain yogurt **OR** a combination

White Bean Soup with Potatoes and Greens

35 minutes / Servings: 4

This substantial soup draws inspiration from caldo gallego, a classic dish from Galicia in northwestern Spain. The bacon plus smoked paprika (and cumin, if you have a jar in the pantry) are meant to mimic the flavors of Spanish dry-cured chorizo. (That said, if you wish to add some chorizo, chop about 2 ounces and cook it with the bacon; skip the paprika and/or cumin.) Turnip greens are traditional in caldo gallego, but we use lacinato (also called dinosaur or Tuscan) kale or curly kale, which is more likely to be in your refrigerator and is easier to find in the grocery store.

1 tablespoon extra-virgin olive oil, plus more to serve

6 ounces bacon, chopped

2 medium garlic cloves, smashed and peeled

½ teaspoon smoked paprika OR ground cumin OR both

1 pound Yukon Gold potatoes, peeled and cut into ¾-inch chunks

½ teaspoon dried thyme OR 1 sprig fresh thyme

6 cups low-sodium chicken broth

1 bunch lacinato kale OR curly kale, stemmed and leaves cut or torn into bite-size pieces (6 cups lightly packed)

15½-ounce can cannellini OR great northern beans, rinsed and drained

In a large saucepan over medium, combine the oil and bacon; cook, stirring occasionally, until the bacon is well browned, 5 to 6 minutes. Add the garlic and paprika (and/or cumin), then cook, stirring, until fragrant, about 30 seconds. Add the potatoes, thyme and broth.

Bring to a simmer over medium-high, stirring occasionally, then stir in the kale and return to a simmer. Cover, reduce to medium-low and simmer, stirring occasionally, until the potatoes are just tender, about 15 minutes.

Add the beans, bring to a simmer over medium and cook, uncovered, and stirring occasionally, until heated through, about 5 minutes. Off heat, discard the garlic and thyme sprig (if used). Taste and season with salt and pepper. Serve drizzled with additional oil.

Pinto Beans with Bacon and Chipotle

40 minutes / Servings: 4 to 6

Mexican frijoles charros, or "cowboy beans," often is made by simmering pinto beans and fresh tomatoes with multiple varieties of pork, including sausage, ham, pork rind, and shoulder or foot. We keep things simple—but make them smoky—by using bacon. We add spiciness and even more smoky notes with chipotle chili in adobo sauce. Serve these hearty, stewy beans with warm tortillas.

6 ounces bacon,
chopped

1 medium red onion,
¾ chopped, ¼ finely
chopped, reserved
separately

3 medium garlic cloves,
finely chopped

1 chipotle chili in
adobo, chopped, plus
2 teaspoons adobo sauce

2 teaspoons ground
cumin

2 teaspoons
chili powder

Two 15½-ounce cans
pinto beans, rinsed
and drained

3 cups low-sodium
chicken broth

14½-ounce can
crushed tomatoes

Kosher salt and
ground black pepper

In a large pot over medium, cook the bacon, stirring occasionally, until lightly browned and beginning to crisp, 4 to 6 minutes. Add the chopped onion; cook, stirring occasionally, until softened and beginning to brown, 4 to 5 minutes.

Add the garlic, chipotle and adobo sauce, cumin and chili powder; cook, stirring, until fragrant, 1 to 2 minutes. Add the beans, broth and tomatoes. Bring to a simmer scraping up any browned bits, then reduce to medium-low and cook, stirring occasionally, until the mixture is slightly thickened, about 20 minutes.

Off heat, taste and season with salt and pepper. Serve sprinkled with the finely chopped onion.

Optional garnish: Chopped fresh cilantro **OR** sliced radishes **OR** both

Smashed Chickpeas with Lemon and Scallions

35 minutes / Servings: 4

This substantial, flavor-filled chickpea "mash" requires just a handful of ingredients and comes together fast. Roughly smashing most of the canned chickpeas—and leaving the remainder whole—creates a chunky-creamy texture that's hearty and satisfying. To brighten the chickpeas' earthy flavors, we add a full bunch of scallions and both lemon zest and juice. Serve as a side dish to roasted or grilled meats or chicken, or make the mash into a meal with a dollop of plain yogurt, soft-cooked eggs and/or warmed pita bread.

1½ teaspoons cumin seeds, coarsely ground

1½ teaspoons fennel seeds, coarsely ground

Kosher salt and ground black pepper

Two 15½-ounce cans chickpeas, rinsed and drained

4 tablespoons extra-virgin olive oil, divided, plus more to serve

1 bunch scallions, thinly sliced

2 teaspoons grated lemon zest, plus ¼ cup lemon juice

In a small bowl, stir together the coarsely ground cumin and fennel, ¾ teaspoon salt and 1 teaspoon pepper; set aside. Add three-quarters of the chickpeas to a large bowl. Using a potato masher, roughly mash them, then stir in the remaining whole chickpeas.

In a 12-inch cast-iron or nonstick skillet over medium-high, heat 2 tablespoons of oil until barely smoking. Stir in the chickpeas and half the spice mixture, then distribute in an even layer. Cook without stirring until browned and lightly crisped on the bottom, 2 to 3 minutes. Add half the scallions and the remaining 2 tablespoons oil. Stir to combine, then cook without stirring until heated through, about 1 minute.

Stir in the lemon zest and juice, the remaining spice mixture and the remaining scallions. Taste and season with salt and pepper. Transfer to a serving bowl and drizzle with additional oil.

Fried White Beans with Bacon, Garlic and Spinach

25 minutes / Servings: 4

This simple recipe takes full advantage of the starchiness of cannellini beans. Frying the beans in the fat rendered from bacon combined with some fruity olive oil blisters, browns and crisps their exteriors, creating a pleasing contrast to the soft, creamy interiors. Garlic, smoked paprika and lemon juice are perfect flavor accents, and baby spinach wilted into the mix at the end of cooking rounds out the dish. For best crisping and to minimize splatter, pat the beans dry after draining them. And when frying, stir the beans only every minute or so.

4 ounces bacon, chopped

1 tablespoon extra-virgin olive oil, plus more to serve

4 medium garlic cloves, minced

½ teaspoon smoked paprika

Kosher salt and ground black pepper

Two 15½-ounce cans cannellini beans, rinsed, drained and patted dry

5-ounce container baby spinach

2 tablespoons lemon juice, plus lemon wedges to serve

In a 12-inch skillet combine the bacon and 1 tablespoon oil. Cook over medium, stirring occasionally, until the bacon is crisp, 5 to 6 minutes. Using a slotted spoon, transfer to a paper towel–lined plate; set aside.

To the fat remaining in the skillet, add the garlic, paprika and 1 teaspoon pepper. Cook over medium-high, stirring, until fragrant, about 30 seconds. Add the beans and cook, stirring only about once every minute or so, until the skins begin to split and crisp and are lightly browned, 5 to 6 minutes.

Add the spinach and stir just until wilted. Remove the pan from the heat and stir in the lemon juice, then taste and season with salt and pepper. Transfer to a serving dish, drizzle with additional oil and sprinkle with the bacon. Serve with lemon wedges.

Turkish White Bean Salad

40 minutes (10 minutes active) / Servings: 4 to 6

Fasülye piyazi, a simple white bean salad with tomatoes, herbs, olives and eggs, is a classic in Turkey. To infuse the beans with flavor, we toss them with salt and optional dried mint, then heat them in the microwave before combining them while hot with onion, vinegar and pepper. As the beans cool, they absorb the seasonings. Chopped hard-cooked eggs often accompany this salad, so feel free to add some as a garnish. If you have Aleppo pepper in your pantry, a sprinkling will lend mild, smoky heat to the finished salad.

Two 15½-ounce cans great northern beans OR navy beans, rinsed and drained

½ teaspoon dried mint (optional)

Kosher salt and ground black pepper

1 small red onion, halved and thinly sliced

3 tablespoons red wine vinegar

1 cup cherry OR grape tomatoes, halved

½ cup pitted green OR black olives OR a combination, roughly chopped

1 or 2 Fresno OR serrano chilies, stemmed and sliced into thin rings

1 teaspoon grated lemon zest OR ground sumac

Extra-virgin olive oil, to serve

In a large microwave-safe bowl, toss the beans with the dried mint (if using) and ½ teaspoon salt. Cover and microwave on high until hot, 3 to 3½ minutes, stirring once halfway through. Add the onion, vinegar and ¾ teaspoon pepper to the hot beans, toss, then let stand for about 30 minutes, stirring once or twice.

Stir in the tomatoes, olives, chilies and lemon zest. Taste and season with salt and pepper, then transfer to a serving dish. Serve drizzled with oil.

Optional garnish: Chopped hard-cooked eggs OR Aleppo pepper OR torn fresh mint OR a combination.

Egyptian-Style Pinto Beans

35 minutes / Servings: 4

Ful medammes, or cooked dried fava beans finished with various garnishes that add color as well as flavor and texture (chopped tomatoes, parsley, onion and hard-cooked eggs are typical), often is considered the national dish of Egypt, though it is common throughout the Middle East and North Africa. We swap canned pinto beans, which have a dense, creamy, buttery quality, for the dried favas, and we cook them briefly with seasonings before lightly mashing and garnishing them. Serve with warm pita bread for scooping.

Two 15½-ounce cans pinto beans, rinsed and drained

¼ cup lemon juice, plus lemon wedges to serve

¼ cup extra-virgin olive oil, plus more to serve

2 medium garlic cloves, finely grated

¼ teaspoon red pepper flakes OR 1 teaspoon Aleppo pepper

¾ teaspoon ground cumin

Kosher salt and ground black pepper

1 ripe medium tomato, cored and chopped

2 hard-cooked large eggs, peeled and cut into wedges

½ cup lightly packed fresh flat-leaf parsley, roughly chopped

In a medium saucepan over medium, combine the beans, lemon juice, oil, garlic, pepper flakes, cumin, ½ teaspoon black pepper and ½ cup water. Cook, stirring occasionally, until the beans have softened and the mixture is slightly soupy, about 10 minutes.

Off heat, use a potato masher to lightly mash the beans so the mixture thickens slightly but keep them mostly whole. Taste and season with salt and pepper.

Transfer the beans to a serving bowl or divide among individual bowls. Garnish with the tomato, eggs and parsley. Drizzle with additional oil and serve with lemon wedges.

Optional garnish: Chopped cucumber OR thinly sliced scallions OR both

Quick Creamy Hummus

30 minutes / Makes 4 cups

You can make a serviceable hummus simply by emptying canned chickpeas into a food processor and letting the machine run. But if you simmer the canned legumes with a little baking soda and puree them while warm, as we do in this recipe, you'll end up with hummus that's remarkably smooth and creamy, as well as wonderfully light. Traditionally, hummus is served warm and garnished with paprika, cumin, chopped fresh parsley and a drizzle of extra-virgin olive oil. Sometimes a sliced hard-cooked egg is added. Leftover hummus can be refrigerated for up to five days. To reheat, transfer to a microwave-safe bowl, cover and heat for 1 to 2 minutes, stirring halfway through; add a few tablespoons of water as needed to reach the proper consistency.

Three 15½-ounce cans chickpeas, drained, 2 cups liquid reserved

Kosher salt

¼ teaspoon baking soda

½ cup tahini

¼ cup lemon juice

⅛ teaspoon cayenne pepper

1 to 2 tablespoons extra-virgin olive oil

1 tablespoon chopped fresh flat-leaf parsley

½ teaspoon ground cumin, toasted

½ teaspoon sweet paprika

In a large saucepan, combine the chickpeas, the reserved chickpea liquid, ½ teaspoon salt, the baking soda and 3 cups water. Bring to a boil over high, then reduce to medium and simmer, stirring occasionally, until the chickpeas are very tender and their skins begin to fall off, 15 to 20 minutes.

Drain the chickpeas in a colander set in a large bowl; reserve ¾ cup of the chickpea cooking water. Let drain for about 1 minute. Set aside about 2 tablespoons of the chickpeas for garnish, then transfer the remainder to a food processor. Add ½ teaspoon salt, then process until completely smooth, about 3 minutes.

Stop the food processor and add the tahini. Process until the mixture has lightened and is very smooth, about 1 minute. Use a rubber spatula to scrape the sides and bottom of the processor bowl. With the machine running, add the reserved cooking liquid, the lemon juice and cayenne. Process until combined, about 1 minute. Taste and season with salt.

Transfer the hummus to a shallow serving bowl and use a large spoon to swirl a well in the center. Drizzle with the olive oil, then top with the reserved 2 tablespoons chickpeas, the parsley, cumin and paprika.

White Beans and Tomatoes with Anchovies and Vinegar

25 minutes / Servings: 4

This simple and remarkably flavorful bean dish was inspired by a classic from Italy's Veneto region, fagioli in salsa (or fasoi in salsa), which usually is made with borlotti beans, extra-virgin olive oil, anchovies and garlic. We use canned cannellini or pinto beans and include a generous amount of vinegar, as is traditional, to lend a pleasant sharpness. Cherry or grape tomatoes add juiciness, sweetness and color, and lots of chopped parsley lends fresh, grassy notes. Depending on what you have in your refrigerator, feel free to swap in another herb, such as basil, or a big handful of peppery arugula.

¼ cup extra-virgin olive oil, plus more to serve

3 medium garlic cloves, thinly sliced

1 large carrot, peeled and finely chopped

4 to 6 oil-packed anchovy fillets

½ cup white **OR** red wine vinegar

Two 15½-ounce cans cannellini beans **OR** pinto beans, rinsed and drained

1 pint cherry **OR** grape tomatoes, halved

1 cup finely chopped fresh flat-leaf parsley

Kosher salt and ground black pepper

In a 12-inch skillet, combine the oil and garlic. Cook over medium, stirring occasionally, until the garlic starts to brown, 1 to 2 minutes. Add the carrot and anchovies; cook, stirring, until the anchovies are completely broken down, 1 to 2 minutes.

Add the vinegar, reduce to medium-low and cook, stirring, until the vinegar is reduced by about half, about 5 minutes. Add the beans and tomatoes; cook, stirring, until heated through and the tomatoes are slightly softened, 5 to 8 minutes.

Off heat, stir in the parsley. Taste and season with salt and pepper. Serve drizzled with additional oil.

Pasta e Fagioli

40 minutes / Servings: 6

This classic Italian pasta and bean soup can be made with a few pantry staples. Simple techniques, like browning the onion and cooking canned tomato juices until concentrated, deepen the flavor. For even more umami, toss in a Parmesan rind as the soup simmers.

2 tablespoons extra-virgin olive oil, plus more to serve

1 medium yellow onion, chopped

Kosher salt and ground black pepper

1 medium carrot, peeled and chopped

3 medium garlic cloves, minced

1 teaspoon dried rosemary **OR** 1 fresh rosemary sprig

28-ounce can whole peeled tomatoes, juices drained and reserved, tomatoes crushed by hand

Two 15½-ounce cans cannellini beans **OR** great northern beans **OR** navy beans **OR** Roman beans **OR** pinto beans, rinsed and drained

1 quart low-sodium chicken broth **OR** vegetable broth

¾ cup elbow macaroni **OR** ditalini pasta

In a large pot over medium-high, heat the oil until shimmering. Add the onion and ½ teaspoon salt, then cook, stirring occasionally, until the onion is lightly browned, 8 to 10 minutes. Add the carrot, garlic and rosemary; cook, stirring, until the garlic is fragrant, about 30 seconds. Add the tomato juices and cook, stirring occasionally, until a spatula leaves a trail when drawn through the mixture, 6 to 8 minutes.

Stir in the beans, crushed tomatoes, broth, ½ teaspoon salt and 1 teaspoon pepper. Bring to a simmer, then reduce to medium and simmer, uncovered and stirring occasionally, until the carrot is almost tender, about 10 minutes. Add the pasta and cook until al dente.

Off heat, taste and season with salt and pepper. Remove and discard the rosemary sprig (if used). Serve drizzled with additional olive oil.

Optional garnish: Finely grated Parmesan cheese **OR** pecorino Romano **OR** red pepper flakes **OR** chopped fresh basil **OR** basil pesto **OR** a combination

Can-Do
TOMATOES

Indian-Style Tomato-Ginger Soup / 24

Double-Tomato Soup with Cilantro, Lime and Fried Garlic / 25

Shakshuka / 26

Cream-Free Tomato Bisque with Parmesan Croutons / 27

Tomato-Rice Soup with Caramelized Onion / 28

Pasta al Pomodoro / 29

Tomato-Mushroom Curry / 30

Chilaquiles Rojos / 32

One-Pot Pasta all'Arrabbiata / 33

Pasta with Roasted Tomato and Anchovy Sauce / 35

Indian-Style Tomato-Ginger Soup

25 minutes / Servings: 4 to 6

This recipe was inspired by Indian soups known as shorba. ("Shorba" comes from the Arabic word "shurba," meaning "soup.") Often simple, brothy, pureed soups, they are considered comfort food—the kind of soothing dish you'd find in home kitchens rather than in restaurants. In our version, we stir in garam masala, a blend of sweet, warming spices, to add depth of flavor and to complement the slightly acidic tomatoes and yogurt. If you happen to have ghee on hand, use it in place of butter for a subtly richer, more nuanced flavor. We like this soup served with warm naan for dipping.

2 tablespoons salted butter OR ghee

2 tablespoons minced fresh ginger

1 small bunch cilantro, tender stems finely chopped, leaves roughly chopped, reserved separately

4 teaspoons garam masala

28-ounce can whole peeled tomatoes

Kosher salt and ground black pepper

½ cup plain whole-milk yogurt, plus more to serve

In a large saucepan over medium-high, melt the butter. Add the ginger and cilantro stems; cook, stirring occasionally, until the ginger begins to stick to the pot and brown lightly, about 2 minutes. Add the garam masala and cook, stirring, until fragrant, 30 to 60 seconds. Stir in the tomatoes with juices, 3 cups water and ½ teaspoon each salt and pepper.

Bring to a simmer, scraping up any browned bits, then cover and cook, stirring occasionally and breaking up the tomatoes with a wooden spoon, until the tomatoes have softened, about 10 minutes. Remove the pan from the heat and let cool, uncovered, for about 5 minutes.

Using a blender and working in batches so the jar is never more than half full, puree the tomato mixture until smooth, about 20 seconds, then return to the saucepan. (Alternatively, use an immersion blender to puree the soup directly in the saucepan.) Stir in half of the cilantro leaves and cook over medium, stirring occasionally, until heated through, about 3 minutes.

Off heat, whisk in the yogurt, then taste and season with salt and pepper. Serve sprinkled with the remaining cilantro leaves and topped with yogurt.

Double-Tomato Soup with Cilantro, Lime and Fried Garlic

45 minutes / Servings: 6

We combine tomatoes in two forms—both pantry staples—to make this flavor-filled vegetarian soup. Browning a full can of tomato paste in garlic-infused olive oil creates an umami-rich base and perfect backdrop for bold ingredients such as fresh chili, herbal cilantro and tangy lime juice. And for texture, we add a can of roughly chopped whole tomatoes. If you'd like a little heat, leave the seeds in the jalapeño. Sour cream dolloped onto individual bowlfuls lends creamy richness, but try one or more of the garnishes listed below for even more complexity.

2 tablespoons extra-virgin olive oil	1 quart low-sodium vegetable broth
3 medium garlic cloves, thinly sliced	Kosher salt and ground black pepper
6-ounce can tomato paste (⅔ cup)	½ cup lightly packed fresh cilantro, finely chopped, plus cilantro leaves to serve
1 jalapeño chili, stemmed, seeded (if desired) and minced	
14½-ounce can whole peeled tomatoes, chopped, OR 14½-ounce can diced tomatoes	2 tablespoons lime juice, plus lime wedges to serve
	Sour cream, to serve

In a large saucepan over medium, cook the oil and garlic, stirring occasionally, until the garlic is golden brown, 2 to 3 minutes. Using a slotted spoon, transfer the garlic to a small plate and set aside. Add the tomato paste and jalapeño to the pan and cook, stirring often, until the paste browns and slightly sticks to the pot, 2 to 3 minutes.

Add the tomatoes with juices, the broth and ½ teaspoon each salt and pepper. Bring to a simmer over medium-high, scraping up any browned bits, then reduce to medium and simmer, uncovered and stirring occasionally, until the soup is slightly reduced, about 20 minutes.

Off heat, stir in the cilantro and lime juice, then taste and season with salt and pepper. Ladle the soup into bowls. Sprinkle with the reserved garlic chips and cilantro leaves, then spoon on a dollop of sour cream. Serve with lime wedges.

Optional garnish: Thinly sliced radishes OR crushed tortilla chips OR shredded cheddar cheese OR a combination

Shakshuka

30 minutes / Servings: 4 to 6

This is a classic version of shakshuka, or eggs poached in a sauce of tomatoes and bell pepper. We use harissa, a North African spice paste and a must-have ingredient in our pantry, to lend bold, rich flavor. Serve with warm, crusty bread.

2 tablespoons extra-virgin olive oil, plus more to serve

1 medium red bell pepper, stemmed, seeded and thinly sliced **OR** ½ cup drained and thinly sliced roasted red peppers

1 medium red onion, halved and thinly sliced

Kosher salt and ground black pepper

28-ounce can whole peeled tomatoes, crushed by hand

2 tablespoons harissa paste

6 large eggs

¼ cup finely chopped fresh flat-leaf parsley **OR** cilantro

In a 12-inch nonstick skillet over medium-high, heat the oil until shimmering. Add the pepper, onion and ½ teaspoon each salt and pepper. Cook, stirring occasionally, until the onion is light golden brown, about 5 minutes.

Stir in the tomatoes with juices, the harissa and ½ cup water. Bring to a simmer and cook, uncovered, stirring occasionally, until the pepper and onion are fully softened, 6 to 8 minutes. Taste and season with salt and pepper.

Reduce to medium-low, then use the back of a large spoon to make 6 evenly spaced indentations in the tomatoes and sauce, each about 2 inches in diameter. Crack 1 egg into each well, then sprinkle with salt and pepper. Cover and cook until the egg whites are set but the yolks are still runny, 5 to 8 minutes, rotating the skillet halfway through. Remove from the heat, sprinkle with parsley and drizzle with additional oil.

Optional garnish: Crumbled feta cheese **OR** plain yogurt **OR** chopped pitted black or green olives **OR** a combination

Cream-Free Tomato Bisque with Parmesan Croutons

40 minutes (20 minutes active) / Servings: 4

In our grown-up twist on that childhood favorite—a bowl of creamy tomato soup with grilled cheese for dipping—we created a silky bisque and serve it topped with crisp Parmesan croutons in place of a sandwich. Rather than thicken the soup with heavy cream, we simmer pieces of torn bread in the tomato broth, then blend everything to produce a satisfying soup with a velvety texture. Canned crushed tomatoes keep prep time to a minimum.

4 tablespoons salted butter, cut into 1-tablespoon pieces, divided

5 tablespoons extra-virgin olive oil, divided

8 ounces country-style white bread, crusts removed, torn into bite-size pieces (about 6 cups), divided

¾ teaspoon dried thyme OR dried oregano, divided

Kosher salt and ground black pepper

¼ teaspoon red pepper flakes (optional)

1 ounce Parmesan OR pecorino Romano cheese, finely grated (½ cup), plus more to serve

1 medium yellow onion, finely chopped

2 medium garlic cloves, smashed and peeled

28-ounce can crushed tomatoes

In a large pot over medium-high, melt 2 tablespoons butter with 2 tablespoons oil. Set aside 1½ cups torn bread for thickening the soup. Add the remaining bread, ½ teaspoon thyme, ¼ teaspoon each salt and black pepper, and the pepper flakes (if using) to the pot. Cook, stirring occasionally and lowering the heat as needed to prevent the seasonings from burning, until the bread is golden brown, 2 to 4 minutes. Transfer to a large plate, toss with the Parmesan and spread in a single layer. Set aside to cool and crisp.

In the same pot over medium, melt the remaining 2 tablespoons butter. Add the onion, garlic, ½ teaspoon salt and the remaining ¼ teaspoon thyme; cook, stirring occasionally, until the onion is translucent but not browned, 5 to 7 minutes. Stir in the tomatoes, the 1½ cups reserved bread and 4 cups water. Cook, uncovered and stirring occasionally, until the bread is completely soft and the broth is slightly thickened, about 10 minutes. Remove from the heat and cool for about 5 minutes.

Using a blender and working in batches so the jar is never more than half full, puree the tomato mixture, streaming in the remaining 3 tablespoons oil, until smooth. Return the soup to the pot. (Alternatively, if you own an immersion blender, puree the soup directly in the pot; when almost smooth, slowly stream in the remaining 3 tablespoons oil while blending.) Cook over medium-low, stirring often, until heated through, 2 to 5 minutes. Thin the soup with water, if needed, to reach the desired consistency.

Off heat, taste and season with salt and black pepper. Serve topped with the croutons and sprinkled with additional Parmesan.

Optional garnish: Basil pesto

Tomato-Rice Soup with Caramelized Onion

45 minutes / Servings: 4

To deepen the flavor of this pantry staple soup, we caramelize an onion and simmer some of it into the soup; the rest is reserved for garnish. Though our preference is long-grain white rice (regular, jasmine or basmati), even starchy Arborio rice works. Long-grain brown rice is good, too, but be sure to increase the simmering time to 35 to 40 minutes. No matter what type of rice you use, be sure to rinse and drain it before adding it to the pot.

1 tablespoon extra-virgin olive oil, plus more to serve

1 large yellow onion, halved and thinly sliced

1 teaspoon white sugar

Kosher salt and ground black pepper

1 teaspoon dried thyme

½ cup long-grain white rice, rinsed and drained (see headnote)

14½-ounce can whole peeled tomatoes, crushed by hand

1 quart low-sodium chicken broth OR vegetable broth

½ cup lightly packed fresh flat-leaf parsley OR basil leaves, chopped

In a large saucepan over medium, heat the oil until shimmering. Add the onion, sugar and ½ teaspoon each salt and pepper. Cook, stirring occasionally, until the onion is well browned, 12 to 15 minutes. Transfer half to a small bowl; set aside.

Add the thyme to the remaining onion in the pan and cook, stirring, until fragrant, about 30 seconds. Add the rice, tomatoes with juices and broth. Bring to a simmer over medium-high, then cover, reduce to medium and simmer, stirring occasionally, until the rice is tender, 18 to 20 minutes.

Off heat, stir in the parsley, then taste and season with salt and pepper. Garnish with the reserved onion and a drizzle of additional oil.

Optional garnish: Basil pesto **OR** finely grated Parmesan cheese **OR** both

Pasta al Pomodoro

25 minutes / Servings: 4 to 6

Chances are, you've got everything in your pantry for this simple pasta with tomato sauce. We drain a can of whole peeled tomatoes, then cook the juices down with garlic, red pepper flakes and oregano to create a concentrated base. Before adding the tomatoes to the pot, we crush them by hand rather than finely chop so the sauce has texture. Be sure to boil the pasta as directed in a scant amount of water until just shy of al dente. The noodles will finish cooking directly in the sauce, with some of the starchy liquid to lend body and clingability. Add some warm, crusty bread and dinner is served.

1 pound spaghetti OR linguine OR bucatini

Kosher salt and ground black pepper

¼ cup extra-virgin olive oil, plus more to serve

2 medium garlic cloves, smashed and peeled

½ teaspoon dried oregano OR 2 fresh oregano sprigs

¼ teaspoon red pepper flakes

28-ounce can whole peeled tomatoes, juices drained and reserved, tomatoes crushed by hand

1-inch piece Parmesan rind (optional), plus finely grated Parmesan cheese, to serve

In a large pot, bring 2 quarts water to a boil. Add the pasta and 1 tablespoon salt, then cook, stirring occasionally, until just shy of al dente. Reserve ½ cup of the cooking water, then drain; set aside.

Meanwhile, in a 12-inch skillet over medium-high, combine the oil and garlic; cook, stirring often, until the garlic is lightly golden, 1 to 2 minutes. Add the oregano and pepper flakes, then cook, stirring, until fragrant, about 30 seconds. Add the tomato juices and Parmesan rind (if using). Bring to a simmer and cook, stirring often, until a spatula leaves a trail when drawn through the mixture, about 5 minutes.

Add the crushed tomatoes and cook, stirring often, until heated through, about 2 minutes. Add the pasta and ¼ cup of the reserved cooking water, then reduce to medium and cook, stirring and tossing, until the pasta is al dente and lightly sauced, about 3 minutes; add more cooking water 1 tablespoon at a time as needed if the mixture looks dry.

Off heat, remove and discard the garlic cloves, Parmesan rind (if used) and oregano sprigs (if used). Taste and season with salt and black pepper. Serve drizzled with additional oil and sprinkled with Parmesan.

Optional garnish: Torn fresh basil

Tomato-Mushroom Curry

40 minutes / Servings: 4

Meaty cremini mushrooms play a starring role in this curry inspired by the flavors of tikka masala and butter chicken. Many of those recipes call for copious amounts of butter, yogurt and cream, but we lighten things up by swapping the dairy for cashews pureed with a little water until smooth. The puree lends a creamy texture without making the dish heavy. If you have only white mushrooms on hand, they'll work well, too. For a pop of color, stir ½ cup thawed frozen peas into the curry at the end of cooking. Warm naan or nutty brown rice are wonderful accompaniments.

½ cup roasted salted cashews, plus 2 tablespoons chopped cashews, divided

3 tablespoons grapeseed or other neutral oil

1 medium yellow onion, finely chopped

4 medium garlic cloves, minced

1 tablespoon finely grated fresh ginger

1 tablespoon garam masala

2 teaspoons hot paprika OR 2 teaspoons sweet paprika plus ⅛ teaspoon cayenne pepper

Kosher salt and ground black pepper

14½-ounce can crushed tomatoes

1 pound cremini OR white mushrooms, trimmed, halved if medium, quartered if large

In a blender, combine the ½ cup cashews and ⅓ cup water; soak for about 10 minutes. Puree on high until smooth, scraping the jar as needed, 1 to 2 minutes; set aside.

In a 12-inch skillet over medium, heat the oil until shimmering. Add the onion and cook, stirring occasionally, until beginning to brown, 6 to 9 minutes. Add the garlic, ginger, garam masala, paprika and ½ teaspoon pepper; cook, stirring, until fragrant, about 1 minute. Add the cashew puree and cook, stirring often, until browned and sticking to the bottom of the skillet, about 2 minutes.

Add the tomatoes and ¾ cup water, scraping up the browned bits, then stir in the mushrooms and ¾ teaspoon salt. Cover, reduce to medium-low and cook, stirring occasionally and scraping along the bottom of the pan to prevent sticking, until the mushrooms are very tender and the sauce is creamy, 10 to 15 minutes. Off heat, taste and season with salt and pepper. Serve sprinkled with the chopped cashews.

Optional garnish: Chopped fresh cilantro **OR** lemon wedges **OR** both

Chilaquiles Rojos

35 minutes / Servings: 4

A beloved Mexican breakfast dish that's equally great for lunch or dinner, chilaquiles feature tortilla chips that are lightly cooked in a red or green sauce and topped with melted cheese. It was created as a way to use up leftover tortillas and other ingredients, though the dish works equally well with store-bought chips, as in this recipe. If you have some corn tortillas on hand and want to make your own, see Oven-Baked Tortilla Chips, below. If you like, to round out the meal, serve the chilaquiles with scrambled or fried eggs.

1 medium white OR yellow OR red onion, quartered

2 tablespoons grapeseed or other neutral oil, divided

3 medium garlic cloves, peeled

14½-ounce can diced fire-roasted OR diced regular tomatoes

1 chipotle chili in adobo, plus 1 teaspoon adobo sauce

½ teaspoon ground cumin OR dried oregano OR both

6 cups tortilla chips

Kosher salt and ground black pepper

4 ounces cheddar OR pepper jack OR cotija cheese, shredded (1 cup)

½ cup lightly packed fresh cilantro leaves and tender stems

Finely chop 1 onion quarter; set aside for garnish. In a 12-inch skillet over medium-high, heat 1 tablespoon oil until barely smoking. Add the remaining onion quarters and the garlic and cook, turning occasionally with tongs, until charred all over, 6 to 9 minutes. If the garlic is done before the onion, remove from the skillet. Transfer the onion and garlic to a blender; reserve the skillet. To the blender, add the tomatoes with juices, chipotle and adobo sauce and cumin, then puree until smooth, about 1 minute.

In the same skillet over medium, heat the remaining 1 tablespoon oil until shimmering. Carefully add the puree (it will splatter) and cook, uncovered and stirring often, until slightly darkened and thickened, 5 to 7 minutes. Stir in 1 cup water and bring to a simmer. Add the tortilla chips and toss to coat.

Off heat, taste and season with salt and pepper. Sprinkle with the cheese and stir until beginning to melt, about 2 minutes. Sprinkle with the chopped onion and cilantro and serve directly from the skillet.

Optional garnish: Diced avocado **OR** sour cream **OR** Mexican crema **OR** lime wedges **OR** pickled jalapeños **OR** hot sauce **OR** a combination

Oven-Baked Tortilla Chips

Heat the oven to 450°F with a rack in the middle position. **Cut twelve 6-inch corn tortillas** into 8 wedges each. On a rimmed baking sheet, toss the tortillas with **3 tablespoons grapeseed or other neutral oil,** then sprinkle with **kosher salt and black pepper.** Distribute in an even layer and bake until browned and crisped, about 10 minutes, tossing once about halfway through. Transfer to a large plate.

One-Pot Pasta all'Arrabbiata

20 minutes / Servings: 4 to 6

Pasta all'arrabbiata, from the Lazio region of Italy, features a spicy marriage of tomatoes, garlic and pepper flakes (arrabbiata translates as "angry"). This one-pot version cooks the pasta directly in the sauce, so there's no need to dirty two pots and heat up the kitchen with a gallon of boiling water. We like this made with enough pepper flakes for moderate but not overly assertive heat; adjust the amount to suit your taste.

3 tablespoons extra-virgin olive oil, plus more to serve

4 medium garlic cloves, thinly sliced

½ teaspoon red pepper flakes

14½-ounce can diced tomatoes

Kosher salt and ground black pepper

1 pound penne

1 ounce finely grated Parmesan OR pecorino Romano cheese (½ cup), plus more to serve

In a large pot, combine the oil, garlic and pepper flakes. Cook over medium-high, stirring often, until fragrant, about 1 minute. Add the tomatoes with juices, 1 teaspoon salt and ½ teaspoon black pepper. Add 3 cups water and the pasta; stir to combine. Bring to a boil over medium-high, then reduce to medium, cover and cook, stirring occasionally, until the pasta is al dente, 9 to 11 minutes.

Remove the pot from the heat and stir in the Parmesan. Cover and let stand for 5 minutes. Stir vigorously, then taste and season with salt and black pepper. Serve drizzled with additional oil and sprinkled with additional cheese.

Optional garnish: Chopped fresh basil

Pasta with Roasted Tomato and Anchovy Sauce

35 minutes / Servings: 4 to 6

In this recipe, we cook the tomato-anchovy sauce in the oven rather than on the stovetop. It's our pantry-centric adaptation of a dish we had at Osteria ai Promessi Sposi in Venice, Italy, where chef Claudio Furlanis roasts fresh tomatoes in a scorchingly hot oven before combining them with anchovies and pasta. To balance the acidity of canned tomatoes, we add a small measure of sugar. And when the pasta and sauce are combined, we toss in some butter—its smooth, sweet richness rounds out all the flavors.

28-ounce can whole peeled tomatoes

2 medium garlic cloves, smashed and peeled

5 oil-packed anchovy fillets

1 teaspoon white sugar

¼ to ½ teaspoon red pepper flakes

¼ cup extra-virgin olive oil

1 pound rigatoni OR penne rigate OR ziti

Kosher salt and ground black pepper

2 tablespoons salted butter, cut into 4 pieces

Finely grated Parmesan cheese, to serve

Heat the oven to 450°F with a rack in the lower-middle position. In a 9-by-13-inch baking dish, toss together the tomatoes with juices, the garlic, anchovies, sugar and pepper flakes. Drizzle with the oil, then roast, stirring once about halfway, until the mixture is browned at the edges and thickened, but still saucy, about 30 minutes. Let cool slightly.

Meanwhile, in a large pot, bring 2 quarts water to a boil. Add the pasta and 1 tablespoon salt, then cook, stirring occasionally, until just shy of al dente. Reserve ½ cup of the pasta cooking water and drain. Return the pasta to the pot.

Using a fork or potato masher, roughly mash the tomato mixture, then add it to the pasta along with ¼ cup of the reserved cooking water and the butter. Cook over medium, stirring, until the pasta is al dente and lightly sauced, about 3 minutes; add more cooking water 1 tablespoon at a time as needed if the mixture looks dry. Taste and season with salt and pepper. Serve sprinkled with the cheese.

Optional garnish: Torn fresh basil

Tuesday Night TUNA

Portuguese-Style Tuna with Chickpeas / 38

Potato Salad with Capers, Olives and Olive Oil Tuna / 39

Pan-Fried Tuna Cakes with Yogurt-Caper Sauce / 41

Spaghetti with Tuna and Mushrooms / 42

Tuna Gochujang Noodles / 43

Harissa-Spiced Tuna Tartines / 45

Tuna Tostadas with Chipotle, Corn and Quick-Pickled Onion / 46

Deviled Eggs with Tuna, Olives and Capers / 47

Portuguese-Style Tuna with Chickpeas

25 minutes / Servings: 4

The Portuguese classic, salada de bacalhau com grão de bico—or bacalao salad with chickpeas—was the inspiration for this ultra-easy dish that requires no stovetop cooking, only a microwave. The chickpeas are dressed while hot so that as they cool, they absorb the seasonings, ensuring every bite is flavorful. Be sure to use tuna packed in olive oil, as it is richer and silkier than the water-packed variety. Parsley, cilantro or arugula adds green, grassy flavor; use whichever you prefer or have on hand, or even a combination. Just be sure to toss in the greens right before serving, or they will go limp.

¼ cup cider vinegar OR lemon juice

1 medium shallot, sliced into thin rings OR ½ small red onion, thinly sliced

1 medium garlic clove, finely grated

Kosher salt and ground black pepper

15½-ounce can chickpeas, rinsed and drained

Two 5-ounce cans olive oil–packed tuna, drained

1½ cups lightly packed fresh flat-leaf parsley OR cilantro OR baby arugula OR a combination, torn if large

2 hard-cooked large eggs, peeled and cut into wedges

½ cup roasted red peppers, patted dry and thinly sliced

Extra-virgin olive oil, to serve

In a small bowl, stir together the vinegar, shallot, garlic, ¼ teaspoon salt and ½ teaspoon pepper; set aside.

In a large microwave-safe bowl, toss the chickpeas with ¼ teaspoon salt. Cover and microwave on high until hot, 2 to 3 minutes, stirring once halfway through. Add the vinegar-shallot mixture to the hot beans, toss, then let stand for at least 15 minutes or up to 1 hour.

Add the tuna and parsley; gently toss to combine. Taste and season with salt and pepper, then transfer to a serving dish. Top with the eggs and roasted peppers; drizzle with oil.

Potato Salad with Capers, Olives and Olive Oil Tuna

25 minutes / Servings: 4 to 6

This mayo-free potato salad was inspired by classic salade Niçoise. It combines big, bold Mediterranean ingredients and uses a generous amount of capers to add pops of savory, briny flavor in every forkful (you'll need two 4-ounce jars to obtain the ½ cup capers called for in the recipe). The tuna makes the salad hearty enough to serve as a light main, especially if it's served on top of a bed of greens.

½ small red onion, thinly sliced

¾ teaspoon dried oregano

3 tablespoons red wine vinegar

1½ pounds Yukon Gold potatoes OR red potatoes OR a combination, unpeeled, cut into 1-inch chunks

Kosher salt and ground black pepper

½ cup drained capers, plus 1 tablespoon caper brine

⅓ cup pitted black olives, chopped

¼ cup extra-virgin olive oil

5-ounce can olive oil–packed tuna, drained and broken into large flakes

½ cup lightly packed fresh flat-leaf parsley OR basil OR a combination, roughly chopped

In a large bowl, stir together the onion, oregano and vinegar; set aside. Add the potatoes and 2 teaspoons salt to a large saucepan and add water to cover by about 1 inch. Bring to a boil over medium-high, then reduce to medium-low and cook, stirring occasionally, until a skewer inserted into the potatoes meets no resistance, 8 to 10 minutes.

Drain the potatoes in a colander. To the bowl with the onion-vinegar mixture, stir in the capers and brine, the olives, oil, ¼ teaspoon salt and ½ teaspoon pepper. Add the hot potatoes and toss to coat. Add the tuna and toss to combine. Taste and season with salt and pepper, then add the parsley and toss again.

Pan-Fried Tuna Cakes with Yogurt-Caper Sauce

45 minutes / Servings: 4

This recipe was inspired by Israeli seasoned fish cakes known as ktzitzot dagim. Traditional versions usually are prepared with fresh fish and might be fried, baked or cooked directly in a sauce. We've opted for canned tuna, making this an easy recipe for weeknight dinners. We use yogurt two ways: to add tanginess to the fish cakes and as a creamy dipping sauce served alongside. Choose good-quality, water-packed tuna, as its flavor is purer and lighter than the oil-packed variety. Be sure to drain the tuna, then give it a light squeeze before adding it to the mixture; this prevents the patties from becoming soggy.

¾ cup plain whole-milk yogurt, divided

2 tablespoons drained capers, chopped

Kosher salt and ground black pepper

4 tablespoons grapeseed or other neutral oil, divided

2 medium shallots OR ½ medium yellow onion, finely chopped

Two 5-ounce cans water-packed tuna, drained, flaked and lightly squeezed to remove excess water

1 large egg, beaten

½ cup panko breadcrumbs

2 teaspoons grated lemon zest, plus lemon wedges to serve

1 teaspoon ground cumin

In a small bowl, stir together ½ cup of the yogurt, the capers and ¼ teaspoon pepper; set aside. In a 12-inch nonstick skillet over medium, heat 1 tablespoon oil until shimmering. Add the shallots and ½ teaspoon salt, then cook, stirring occasionally, until softened, 6 to 8 minutes. Transfer to a medium bowl; reserve the skillet.

To the bowl with the shallots, add the tuna, egg, panko, lemon zest, cumin, ¼ teaspoon pepper and the remaining ¼ cup yogurt. Stir until well combined. Form into 8 balls and place on a baking sheet. Using your hands, press each ball into a 2½-inch patty.

In the same skillet over medium-high, heat the remaining 3 tablespoons oil until shimmering. Add the patties, reduce to medium and cook until golden brown on the bottoms, 2 to 3 minutes. Using a wide spatula, flip the patties and cook until golden brown on the second sides, about another 3 minutes. Transfer to a paper towel–lined plate and sprinkle lightly with salt.

Transfer the tuna cakes to a serving platter and serve with the yogurt sauce and lemon wedges.

Optional garnish: Hot sauce OR finely chopped fresh cilantro OR both

Spaghetti with Tuna and Mushrooms

40 minutes/ Servings: 6

This is our take on the Italian dish known as spaghetti alla carrettiera ("in the style of cart drivers"). We were inspired by the Roman version, which uses tomatoes, tuna and dried porcini mushrooms, but we used cremini mushrooms. Olive oil–packed tuna is traditional; the oil often is added to the sauce, as we've done.

1 pound spaghetti
OR linguine

Kosher salt and ground
black pepper

3 tablespoons extra-
virgin olive oil, plus more
to serve

8 ounces cremini
OR white mushrooms,
trimmed and sliced

1 small red onion,
halved and thinly sliced

4 medium
garlic cloves, minced

¼ to ½ teaspoon
red pepper flakes

Two 5-ounce cans
olive oil–packed tuna,
drained, oil reserved

14½-ounce can diced
tomatoes

In a large pot, bring 4 quarts water to a boil. Add the pasta and 1 tablespoon salt, then cook, stirring occasionally, until al dente. Reserve 1 cup of the cooking water, then drain; set aside.

In the same pot over medium-high, heat the oil until shimmering. Add the mushrooms, onion and ½ teaspoon salt. Cook, stirring occasionally, until the mushrooms are browned, 5 to 6 minutes. Add the garlic, pepper flakes, ½ teaspoon black pepper and the reserved oil from the tuna; cook, stirring, until fragrant. Stir in the tomatoes with juices and ½ cup of the reserved cooking water. Bring to a simmer and cook until a spatula leaves a trail when drawn through the mixture, about 5 minutes.

Add the pasta and tuna. Toss until the pasta is heated through and the sauce clings lightly, breaking up any large tuna chunks and adding more cooking water as needed. Off heat, taste and season with salt and black pepper. Serve drizzled with additional oil.

Optional garnish: Finely chopped fresh flat-leaf parsley

Tuna Gochujang Noodles

25 minutes / Servings: 4

Our inspiration for this simple recipe comes from bimbim guksu, a Korean cold noodle dish that pairs delicate somen with kimchi and a spicy sauce. Gochujang, a fermented chili paste, supplies savory, umami-rich flavor and canned tuna turns the noodles into a satisfying, but not heavy, meal in a bowl. Fine pasta, such as angel hair or capellini, work well here, but if you happen to have somen, by all means, use it. And if you have lettuce on hand, shred several leaves and divide them among the bowls, creating a bed for the noodles; toss well before eating.

8 ounces capellini **OR** somen noodles

2 to 3 tablespoons gochujang

2 tablespoons toasted sesame oil

2 tablespoons soy sauce

2 tablespoons white sugar **OR** packed light brown sugar

4 teaspoons unseasoned rice vinegar

2 teaspoons finely grated garlic **OR** finely grated fresh ginger **OR** 1 teaspoon each

Kosher salt and ground black pepper

Two 5-ounce cans water-packed **OR** oil-packed tuna, drained

In a large pot of boiling water, cook the noodles until tender. Meanwhile, in a large bowl, whisk together the gochujang, sesame oil, soy sauce, sugar, vinegar, garlic and ¼ teaspoon each salt and pepper. In a small bowl, combine the tuna, a pinch each of salt and pepper and 1½ tablespoons of the gochujang mixture; toss to coat, leaving the tuna in largish flakes.

When the noodles are tender, drain in a colander, rinse under cold running water until the noodles are cool to the touch, then drain again. Add the noodles to the large bowl and toss to coat with the gochujang mixture. Divide the noodles among individual bowls, then top with the tuna, dividing it evenly.

Optional garnish: Toasted sesame seeds **OR** scallions, thinly sliced on the diagonal **OR** chopped cabbage kimchi **OR** thinly sliced radishes **OR** a combination

Harissa-Spiced Tuna Tartines

25 minutes / Servings: 4

A tartine is a slice of bread with toppings—basically, an open-faced sandwich. Here, instead of basic tuna salad sandwiches, we make tartines and give them a Mediterranean spin by spicing things up with harissa, a North African chili sauce and an essential Milk Street pantry ingredient. Olives lend brininess, orange zest brightens the flavors and coriander adds floral notes. In a nod to the classic, we keep the familiar crunch of celery; feel free to swap in fresh fennel if you have it. Instead of stirring mayonnaise into the tuna mixture, we spike mayonnaise with harissa and citrus juice, then drizzle it over the open-faced sandwiches.

10- to 12-ounce baguette OR two 8-inch crusty rolls or ciabatta rolls

5 tablespoons extra-virgin olive oil, divided

Three 5-ounce cans olive oil–packed tuna OR water-packed tuna, drained and flaked

½ cup pitted green olives OR pimento-stuffed green olives, chopped

2 medium celery stalks, chopped OR 1 small fennel bulb, trimmed, halved lengthwise, cored and thinly sliced

5 to 6 teaspoons harissa paste, divided

2 teaspoons grated orange OR lemon zest, plus 1½ tablespoons orange OR lemon juice

½ teaspoon ground coriander OR ground cumin

Kosher salt and ground black pepper

¼ cup mayonnaise OR plain whole-milk yogurt

Heat the broiler with a rack about 6 inches from the element. Cut the baguette in half crosswise, then split each half horizontally to create 4 similarly sized pieces. If using rolls, cut in half horizontally. Pull out some of the interior crumb from each piece, slightly hollowing out the centers and creating boat shapes. Place the bread cut side up on a broiler-safe rimmed baking sheet. Brush with 3 tablespoons oil.

In a medium bowl, stir together the tuna, olives, celery, 2 to 3 teaspoons harissa, the orange zest, coriander and the remaining 2 tablespoons oil. Taste and season with salt and pepper. In a small bowl, whisk together the mayonnaise, orange juice and remaining 3 teaspoons harissa; set aside for serving.

Divide the tuna mixture evenly among the baguette pieces. Broil until the edges of the bread are golden brown and crisp, about 2 minutes. Remove the baking sheet from the oven. Drizzle the tartines with the mayonnaise mixture and serve.

Optional garnish: Fresh flat-leaf parsley OR fresh dill OR thinly sliced radishes OR a combination

Tuna Tostadas with Chipotle, Corn and Quick-Pickled Onion

Start to finish: 30 minutes / Servings: 4

A tostada is a tortilla that's fried until crisp, then topped with ingredients of any sort. We use the oven rather than a skillet to make tostadas; this technique requires less oil and allows you to toast more than one at a time. For topping the tostadas, canned tuna combined with sweet corn, smoky chipotle, citrus juice and zest, and quick-pickled onion, plus a little mayonnaise as binder, is a refreshing take on tuna salad.

½ medium red onion, thinly sliced

1 teaspoon grated lemon **OR** lime zest, plus 2 tablespoons lemon **OR** lime juice

Kosher salt and ground black pepper

Four 6-inch corn tortillas

1 tablespoon grapeseed or other neutral oil

5-ounce can albacore tuna in water, drained and flaked

1 tablespoon mayonnaise

1 tablespoon extra-virgin olive oil

½ cup frozen corn kernels, thawed and patted dry

1 chipotle chili in adobo, finely chopped

Roughly chopped fresh cilantro, to serve

Heat the oven to 400°F with a rack in the upper-middle position. In a medium bowl, stir together the onion, lemon juice and ¼ teaspoon salt; set aside.

Brush the tortillas on both sides with the neutral oil, then place them in a single layer on a rimmed baking sheet. Bake until golden brown and crisp, 8 to 10 minutes, flipping them once about halfway through. Let the tostadas cool on the baking sheet.

To the pickled onion, add the tuna, mayonnaise, olive oil, corn, chipotle, lemon zest and ¼ teaspoon pepper; stir to combine. Taste and season with salt and pepper.

Place the tostadas on individual plates. Top with the tuna mixture, dividing it evenly, then sprinkle with cilantro.

Optional garnish: Sliced avocado **OR** shredded lettuce **OR** pickled jalapeños **OR** sour cream **OR** a combination

Deviled Eggs with Tuna, Olives and Capers

2½ hours (20 minutes active) / Makes 12 deviled eggs

For this recipe, look for tuna packed in olive oil, not water; it's richer and more flavorful. Mixed with egg yolks, capers, mustard, olives and roasted red pepper, the tuna makes a bold filling for a classic hors d'oeuvre.

6 large eggs

2 tablespoons extra-virgin olive oil, plus more to serve

1½ tablespoons lemon juice

1 teaspoon Dijon mustard

5-ounce can olive oil–packed tuna, well drained and finely flaked

2 tablespoons finely chopped fresh flat-leaf parsley OR chives, plus more to serve

2 tablespoons finely chopped pitted black olives, plus more to serve

2 tablespoons finely chopped roasted red pepper, plus more to serve

1 tablespoon drained capers, finely chopped

Kosher salt and ground black pepper

Fill a medium saucepan with about 1 inch of water. Place a steamer basket in the pan, cover and bring the water to a boil over medium-high. Add the eggs to the basket, cover and cook for 11 minutes. Meanwhile, fill a medium bowl with ice water. Using tongs, transfer the eggs to the ice water and let stand until cool to the touch. Peel the eggs, then refrigerate until well-chilled, at least 2 hours or up to 2 days.

Halve each egg lengthwise. Remove the yolks and place in a medium bowl. Add the oil, lemon juice and mustard to the yolks, then mash to a smooth paste. Add the flaked tuna, parsley, olives, roasted red pepper and capers; stir until well combined. Taste and season with salt, pepper and hot sauce (if using).

Using a spoon, mound the filling onto the egg white halves. Garnish with parsley, olives and roasted red pepper, then drizzle with additional oil.

Optional garnish: Hot sauce

Shelf
STALWARTS

Pantry
PASTAS

Hoisin-Ginger Noodles / 52

Pasta with Fennel, Green Olive and Pistachio Pesto / 53

Couscous Cakes with Harissa and Olives / 54

Pasta with Parsley, Walnut and Caper Pesto / 55

Pasta with Pesto Rosso / 56

Spaghetti with Garlic, Oil and Lemon-Parmesan Breadcrumbs / 57

Farfalle with Cabbage, Walnuts and Parmesan / 58

Garlicky Peanut Noodles / 59

Toasted Pearl Couscous with Sweet Potato and Cranberries / 60

Pearl Couscous "Risotto" with Chicken and Spinach / 61

Egg Noodles with Cabbage, Bacon and Sour Cream / 62

Pasta with Chicken, Green Beans and Harissa / 63

Spaghetti with Lemon Pesto / 65

Pasta with Tomato, Onion and Butter / 66

Hoisin-Ginger Noodles

20 minutes / Servings: 4 to 6

A satisfying, flavor-filled noodle dinner doesn't come together more easily and quickly than this. Hoisin provides salty-sweet umami in the no-cook sauce, ginger provides fresh, peppery punch, and chili-garlic sauce (or Sriracha) adds balancing heat along with allium notes. We use linguine here because its shape resembles udon, a type of thick, chewy Japanese wheat noodle; if you happen to have udon in the pantry, by all means, use it. Dried lo mein works well, too.

12 ounces linguine OR dried udon noodles OR dried lo mein

¼ cup plus 2 tablespoons hoisin sauce

¼ cup chili-garlic sauce OR Sriracha sauce

2 tablespoons toasted sesame oil

2 tablespoons soy sauce

1 tablespoon finely grated fresh ginger

3 scallions, thinly sliced

In a large pot, bring 4 quarts water to a boil. Stir in the pasta, then cook, stirring occasionally, until the noodles are tender. Meanwhile, in a medium bowl, whisk together the hoisin, chili-garlic sauce, sesame oil, soy sauce and ginger.

When the noodles are done, drain well in a colander, then return them to the pot. Add the hoisin mixture and toss until evenly coated. Serve sprinkled with the scallions.

Optional garnish: Chopped roasted salted peanuts

Pasta with Fennel, Green Olive and Pistachio Pesto

35 minutes / Servings: 4 to 6

With green olives and Parmesan cheese, this pesto is especially rich in umami, and the pistachios balance the saltiness with their gentle sweetness. It's not only for pasta, though—it's also delicious spread onto sandwiches or served as a relish with roasted vegetables or chicken. If you like, make the pesto ahead; it will keep in an air-tight container in the refrigerator for up to two days.

1 pound penne OR ziti OR rigatoni pasta

Kosher salt and ground black pepper

½ cup raw pistachios

2 ounces (without rind) Parmesan cheese, cut into rough 1-inch pieces, plus finely grated Parmesan to serve

½ cup pitted green olives

½ cup lightly packed fresh flat-leaf parsley

½ cup extra-virgin olive oil

1 medium garlic clove, smashed and peeled

1 teaspoon fennel seeds, toasted

In a large pot, bring 4 quarts water to a boil. Stir in the pasta and 1 tablespoon salt, then cook, stirring occasionally, until al dente. Reserve about ½ cup of the cooking water, then drain in a colander and return to the pot.

While the pasta cooks, in a food processor, combine the pistachios, Parmesan and ½ teaspoon each salt and pepper. Process until the mixture resembles coarse sand, 10 to 20 seconds. Add the olives, parsley, oil, garlic and fennel seeds; process, scraping the bowl as needed, until almost completely smooth, about another 20 seconds.

Add the pesto to the pasta in the pot along with 3 tablespoons of the reserved pasta water, then toss; add more reserved pasta water as needed so the pesto coats the noodles. Taste and season with salt and pepper. Serve sprinkled with grated Parmesan.

Couscous Cakes
with Harissa and Olives

50 minutes (15 minutes active) / Servings: 4

Couscous typically plays a supporting role to tagines or other stews, but here we transform the tiny pasta into crisp, pan-fried cakes that can be the center of a meal. Chopped olives and harissa, a North African spiced pepper paste and a must-have ingredient in our pantry, lend a decidedly Mediterranean flavor. And to add a little gooey richness, we also mix in some shredded mozzarella cheese. Serve the cakes atop a bed of greens or sandwich them between buns.

¾ cup couscous

3 tablespoons extra-virgin olive oil, divided

2 teaspoons ground cumin

Kosher salt and ground black pepper

1¼ cups boiling water

¼ cup chopped pitted black **OR** green olives **OR** a combination

3 tablespoons harissa paste

1 medium garlic clove, finely grated

3 ounces whole-milk mozzarella cheese, shredded (¾ cup)

2 large eggs, lightly beaten

¼ cup all-purpose flour

In a medium bowl, stir together the couscous, 1 tablespoon oil, the cumin, ¾ teaspoon salt and ½ teaspoon pepper. Stir in the boiling water; cover and let stand until the water is absorbed, 15 to 20 minutes.

Into the couscous, stir the olives, harissa, garlic and mozzarella. Add the eggs and flour, then stir until well combined; the mixture will be fairly wet. Refrigerate uncovered for at least 15 minutes or up to 1 hour.

In a 12-inch nonstick skillet over medium-high, heat the remaining 2 tablespoons oil until shimmering. Using your hands, form the couscous mixture into 4 balls; place them in the skillet as they are shaped. Using a spatula, press each into a patty about 4 inches wide. Cook until golden brown on the bottoms, 3 to 5 minutes. Using the spatula, flip the patties, then reduce to medium and cook until golden brown on the second sides, another 3 to 5 minutes. Transfer to a paper towel–lined plate. Sprinkle with salt and serve hot.

Optional garnish: Lemon (or lime or orange) wedges **OR** fresh flat-leaf parsley (or cilantro) leaves **OR** both

Couscous Cakes with Chipotle Chilies

Follow the recipe, substituting chili powder for the ground cumin, **2 tablespoons chopped pickled jalapeños** for the olives and **1 or 2 chipotle chilies in adobo (minced)**, plus **2 teaspoons adobo sauce** for the harissa paste.

Pasta with Parsley, Walnut and Caper Pesto

30 minutes / Servings: 4 to 6

This pesto is a classic combination of herb, cheese and nuts, but the addition of a few tablespoons of capers adds a brininess that complements the grassiness of the parsley and the umami of the walnuts and Parmesan. Instead of tossing it with pasta, also try spreading it onto sandwiches or offer it as a sauce for a seared or grilled steak. The pesto can be made ahead and stored in an airtight container in the refrigerator for up to two days.

1 pound campanelle OR fusilli OR other short pasta shape

Kosher salt and ground black pepper

½ cup walnuts

2 ounces (without rind) Parmesan cheese, cut into rough 1-inch pieces, plus finely grated Parmesan to serve

4 cups lightly packed fresh flat-leaf parsley (about 1 bunch)

½ cup extra-virgin olive oil

3 tablespoons drained capers

In a large pot, bring 4 quarts water to a boil. Stir in the pasta and 1 tablespoon salt, then cook, stirring occasionally, until al dente. Reserve about ½ cup of the cooking water, then drain in a colander and return to the pot.

While the pasta cooks, in a food processor, combine the walnuts, Parmesan, ¼ teaspoon salt and ½ teaspoon pepper. Process until the mixture resembles coarse sand, 10 to 20 seconds. Add the parsley, oil and capers; process, scraping the bowl as needed, until almost completely smooth, about another 30 to 40 seconds.

Add the pesto to the pasta in the pot along with ¼ cup of the reserved pasta water, then toss; add more reserved pasta water as needed so the pesto coats the noodles. Taste and season with salt and pepper. Serve sprinkled with grated Parmesan.

Pasta with Pesto Rosso

30 minutes / Servings: 4 to 6

This rich, intensely flavored red pesto gets savoriness from pecorino and garlic, sweetness from roasted peppers and sun-dried tomatoes, and richness from nuts and olive oil. Though great tossed with pasta, also try stirring it into risotto or other cooked grains. You can make the pesto in advance and store it in an airtight container in the refrigerator for up to two days.

1 pound farfalle **OR** fusilli **OR** other short pasta shape

Kosher salt and ground black pepper

1½ cups roasted red peppers, patted dry and roughly chopped

2 ounces (without rind) pecorino Romano cheese, cut into rough 1-inch pieces, plus finely grated pecorino Romano to serve

1 medium garlic clove, smashed and peeled

½ cup extra-virgin olive oil, plus more to serve

½ cup pine nuts **OR** slivered almonds

¼ cup drained oil-packed sun-dried tomatoes, roughly chopped

½ teaspoon red pepper flakes

In a large pot, bring 4 quarts water to a boil. Stir in the pasta and 1 tablespoon salt, then cook, stirring occasionally, until al dente. Reserve about ½ cup of the cooking water, then drain and return to the pot.

While the pasta cooks, in a food processor, combine the roasted peppers, pecorino, garlic, oil, pine nuts, sun-dried tomatoes, red pepper flakes and ¼ teaspoon each salt and pepper. Process until almost completely smooth, scraping the bowl as needed, about 30 seconds.

Add the pesto to the pasta in the pot along with ¼ cup of the reserved pasta water, then toss; add more reserved pasta water as needed so the pesto coats the noodles. Taste and season with salt and pepper. Serve drizzled with additional oil and sprinkled with grated pecorino.

Optional garnish: Chopped or shredded fresh basil

Spaghetti with Garlic, Oil and Lemon-Parmesan Breadcrumbs

30 minutes / Servings: 4 to 6

Spaghetti aglio e olio—or spaghetti with garlic and oil—is a classic Italian dish and one of the quickest, tastiest dinners you can make with a handful of staple ingredients. We top ours with garlicky toasted bread-crumbs mixed with fresh parsley, lemon zest and Parmesan. The crumbs bring a crispness that contrasts the al dente pasta as well as adds another layer of flavor. Be sure to use light, airy panko breadcrumbs, not fine dry breadcrumbs, which won't add texture.

¼ cup finely chopped fresh flat-leaf parsley

1 teaspoon grated lemon zest, plus 2 tablespoons juice

1 ounce Parmesan cheese, finely grated (½ cup), plus more to serve

4 tablespoons extra-virgin olive oil, divided, plus more to serve

6 medium garlic cloves, minced

¾ cup panko breadcrumbs

1 pound spaghetti

Kosher salt and ground black pepper

¼ teaspoon red pepper flakes

In a medium bowl, toss together the parsley, lemon zest and cheese. Set aside. In a large pot, combine 1 tablespoon oil and half of the garlic; cook over medium-high, stirring, until lightly browned, about 1 minute. Add the panko and cook, stirring often, until golden brown, about 2 minutes. Add the panko to the parsley mixture and toss to combine; set aside.

Rinse the pot, fill with 2 quarts water and bring to a boil. Add the spaghetti and 2 teaspoons salt, then cook, stirring occasionally, until just shy of al dente. Reserve 2 cups of the cooking water, then drain; set aside.

To the pot, add the remaining 3 tablespoons oil, the remaining garlic and the pepper flakes. Cook over medium, stirring occasionally, until the garlic begins to brown, 30 to 60 seconds. Add the lemon juice and 1½ cups of the reserved pasta water and bring to a simmer over medium-high. Add the pasta and cook, tossing with tongs, until al dente and lightly sauced, adding more cooking water 1 tablespoon at a time as needed if the mixture looks dry. Taste and season with salt and black pepper. Serve drizzled with additional oil and sprinkled with the breadcrumbs and additional cheese.

Farfalle with Cabbage, Walnuts and Parmesan

40 minutes / Servings: 4 to 6

This recipe was loosely inspired by northern Italian pizzoccheri, a hearty dish that pairs buckwheat pasta with potatoes, cabbage, butter and cheese. To develop deep, complex flavor, we brown the cabbage well, which adds a pleasant bitterness to the subtly sweet vegetable, and at the same time, the butter takes on rich, nutty notes. Walnuts and Parmesan contribute umami, while a squeeze of lemon juice brightens the flavors. For a richer, creamier dish, swap out the Parmesan for blue cheese, if you have some on hand. Short pasta shapes, such as farfalle, fusilli or gemelli, work best.

1 pound farfalle OR fusilli OR gemelli pasta

Kosher salt and ground black pepper

½ cup walnuts

2 tablespoons extra-virgin olive oil

2 medium garlic cloves, thinly sliced

8 ounces green OR red OR Savoy cabbage, cored and cut crosswise into ½-inch ribbons (about 4 cups)

2 tablespoons salted butter, cut into 4 or 5 pieces

1 tablespoon lemon juice

½ cup lightly packed fresh flat-leaf parsley, chopped

Shaved Parmesan cheese OR crumbled blue cheese

In a large pot, bring 4 quarts water to a boil. Add the pasta and 1 tablespoon salt, then cook, stirring occasionally, until al dente. Reserve 1 cup of the cooking water, then drain; set aside.

Meanwhile, in a 12-inch skillet over medium, toast the walnuts, stirring often, until fragrant and lightly browned, about 3 minutes. Transfer to a cutting board; reserve the skillet. Let the nuts cool slightly, then finely chop; set aside.

In the same skillet over medium-high, combine the oil and garlic; cook, stirring often, until the garlic begins to brown, about 30 seconds. Stir in the cabbage, butter, ½ teaspoon salt and ¼ teaspoon pepper. Distribute the cabbage in an even layer, then cook, stirring only once or twice, until well browned and tender-crisp, 2 to 4 minutes.

Stir the pasta into the cabbage mixture, then add half of the walnuts and ½ cup of the reserved cooking water. Reduce to medium and cook, stirring constantly and vigorously, until the pasta is lightly sauced, 1 to 3 minutes, adding more cooking water as needed to make a silky sauce.

Off heat, stir in the lemon juice and half the parsley. Taste and season with salt and pepper. Serve sprinkled with the remaining walnuts and parsley, Parmesan and generous grindings of pepper.

Garlicky Peanut Noodles

20 minutes / Servings: 4

This Asian-inspired noodle dish comes together in a flash. We use peanut butter for a rich, flavorful sauce, while soy sauce (or fish sauce) and miso provide a double-dose of umami, and chili-garlic sauce (or Sriracha) adds a bright hit of heat. The noodles are delicious warm or at room temperature, topped with garnishes of your choice; see the suggestions below. We especially like a drizzle of chili crisp, an oil-based condiment infused with red pepper flakes and other spices.

12 ounces linguine OR spaghetti OR dried lo mein

¼ cup crunchy OR creamy peanut butter

3 medium garlic cloves, finely grated

2 tablespoons unseasoned rice vinegar

2 tablespoons soy sauce OR fish sauce

1 to 2 tablespoons chili-garlic sauce OR Sriracha sauce

1 tablespoon white miso

4 scallions, quartered lengthwise, then cut into 1-inch lengths

Kosher salt

In a large pot, bring 4 quarts water to a boil. Reserve ½ cup of the hot water; set aside. Add the pasta to the pot, then cook, stirring occasionally, until tender.

Meanwhile, in a small bowl, whisk together the peanut butter, garlic, vinegar, soy sauce, chili-garlic sauce, miso and ¼ cup of the reserved water.

When the pasta is done, drain and return to the pot. Off heat, add the peanut butter mixture and toss until evenly coated. If needed, add more of the reserved water 1 tablespoon at a time to thin the sauce. Stir in the scallions, then taste and season with salt.

Optional garnish: Chopped roasted peanuts **OR** cucumber matchsticks **OR** chili oil **OR** chili crisp

Toasted Pearl Couscous with Sweet Potato and Cranberries

Start to finish: 1 hour (25 minutes active)
Servings: 4 to 6

This salad combines couscous with cinnamon-roasted pecans and chunks of tender sweet potato. Quick-pickled onion and dried cranberries lend pops of color and tangy flavor. To bring out its wheaty, nutty taste, we first toast the couscous with a little olive oil before simmering with water. This autumnal salad is easy enough for a weeknight meal, but also is a perfect addition to a holiday dinner, especially since it's delicious served at room temperature. If you like, garnish with crumbled goat cheese.

½ teaspoon ground cinnamon

Kosher salt and ground black pepper

½ cup pecans OR whole almonds, roughly chopped

5 tablespoons extra-virgin olive oil, divided

10 to 12 ounces sweet potato, peeled and cut into ½-inch cubes

½ small red OR yellow onion, finely chopped

2 tablespoons cider vinegar

1 cup pearl couscous

½ cup dried cranberries, chopped

2 cups lightly packed baby arugula OR baby kale

Heat the oven to 400°F with a rack in the upper-middle position. In a small bowl, stir together the cinnamon, 1 teaspoon salt and ½ teaspoon pepper. In a large bowl, toss together the pecans, 1 tablespoon oil and 1 teaspoon of the cinnamon mixture. Distribute in an even layer on a rimmed baking sheet; reserve the bowl. Toast the pecans until lightly browned, 4 to 5 minutes. Transfer to a small bowl; set aside. Reserve the baking sheet.

In the reserved bowl, toss together the sweet potato, 1 tablespoon oil and the remaining cinnamon mixture. Distribute in an even layer on the same baking sheet; reserve the bowl once again. Roast the sweet potato, stirring halfway through, until browned and tender, 20 to 25 minutes. Remove from the oven and set aside.

Meanwhile, in the reserved bowl, stir together the onion, vinegar, 2 tablespoons oil and ¼ teaspoon each salt and pepper; set aside. In a large saucepan over medium, combine the remaining 1 tablespoon oil and the couscous. Cook, stirring, until golden brown, 2 to 3 minutes. Add the cranberries, ½ teaspoon each salt and pepper and 2 cups water. Bring to a simmer over medium-high, then reduce to low. Cover and simmer, stirring once or twice, until the couscous is tender, 8 to 10 minutes. Remove from the heat, uncover and cool slightly.

To the bowl with the onion, stir in the couscous, sweet potato, arugula and half the pecans. Taste and season with salt and pepper. Serve sprinkled with the remaining pecans.

Pearl Couscous "Risotto" with Chicken and Spinach

Start to finish: 40 minutes / Servings: 4

Classic risotto is made with starchy medium-grain Italian rice, such as Arborio or carnaroli. But this "risotto" uses pearl couscous (which actually is a pasta) instead of rice and a cooking method that produces "grains" with a creamy consistency. Scallions, carrot and sun-dried tomatoes are sautéed to develop a rich, subtly sweet flavor base. Cooked shredded chicken, stirred in at about the midpoint, turns the dish into a one-pot meal. You can use chicken you've cooked yourself, or for ease, grab a store-bought rotisserie bird.

2 tablespoons extra-virgin olive oil, plus more to serve

1 bunch scallions, thinly sliced, white and green parts reserved separately OR 6 medium garlic cloves, minced

1 medium carrot, peeled and finely chopped

¼ cup drained oil-packed sun-dried tomatoes, finely chopped

Kosher salt and ground black pepper

1 cup pearl couscous

½ cup dry white wine

3 cups shredded cooked chicken

5-ounce container baby spinach

In a large pot over medium, heat the oil until shimmering. Add the scallion whites, carrot, sun-dried tomatoes and ½ teaspoon salt; cook, stirring occasionally, until the vegetables have softened, 3 to 5 minutes. Stir in the couscous, then add the wine and cook, scraping up any browned bits, until the pan is almost dry, 1 to 2 minutes.

Add the shredded chicken and 4 cups water, then bring to a simmer over medium-high. Cook, stirring often and vigorously, until the couscous is tender and almost all the liquid has been absorbed, 11 to 14 minutes.

Reduce to low and add the spinach. Cook, stirring constantly, until the spinach is just wilted, 1 to 2 minutes. Taste and season with salt and pepper, then stir in the scallion greens.

Optional garnish: Finely grated Parmesan **OR** pecorino Romano cheese

Egg Noodles with Cabbage, Bacon and Sour Cream

Start to finish: 45 minutes / Servings: 4 to 6

Originating in Poland, where it's known as haluski, this dish combines a few pantry staples into comforting fare that's more than the sum of its parts. Traditional recipes call for cooking the onion and cabbage in ample butter; sometimes bacon is included, which we've done here. In place of butter, we slowly cook the vegetables in the rendered bacon fat until they're tender, caramelized and infused with smoky, meaty flavor. A dash of Worcestershire lends sweet-salty notes that complement the cabbage. Sour cream plus a little starchy noodle cooking water create a tangy, luscious sauce.

4 ounces bacon, chopped

2 tablespoons grapeseed or other neutral oil

1 medium yellow onion, halved and thinly sliced

Kosher salt and ground black pepper

2-pound head green cabbage, quartered lengthwise, cored and chopped into 1-inch pieces

2 tablespoons Worcestershire sauce

12 ounces egg noodles

½ cup sour cream

In a large Dutch oven over medium-high, combine the bacon and oil. Cook, stirring occasionally, until browned and crisp, about 5 minutes. Using a slotted spoon, transfer the bacon to a paper towel–lined plate; set aside.

To the fat in the pot, add the onion and ½ teaspoon salt, then cook, stirring occasionally, until golden brown, 5 to 7 minutes; reduce the heat as needed if the onion browns too quickly. Stir in the cabbage and Worcestershire, cover and cook over medium, stirring occasionally, until the cabbage has softened, 20 to 25 minutes.

In a large saucepan, bring 2 quarts water to a boil. Add the noodles and 1½ teaspoons salt, then cook, stirring occasionally, until al dente. Reserve 1 cup of the cooking water, then drain; set aside.

When the cabbage mixture has softened, reduce to medium-low and stir in the noodles, sour cream, ½ cup of the reserved cooking water and 1 teaspoon pepper. Cook, stirring occasionally, until warmed through and creamy, about 2 minutes, adding more cooking water as needed if the mixture looks dry. Off heat, taste and season with salt and pepper. Serve sprinkled with the reserved bacon.

Optional garnish: Chopped fresh chives **OR** dill

Pasta with Chicken, Green Beans and Harissa

Start to finish: 40 minutes / Servings: 4 to 6

The idea for this one-pot dinner came from macroona mbakbka, which sometimes is called the national dish of Libya. Pasta made its way into Libyan cooking as a result of Italian colonization during the early to mid-20th century, and for mbakbka, it's paired with spices, tomato and chicken (sometimes other types of meat). For our version, we use harissa, a North African spice paste, as a simple way to incorporate both chili heat and a mixture of aromatic spices. We also add green beans to round out the dish. For mild palates or if the harissa you purchase is especially spicy, use the lesser amount; for bolder heat, use the larger quantity, and offer more at the table, too.

1½ pounds boneless, skinless chicken thighs, trimmed and cut into 1-inch pieces

1 to 2 tablespoons harissa paste

Kosher salt and ground black pepper

3 tablespoons extra-virgin olive oil

⅓ cup tomato paste

1 medium yellow onion, chopped

4 medium garlic cloves, minced

¾ teaspoon ground allspice

1 pound medium pasta shells

8 ounces green beans, trimmed and cut into 1-inch pieces

3 cups boiling water

In a large bowl, stir together the chicken, harissa and ¼ teaspoon salt. In a large Dutch oven over medium-high, heat the oil until barely smoking. Add the chicken and cook, stirring occasionally, until the chicken is no longer pink on the surface, about 5 minutes. Using a slotted spoon, return the chicken to the bowl.

To the pot over medium, add the tomato paste and cook, stirring occasionally, until it begins to darken and stick to the bottom, 3 to 5 minutes. Add the onion and ¼ teaspoon salt, then cook, stirring occasionally, until it has softened, about 5 minutes. Stir in the garlic and allspice and cook until fragrant, about 30 seconds.

Add the chicken and any accumulated juices, the pasta and green beans, then stir well. Stir in the boiling water and 1 teaspoon salt. Bring to a boil over medium-high, cover and cook, stirring occasionally, until the pasta is al dente and the mixture is saucy. Taste and season with salt and pepper.

Optional garnish: Chopped fresh flat-leaf parsley **OR** mint

Spaghetti with Lemon Pesto

Start to finish: 25 minutes / Servings: 4

This pasta dish is modeled on the spaghetti al pesto di limone that Giovanna Aceto made for us on her family's farm in Amalfi, Italy. The lemons commonly available in the U.S. are more acidic than Amalfi's lemons, so to make a lemon pesto that approximates the original, we use a little sugar to temper the flavor. For extra citrus complexity, we add lemon zest to the pasta cooking water; the oils from the zest lightly perfume the spaghetti, reinforcing the lemony notes of the pesto.

4 lemons

Kosher salt and ground black pepper

1½ teaspoons white sugar, divided

1 pound spaghetti

½ cup slivered almonds

1 ounce (without rind) Parmesan cheese, cut into rough 1-inch pieces, plus finely grated Parmesan to serve

⅓ cup extra-virgin olive oil, plus more to serve

Using a vegetable peeler (preferably a Y-style peeler), remove the zest from the lemons in long, wide strips; try to remove only the colored portion of the peel, not the bitter white pith just underneath. You should have about ⅔ cup zest strips.

In a large pot, combine 2 quarts water, 1½ teaspoons salt, 1 teaspoon of sugar and half of the zest strips. Bring to a boil and cook for 2 minutes, then remove and discard the zest. Add the spaghetti and cook until al dente. Reserve 1½ cups of the cooking water, then drain the pasta and return it to the pot.

Meanwhile, in a food processor, combine the remaining zest strips, the almonds, Parmesan, the remaining ½ teaspoon sugar and ¼ teaspoon each salt and pepper. Process until the mixture resembles coarse sand, 10 to 20 seconds. Add the oil and process just until the oil is incorporated (the mixture will not be smooth), about another 10 seconds; set aside until the pasta is ready.

To the spaghetti in the pot, add the pesto and ¾ cup of the reserved pasta water, then toss to combine; add more reserved pasta water as needed so the pesto coats the noodles. Taste and season with salt and pepper. Serve drizzled with additional oil and with additional grated Parmesan on the side.

Optional garnish: Finely chopped fresh chives

Pasta with Tomato, Onion and Butter

Start to finish: 35 minutes / Servings: 4 to 6

Marcella Hazan's famous tomato sauce with onion and butter, from her book "The Essentials of Classic Italian Cooking," transforms three simple ingredients into a luscious sauce. Our pantry-focused version replaces the fresh tomatoes with a can of tomato paste to create a dish that can be on the table in minutes. To enhance the sweetness and umami, we finish the sauce with a splash of balsamic vinegar and nutty Parmesan cheese. If you don't have spaghetti, use another type of pasta, such as fettuccine or linguine. Fresh basil, though an optional garnish, is a great addition; if you have it on hand, toss some into the pasta just before serving.

1 pound spaghetti

Kosher salt and ground black pepper

4 tablespoons salted butter, cut into 1-tablespoon pieces, divided

1 small yellow onion, chopped

6-ounce can tomato paste

1 tablespoon balsamic vinegar OR white balsamic vinegar

1 ounce Parmesan cheese, finely grated (½ cup), plus more to serve

In a large pot, bring 4 quarts water to a boil. Add the pasta and 1 tablespoon salt, then cook, stirring occasionally, until al dente. Reserve 2 cups of the cooking water, then drain; set aside.

In the same pot over medium, melt 2 tablespoons butter. Add the onion, reduce to low, cover and cook, stirring occasionally, until the onion has softened, 12 to 14 minutes.

Add the tomato paste, ½ teaspoon pepper and 1½ cups of the reserved cooking water, then whisk until smooth. Add the pasta, the remaining 2 tablespoons butter and the vinegar. Using tongs, toss until the sauce clings to the pasta, the pasta is heated through and the butter is melted, adding more cooking water if needed so the noodles are lightly sauced.

Off heat, toss in the Parmesan, then taste and season with salt and pepper. Serve sprinkled with additional Parmesan.

Optional garnish: Chopped fresh basil

Go-To
GRAINS

Vietnamese Rice Soup with Chicken (Cháo Gà) / 70

Garlic Fried Rice with Chicken / 71

Toasted Bulgur with Walnuts and Pickled Grapes / 72

Two-Cheese Baked Farro with Kale and Tomatoes / 73

Quinoa and Black Bean Burgers / 75

Quinoa Salad with Oranges, Olives and Arugula / 76

Toasted Farro and Apple Salad with Mustard Vinaigrette / 78

Greek-Style Spinach and Tomato Rice / 79

Farro Soup with Celery and Parmesan / 80

Quinoa Chaufa with Mixed Vegetables / 82

Curried Fried Rice with Shrimp and Pineapple / 83

Persian-Style Barley and Carrot Soup / 84

Stir-Fried Grains with Charred Cabbage and Tomatoes / 85

Vietnamese Rice Soup with Chicken (Cháo Gà)

Start to finish: 55 minutes (30 minutes active)
Servings: 4

This hearty bowl of soupy rice is known as cháo in Vietnam and frequently is eaten for breakfast. Seasoned with modest amounts of garlic, ginger and fish sauce, our version is built from simple, satisfying flavors. The soup will continue to thicken as it stands; to adjust the consistency, stir in water or broth a few tablespoons at a time.

2 quarts low-sodium chicken broth	Kosher salt and ground black pepper
1 cup Japanese-style short-grain rice	Two 8- to 10-ounce boneless, skinless chicken breasts
3 medium garlic cloves, finely grated	1 tablespoon fish sauce
2 teaspoons finely grated fresh ginger	½ cup lightly packed fresh cilantro, chopped
1 bunch scallions, thinly sliced, white and green parts reserved separately	

In a large pot over medium-high, combine the broth, rice, garlic, ginger, scallion whites and ½ teaspoon black pepper. Bring to a boil, then add the chicken breasts. Cover, reduce to low and cook, adjusting the heat to maintain a gentle simmer, until the thickest part of the chicken reaches 160°F, 18 to 24 minutes.

Using tongs, transfer the chicken to a medium bowl and set aside. Bring the rice mixture to a rapid simmer over medium, then stir in the fish sauce. Cover and continue to cook, stirring occasionally and adjusting the heat as needed to maintain a simmer, until the broth is thickened and the grains of rice no longer settle beneath the surface, about 20 minutes.

While the rice continues to cook, shred the chicken and set aside. When the rice and broth are ready, taste and season with salt and pepper, then ladle into individual bowls. Top with shredded chicken, scallion greens, cilantro and additional pepper.

Garlic Fried Rice
with Chicken

Start to finish: 35 minutes / Servings: 4

This is our take on the Filipino dish known as sinangag, a stir-fried rice chock-full of crisp, toasted garlic. Sliced garlic is browned slowly, creating golden garlic chips to mix into the rice at the end, along with a flavorful oil that infuses the entire dish. Sinangag typically is served as a side, but we add chicken to transform it into a main. For best texture, use cooked rice that's been refrigerated until firm. To make enough rice for this recipe, in a large saucepan, combine 2 cups water and 1½ cups jasmine rice (or regular long-grain white rice), rinsed and drained. Bring to a simmer over medium-high, then reduce to low, cover and cook for 15 to 18 minutes. Let stand, covered, for 10 minutes, then transfer to a wide, shallow bowl. Cool to room temperature, then cover and refrigerate until well chilled.

8 ounces boneless, skinless chicken thighs, trimmed and cut into ½- to ¾-inch pieces

2 tablespoons soy sauce, divided

½ teaspoon white sugar

Kosher salt and ground black pepper

3 tablespoons grapeseed or other neutral oil, divided

8 medium garlic cloves, thinly sliced

3 scallions, thinly sliced, white and green parts reserved separately

4 cups cooked and chilled long-grain white rice, preferably jasmine rice (see headnote)

In a medium bowl, stir together the chicken, 1 tablespoon soy sauce, the sugar and ¼ teaspoon salt. In a 12-inch nonstick skillet over medium-high, heat 1 tablespoon oil until shimmering. Add the chicken in an even layer and cook without stirring until browned on the bottom, 2 to 3 minutes. Stir the chicken, then cook, stirring occasionally, until well browned all over and cooked through, another 2 to 3 minutes. Transfer the chicken to a plate; set aside.

Wash and dry the skillet. Set it over medium-low and add the remaining 2 tablespoons oil and the garlic. Cook, stirring only occasionally at first then more often once the garlic begins to color, until some of the slices are light golden brown, about 5 minutes. Add the scallion whites and cook, stirring, until most of the garlic is golden brown, about 2 minutes.

Add the rice, breaking up any clumps, followed by the remaining 1 tablespoon soy sauce and ¼ teaspoon salt. Cook over medium-high, stirring and scraping the bottom of the pan to incorporate the garlic and any browned bits, until the rice is heated through, about 2 minutes. Add the chicken and any accumulated juices; cook, stirring, until warmed through, about 1 minute.

Off heat, taste and season with salt. Transfer to a serving dish, then sprinkle with the scallion greens and pepper.

Toasted Bulgur with Walnuts and Pickled Grapes

Start to finish: 40 minutes / Servings: 4 to 6

We combine bulgur with quick-pickled grapes and red onion for pops of sweet-tart flavor. Both the bulgur and the walnuts are toasted to bring out their nutty taste. The recipe calls for coarse bulgur, which has a pleasantly chewy bite. Serve at room temperature alongside roasted or grilled chicken, meat or fish.

8 ounces seedless red OR green grapes, halved (1½ cups)

1 small red OR yellow onion, halved and thinly sliced

3 tablespoons cider vinegar

Kosher salt and ground black pepper

½ cup walnuts OR pecans OR almonds

1 cup coarse bulgur

2 tablespoons extra-virgin olive oil

2 cups lightly packed fresh flat-leaf parsley OR mint, roughly chopped

In a large bowl, stir together the grapes, onion, vinegar and ½ teaspoon each salt and pepper; set aside.

In a large saucepan over medium, toast the walnuts, stirring often, until fragrant and lightly browned, 2 to 3 minutes. Transfer to a cutting board; reserve the saucepan. Let the nuts cool slightly, then roughly chop; set aside.

In the same saucepan over medium, toast the bulgur, stirring often, until fragrant, about 1 minute. Add 2 cups water and bring to a simmer over medium-high, stirring occasionally. Cover, reduce to low and cook until all of the water has been absorbed, 12 to 15 minutes. Remove the pan from the heat, uncover and let the bulgur cool slightly, stirring occasionally, for 10 to 15 minutes.

Add the bulgur to the bowl with the grapes and onion; toss to combine. Stir in the oil, parsley and half of the walnuts. Taste and season with salt and pepper. Serve sprinkled with the remaining walnuts.

Optional garnish: Crumbled feta cheese OR blue cheese OR fresh goat cheese (chèvre)

SHELF STALWARTS

Two-Cheese Baked Farro with Kale and Tomatoes

Start to finish: 1 hour 10 minutes (20 minutes active), plus cooling / Servings: 6 to 8

Though it's typically simmered with liquid on the stovetop, farro also does well in the oven—a mostly hands-off approach that's easy on the cook. First, we toast the grains to enhance their nutty taste, then bake them until tender in a tomato sauce seasoned with red pepper flakes and dried herbs. Kale lends earthy flavor to the mix. For lots of cheesy goodness, this one-pot dish is topped with mozzarella and Parmesan.

1½ cups pearled farro

4 tablespoons extra-virgin olive oil, divided

1 bunch lacinato kale OR curly kale, stemmed and chopped into rough 1-inch pieces (8 cups) OR 8 ounces Brussels sprouts, trimmed and sliced (4 cups)

4 medium garlic cloves, thinly sliced

Kosher salt and ground black pepper

28-ounce can crushed tomatoes

1 teaspoon dried oregano OR dried thyme OR 2 bay leaves

¼ to ½ teaspoon red pepper flakes

8 ounces mozzarella OR Swiss OR provolone cheese, shredded (2 cups)

2 ounces Parmesan OR Asiago cheese, finely grated (1 cup)

Heat the oven to 425°F with a rack in the lower-middle position. In a large Dutch oven over medium-high, combine the farro and 2 tablespoons oil. Cook, stirring often, until toasted, 3 to 5 minutes. Add the kale, garlic and ½ teaspoon each salt and pepper. Cook, stirring occasionally, until the kale is bright green and slightly wilted, about 2 minutes. Stir in the tomatoes, oregano, pepper flakes and 3 cups water, then bring to a boil. Cover and transfer to the oven.

Bake for 30 minutes, then remove from the oven and uncover. The mixture will have thickened slightly but still will be soupy. Stir, then sprinkle evenly with the mozzarella and Parmesan. Drizzle with the remaining 2 tablespoons oil. Return to the oven, uncovered, and bake until browned and bubbling and the farro is very tender, about 20 minutes; the mixture will be slightly stewy but will thicken as it cools. Cool for about 10 minutes before serving.

Quinoa and Black Bean Burgers

Start to finish: 1½ hours (20 minutes active)
Servings: 6

Pan-fried until browned and crisp, these vegetarian burgers are terrific sandwiched between buns with your favorite fixings, but also are satisfying on their own with a tossed green salad. Canned black beans lend a meaty, substantial texture and help bind the ingredients together. White, red or rainbow (tricolor) quinoa all work well, so use whatever you have. If you purchased pre-rinsed quinoa, there's no need to rinse and drain it before cooking.

⅓ cup quinoa
(see headnote), rinsed
and drained

Kosher salt and
ground black pepper

15½-ounce can black
beans, drained but
not rinsed

1 large egg, lightly beaten

½ cup panko breadcrumbs

2 scallions,
finely chopped

½ teaspoon ground cumin

½ teaspoon smoked
paprika OR chipotle chili
powder

3 tablespoons grapeseed
or other neutral oil

In a medium saucepan, stir together the quinoa, a pinch of salt and ⅔ cup water. Bring to a boil over medium-high, then cover, reduce to low and cook without stirring until the quinoa absorbs the liquid, 13 to 15 minutes. Remove the pan from the heat, then drape a kitchen towel across the pan and re-cover. Let stand for 10 minutes. Fluff the quinoa with a fork, transfer to a small plate and cool to room temperature, stirring once or twice, about 30 minutes.

In a large bowl, using a fork or a potato masher, coarsely mash the black beans. Add the quinoa, egg, panko, scallions, cumin, paprika and ½ teaspoon each salt and pepper; stir until well combined. Form into six 3-inch patties and place on a large plate. Refrigerate, uncovered, to firm up the patties, about 15 minutes.

In a 12-inch nonstick skillet over medium-high, heat the oil until barely smoking. Add the patties and cook until browned and crisp on the bottoms, about 5 minutes. Using a wide spatula, flip the patties and cook until browned and crisp on the second sides, about another 2 minutes.

Optional garnish: Sliced cheese OR sliced tomato OR sliced onion OR lettuce leaves OR sliced pickles OR mayonnaise OR a combination

Quinoa Salad with Oranges, Olives and Arugula

Start to finish: 1 hour (30 minutes active)
Servings: 4 to 6

Quinoa actually is a seed, but it can be cooked and eaten like a grain. In this salad, sweet, juicy oranges complement the earthy flavor of the quinoa. We add olives for a briny note plus a handful of tender greens for color and freshness. Use whatever type of quinoa you'd like—white, red or rainbow (tricolor) all work well. If the quinoa you purchased is pre-rinsed, there's no need to rinse and drain it before cooking. Serve on its own as a light main or as a side to seafood, chicken or pork.

3 tablespoons red wine vinegar OR cider vinegar

3 tablespoons extra-virgin olive oil

½ teaspoon dried oregano

Kosher salt and ground black pepper

2 oranges

1 small red OR yellow onion, halved and thinly sliced

½ cup pitted black OR green olives, halved

1 cup quinoa (see headnote), rinsed and drained

2½ ounces (4 cups lightly packed) baby arugula OR baby spinach OR spring mix

In a large bowl, whisk together the vinegar, oil, oregano and ½ teaspoon each salt and pepper; set aside.

Using a vegetable peeler (preferably a Y-style peeler), remove 2 pieces of zest from 1 of the oranges in long, wide strips; try to remove only the colored portion of the peel, not the bitter white pith just underneath; set aside. Using a sharp knife, slice ½ inch off the top and bottom of each orange. One at a time, stand an orange on a cut end and cut from top to bottom following the contours of the fruit to remove the peel and white pith. Cut the oranges lengthwise into quarters, then thinly slice crosswise, reserving all of the juices.

Add the orange slices and accumulated juices to the dressing, along with the onion and olives. Toss to combine, then set aside.

In a medium saucepan, stir together the quinoa, zest strips, ½ teaspoon salt and 2 cups water. Bring to a boil over medium-high, then cover, reduce to low and cook without stirring until the quinoa absorbs the liquid, 13 to 15 minutes. Remove the pan from heat, then drape a kitchen towel across the pan and re-cover. Let stand for 10 minutes. Fluff the quinoa with a fork, transfer to a large plate and let cool, stirring once or twice, until barely warm to the touch, about 30 minutes.

Remove and discard the zest strips from the quinoa. Transfer the quinoa to the bowl with the oranges, then toss to combine. Add the arugula and toss again. Taste and season with salt and pepper.

Optional garnish: Crumbled feta cheese OR fresh goat cheese (chèvre) OR toasted walnuts OR toasted sliced almonds

Toasted Farro and Apple Salad with Mustard Vinaigrette

Start to finish: 1 hour (30 minutes active)
Servings: 4 to 6

This autumnal salad matches toothsome farro with tangy-sweet apple, crisp celery and pungent onion that's mellowed by briefly steeping it in the mustard vinaigrette. Be sure the farro is still warm when it's dressed. As it cools, the grains absorb flavor. The salad is delicious served cold or at room temperature.

1 cup pearled farro

Kosher salt and ground black pepper

3 tablespoons cider vinegar OR white wine vinegar

2 teaspoons Dijon mustard OR whole-grain mustard

3 tablespoons extra-virgin olive oil

½ small red OR yellow onion, finely chopped

1 large apple, cored and cut in ½-inch cubes

2 medium celery stalks, chopped

1 cup lightly packed fresh flat-leaf parsley OR mint OR dill OR a combination, roughly chopped

In a large saucepan over medium, toast the farro, stirring, until lightly browned and fragrant, about 3 minutes. Add 1 quart water and 1 teaspoon salt; stir. Bring to a simmer over medium-high, then reduce to medium and simmer, uncovered and stirring once or twice, until the farro is tender with a little chew, 25 to 30 minutes.

Meanwhile, in a large bowl, whisk together the vinegar, mustard, oil and ½ teaspoon each salt and pepper. Stir in the onion; set aside. When the farro is done, drain in a colander; cool for 5 to 10 minutes.

Add the still-warm farro to the dressing mixture and toss. Let stand until cooled to room temperature, tossing once or twice. Add the apple, celery and parsley; toss to combine. Taste and season with salt and pepper.

Optional garnish: Sliced radishes OR crumbled fresh goat cheese (chèvre) OR toasted walnuts OR a combination

Greek-Style Spinach and Tomato Rice

Start to finish: 40 minutes / Servings: 4

Spanakorizo, or spinach rice, is a classic home-style Greek dish. For our version, instead of long-grain rice, we use medium-grain Arborio rice to achieve a creamy, velvety consistency similar to Italian risotto. We also cook the rice using a method similar to our risotto technique, adding boiling liquid to the grains in multiple batches and stirring vigorously to heighten their starchiness. The rice gets depth of flavor and a rusty hue from tomato paste that's sautéed until it begins to caramelize. If you have feta, crumble some on just before serving; the cheese adds a welcome tang and creamy richness.

2 tablespoons
extra-virgin olive oil

1 medium yellow onion,
finely chopped

3 tablespoons
tomato paste

3 medium garlic cloves,
minced

1 cup Arborio rice

Kosher salt and
ground black pepper

4 cups boiling water,
divided

5-ounce container baby
spinach, roughly chopped

2 teaspoons grated lemon
zest, plus 2 tablespoons
lemon juice

¼ cup finely chopped
fresh flat-leaf parsley
OR dill

In a 12-inch nonstick skillet over medium, combine the oil and onion; cook, stirring occasionally, until the onion has softened, about 10 minutes. Add the tomato paste and cook, stirring, until the paste begins to brown, about 2 minutes. Add the garlic and cook, stirring, until fragrant, about 30 seconds.

Add the rice, 1 teaspoon salt and ½ teaspoon pepper; stir until the grains are well combined with the tomato paste. Add 3 cups of the boiling water and bring to a simmer over medium-high. Reduce to medium and cook, uncovered and stirring often and briskly, until most of the liquid has been absorbed, 8 to 10 minutes.

Add ½ cup of the remaining boiling water and simmer, stirring often and briskly, until the rice is al dente and the consistency is creamy but still quite loose, 8 to 10 minutes. If the rice is thick and dry but the grains are still too firm, add some of the remaining boiling water and cook, stirring, until the rice is al dente.

Off heat, add the spinach, lemon zest and juice, and half of the parsley. Stir until the spinach is wilted, then taste and season with salt and pepper. Serve sprinkled with the remaining parsley.

Optional garnish: Crumbled feta cheese

Farro Soup with Celery and Parmesan

Start to finish: 1 hour (25 minutes active)
Servings: 4

This soup is remarkably flavorful, though it's made with just a handful of basic ingredients. It features farro, an ancient wheat grain that boasts a pleasantly chewy texture and nutty taste. Be sure to use pearled farro; the grains have had the bran removed, which speeds up the cooking. Quick-cooking barley is a great alternative to farro. To boost the umami, we first brown tomato paste, then finish the soup with grated Parmesan. If you have a Parmesan rind on hand, add it to the simmering soup to deepen the flavor.

3 tablespoons
extra-virgin olive oil

1 medium yellow onion,
halved and thinly sliced

4 medium celery stalks,
thinly sliced

1 teaspoon dried rosemary
OR dried thyme

Kosher salt and
ground black pepper

2 tablespoons
tomato paste

1 cup pearled farro OR
quick-cooking barley

1-inch piece Parmesan
rind (optional), plus
2 ounces Parmesan
cheese, finely grated
(1 cup)

2 quarts low-sodium
chicken broth OR
vegetable broth

In a large saucepan over medium-high, heat the oil until shimmering. Add the onion, celery, rosemary, ¼ teaspoon salt and ½ teaspoon pepper. Reduce to medium and cook, stirring often, until the vegetables begin to release their moisture, about 2 minutes. Reduce to medium-low, cover and cook, stirring occasionally, until the vegetables are softened but not browned, 10 to 15 minutes.

Add the tomato paste and cook over medium-high, stirring, until the paste browns and slightly sticks to the pan, about 2 minutes. Add the farro and stir until the grains are well combined with the paste. Add the Parmesan rind (if using) and the broth. Bring to a simmer, then reduce to medium and simmer, uncovered, stirring once or twice, until the farro is tender with a little chew, 25 to 30 minutes.

Off heat, remove and discard the Parmesan rind (if used). Taste and season with salt and pepper. Serve sprinkled with the Parmesan and a generous grind of pepper.

Optional garnish: Basil pesto

Quinoa Chaufa with Mixed Vegetables

Start to finish: 45 minutes, plus cooling
Servings: 4 to 6

Chaufa is Peruvian fried rice, a standard dish in chifa cuisine, which fuses Peruvian and Chinese cooking. But these days it's common to find chaufa that replaces the rice with more nutrient-dense quinoa, a seed native to the Andean region. You'll get the lightest, fluffiest texture if the quinoa is cooked and cooled before stir-frying. An efficient way to approach this recipe is to prep the vegetables and other ingredients while the quinoa cools, or if you like to plan ahead, you can prepare the quinoa a day or two in advance and refrigerate it until you're ready to make the chaufa.

¾ cup quinoa, rinsed and drained

Kosher salt and ground black pepper

4 tablespoons grapeseed or other neutral oil, divided

8 ounces broccoli florets, chopped into ½- to 1-inch pieces OR green beans, trimmed and cut into 1-inch lengths OR a combination

1 small red bell pepper, stemmed, seeded and thinly sliced OR 4 ounces snow peas, trimmed

2 tablespoons minced fresh ginger

2 medium garlic cloves, minced OR 1 bunch scallions, whites thinly sliced, greens sliced about ½ inch thick, reserved separately

2 large eggs, beaten

2 tablespoons soy sauce

1 tablespoon hoisin OR oyster sauce

In a medium saucepan, stir together the quinoa, ½ teaspoon salt and 1½ cups water. Bring to a boil over medium-high, then cover, reduce to low and cook without stirring until the quinoa absorbs the liquid, 13 to 15 minutes. Remove the pan from the heat, drape a kitchen towel across the top, then re-cover. Let stand for 10 minutes. Fluff the quinoa with a fork, transfer to a large plate and cool to room temperature, stirring once or twice.

In a 12-inch nonstick skillet over medium-high, heat 2 tablespoons oil until barely smoking. Add the broccoli and cook, stirring just once or twice, until beginning to char at the edges, 2 to 3 minutes. Add the bell pepper, ginger, garlic (or scallion whites) and ½ teaspoon pepper. Cook, stirring occasionally, until the vegetables are lightly browned, 3 to 5 minutes.

Stir in the quinoa, then distribute the mixture in an even layer. Cook without stirring until you hear crackling and sizzling, about 30 seconds. Stir, distribute again in an even layer and cook until you once again hear crackling and sizzling, about another 30 seconds.

Push the mixture to one side of the skillet. Add the remaining 2 tablespoons oil to the clearing and heat until shimmering. Add the eggs to the clearing and cook, stirring just the eggs, until set but still glossy and shiny, 20 to 30 seconds. Now stir the eggs into the quinoa mixture, breaking them into small bits.

Add the soy sauce and hoisin; cook, stirring, until the skillet is dry and the chaufa is sizzling, about 2 minutes. Off heat, stir in the scallion greens (if using), then taste and season with salt and pepper.

Optional garnish: Toasted sesame oil **OR** chopped fresh cilantro **OR** Sriracha sauce **OR** a combination

Curried Fried Rice with Shrimp and Pineapple

Start to finish: 35 minutes / Servings: 4

Fried rice takes to endless variations. In this version, bits of pineapple provide bursts of sweetness and jalapeño chili lends heat, a nice contrast to the briny shrimp. Using chilled rice is key, as the firm grains will separate easily, yielding light and fluffy fried rice. To cook enough rice for this recipe, in a large saucepan, combine 2 cups water and 1½ cups jasmine rice (or regular long-grain white rice), rinsed and drained. Bring to a simmer over medium-high, then reduce to low, cover and cook for 15 to 18 minutes. Let stand, covered, for 10 minutes, then transfer to a wide, shallow bowl. Cool to room temperature, cover and refrigerate until fully chilled.

3 tablespoons grapeseed or other neutral oil, divided

1 bunch scallions, thinly sliced, white and green parts reserved separately

1 jalapeño chili, stemmed and sliced into thin rounds, plus more to serve

2 teaspoons curry powder

8 ounces medium (41/50 per pound) shrimp, peeled, deveined (tails removed), halved crosswise and patted dry

Kosher salt and ground black pepper

1 cup drained juice-packed canned pineapple tidbits OR chunks OR chopped slices OR thawed frozen pineapple chunks OR chopped fresh pineapple

2 tablespoons fish sauce OR soy sauce

4 cups cooked and chilled long-grain white rice, preferably jasmine rice

⅓ cup roasted salted cashews, roughly chopped OR roasted salted peanuts

In a 12-inch nonstick skillet over medium-high, heat 2 tablespoons oil until shimmering. Add the scallion whites and jalapeño; cook, stirring often, until starting to brown, about 2 minutes. Stir in the curry powder, then stir in the shrimp and ¼ teaspoon salt; distribute the shrimp in a single layer. Cook without stirring until beginning to brown, about 1 minute. Stir, then cook without stirring until the shrimp are opaque throughout, another 30 seconds. Transfer the shrimp to a medium bowl; set aside.

In the same skillet over medium-high, heat the remaining 1 tablespoon oil until shimmering. Add the pineapple, fish sauce, rice and ¼ teaspoon salt, breaking up any clumps of rice. Cook, stirring and scraping the bottom of the pan to incorporate any browned bits, until the pineapple and rice are heated through, about 2 minutes. Stir in the shrimp and accumulated juices.

Off heat, stir in the cashews and scallion greens. Taste and season with salt and pepper. Transfer to a serving dish and garnish with additional jalapeño.

Optional garnish: Lime wedges OR chopped fresh cilantro OR both

Persian-Style Barley and Carrot Soup

Start to finish: 35 minutes / Servings: 4

In this riff on Persian soup e jo, we toast the barley in a dry pan to bring out rich, nutty flavor. Be sure to use quick-cooking barley, which resembles rolled oats; it softens much more quickly than pearled barley. Traditional soup e jo often is thickened with a béchamel sauce. We use sour cream, tempering it with a little of the hot broth and whisking it in off heat to prevent curdling. Sometimes pleasantly tart barberries garnish the soup, though easier-to-find dried currants or cranberries also are delicious. For an even heartier dish, rinse and drain a 15½-ounce can of kidney beans, then add them to the broth after the barley has cooked for 5 minutes.

1 cup quick-cooking barley (see headnote)

2 tablespoons extra-virgin olive oil

3 medium carrots, peeled and finely shredded on the small holes of a box grater

Kosher salt and ground black pepper

1 teaspoon ground turmeric

1 quart low-sodium chicken broth

¼ cup dried cranberries, roughly chopped OR dried currants

⅓ cup sour cream, plus more to serve

2 teaspoons lemon juice OR lime juice

In a large saucepan over medium-high, toast the barley, stirring occasionally, until lightly browned, 4 to 5 minutes. Transfer to a small bowl; set aside. In the same pan over medium-low, add the oil, carrots and ¼ teaspoon salt. Cover and cook, stirring often, until the carrots have softened, 5 to 8 minutes.

Stir in the barley, turmeric, broth and 2 cups water. Bring to a boil over medium-high, then reduce to medium-low, cover and simmer, stirring occasionally, until the barley is tender, 10 to 12 minutes.

Remove the pan from the heat and stir in the cranberries. In a small bowl, whisk together the sour cream and about ½ cup of the soup, then slowly whisk this mixture into the pan. Cover and let stand for 5 minutes. Stir in the lemon juice, then taste and season with salt and pepper. Serve topped with additional sour cream.

Optional garnish: Chopped fresh mint **OR** chopped fresh flat-leaf parsley

Stir-Fried Grains with Charred Cabbage and Tomatoes

Start to finish: 30 minutes / Servings: 4

A type of Indian vegetable stir-fry called thoran inspired this mix of grain and vegetables. We like nutty, firm-textured farro, but brown rice also is good. Either way, you'll need 4 cups of cooked grain; be sure to allow it to cool to room temperature or even chill it before stir-frying. Cabbage is our first choice for this dish, but other lower-moisture vegetables, such as green beans or Brussels sprouts, also are good.

4 tablespoons grapeseed or other neutral oil, divided

8 ounces green cabbage, cored and chopped into rough 1-inch pieces (about 4 cups) OR 8 ounces green beans, cut into 1-inch lengths OR 8 ounces Brussels sprouts, trimmed and shredded OR a combination

Kosher salt and ground black pepper

1 small yellow onion, halved and thinly sliced

1 tablespoon cumin seeds OR mustard seeds OR a combination

3 medium garlic cloves, minced

2 teaspoons curry powder

4 cups cooked and cooled farro OR brown rice

1 pint grape OR cherry tomatoes, halved

1 tablespoon lime juice OR lemon juice

In a 12-inch nonstick skillet over medium-high, heat 2 tablespoons oil until barely smoking. Add the cabbage, ¾ teaspoon salt and ½ teaspoon pepper. Cook, stirring only once or twice, until the cabbage is lightly charred, 2 to 3 minutes. Stir in the onion and cumin seeds; cook, stirring occasionally, until the vegetables are well charred, 3 to 5 minutes.

Add the remaining 2 tablespoons oil, the garlic and curry powder. Cook, stirring, until fragrant, about 30 seconds. Stir in the farro, breaking up any lumps. Distribute the mixture in an even layer and cook without stirring until you hear sizzling, about 30 seconds. Stir, distribute again in an even layer and cook until you once again hear sizzling, about another 30 seconds.

Add the tomatoes and cook, stirring occasionally, until the tomatoes are softened, 3 to 4 minutes. Off heat, stir in the lime juice. Taste and season with salt and pepper.

Optional garnish: Chopped toasted nuts **OR** plain yogurt **OR** chopped fresh cilantro **OR** a combination

Lentils
SIX WAYS

Rice and Lentils with Onion Tarka / 88

Lentil Salad with Tahini, Almonds and Pomegranate Molasses / 89

Red Lentil and Coconut Dal with Ginger-Garlic Tarka / 90

Spanish-Style Lentil Stew with Garlic and Smoked Paprika / 92

Braised Sausages and Lentils with Parsley-Caper Relish / 93

Umbrian-Style Lentil Soup / 94

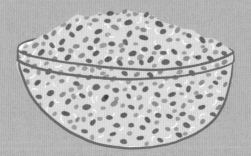

Rice and Lentils with Onion Tarka

Start to finish: 45 minutes (15 minutes active), plus soaking / Servings: 4 to 6

To create this soul-satisfying dish, we took inspiration from the Indian rice and lentil dish known as kitchari. We finish our version with onion tarka, which features spices that are bloomed in hot oil to release their fragrance and flavor. Tarka typically is made with whole spices; we call for a cinnamon stick, cloves and cumin seeds, but feel free to mix and match the seasonings depending on what's in your pantry. Take the time to first soak the rice and lentils in salted water, as this helps them to cook up light and separate.

1 cup long-grain white rice, preferably basmati rice

⅓ cup red lentils **OR** brown lentils **OR** yellow split peas

Kosher salt and ground black pepper

¾ teaspoon ground turmeric, divided

¼ cup grapeseed or other neutral oil **OR** ghee

1 medium red **OR** yellow onion, halved and thinly sliced

1 cinnamon stick **OR** 2 bay leaves **OR** both

2 whole cloves **OR** ¼ teaspoon ground cardamom **OR** both

1 teaspoon cumin seeds **OR** mustard seeds **OR** fennel seeds **OR** a combination, lightly crushed

1 jalapeño **OR** serrano **OR** Fresno chili, stemmed and minced

In a medium bowl, combine the rice, lentils and 1½ teaspoons salt. Add water to cover by 1 inch, then stir. Let stand for at least 30 minutes or up to 2 hours.

Drain the rice and lentils in a fine-mesh strainer, then rinse under cool running water and drain again. Transfer to a medium saucepan; stir in ½ teaspoon turmeric, ½ teaspoon each salt and pepper and 2 cups water. Bring to a boil over medium-high, then cover, reduce to low and cook without stirring until all of the water has been absorbed and the rice and lentils are tender, about 20 minutes. Remove from the heat and let stand, covered, for 10 minutes.

While the rice rests, in a small skillet over medium-high, heat the oil until shimmering or melt the ghee. Add the onion and cinnamon stick, then cook, stirring often, until the onion begins to brown, about 3 minutes. Add the cloves and cumin seeds; cook, stirring occasionally, until the onion is softened and browned, 6 to 8 minutes. Immediately remove from the heat, then stir in the chili and remaining ¼ teaspoon turmeric. Remove and discard the cinnamon or cloves (if used).

Using a fork, fluff the rice-lentil mixture. Taste and season with salt and pepper. Transfer to a serving bowl or to individual bowls, then pour on the spice mixture, including the oil.

Optional garnish: Chopped fresh cilantro **OR** chopped roasted cashews **OR** plain whole-milk yogurt **OR** a combination

Lentil Salad with Tahini, Almonds and Pomegranate Molasses

Start to finish: 1 hour (15 minutes active) / Servings: 4

Made with creamy tahini, toasted almonds and sweet-and-sour pomegranate molasses, this lentil salad boasts layers of complex flavor. Spice cabinet staples like smoked paprika or cumin work beautifully to enhance the earthiness of the lentils. If you have baharat in your pantry, by all means, use it instead. This blend of warm and savory spices, popular in Middle Eastern cooking, usually includes cardamom, coriander, cloves and cumin; you'll find baharat in many supermarkets. We dress the salad while still warm and let it stand so the lentils absorb the seasonings.

¼ cup extra-virgin olive oil

½ medium yellow onion OR 2 medium shallots, halved and thinly sliced

¼ cup sliced almonds

Kosher salt and ground black pepper

1 teaspoon smoked paprika OR ground cumin OR baharat

1 cup brown lentils OR green lentils, rinsed and drained

3 tablespoons tahini

2 tablespoons lemon juice

1 tablespoon pomegranate molasses, plus more to serve

¾ cup chopped fresh flat-leaf parsley OR chopped fresh cilantro OR thinly sliced scallions OR a combination

In a large saucepan over medium-high, heat the oil until shimmering. Add the onion and cook, stirring often, until browned at the edges, about 3 minutes. Add the almonds and a pinch each of salt and pepper, then cook, stirring often, until the almonds are lightly browned, about 2 minutes. Add the paprika and cook, stirring, until fragrant, about 30 seconds. Using a slotted spoon, transfer the onion-almond mixture to a paper towel–lined plate. Pour the spiced oil into a medium bowl; set aside.

In the same saucepan, combine the lentils, ½ teaspoon salt, 1 teaspoon pepper and 5 cups water. Bring to a simmer over medium-high, then reduce to medium and simmer, uncovered and stirring occasionally, until the lentils are tender but still hold their shape, 15 to 20 minutes; drain.

To the spiced oil, whisk in the tahini and 2 tablespoons water until smooth. Whisk in the lemon juice and pomegranate molasses, then stir in the lentils. Let stand for at least 15 minutes.

Stir in half each of the parsley and onion-almond mixture, then taste and season with salt and pepper. Garnish with the remaining parsley, onion-almond mixture and a drizzle of additional pomegranate molasses.

Optional garnish: Seeded and minced jalapeño chili OR pomegranate seeds OR both

Red Lentil and Coconut Dal with Ginger-Garlic Tarka

Start to finish: 40 minutes (20 minutes active)
Servings: 4

Our version of dal, the classic Indian lentil stew, gets creamy richness from coconut milk plus a double dose of garlic and ginger: The aromatics season the lentils as they simmer and also are used to make an infused oil, known as tarka, that's poured over the finished dish to add a final layer of flavor. To prep the ginger for the tarka, first cut thin slices, then stack them and cut them into slender matchsticks. We call for red lentils because they cook quickly and break down into a rustic but velvety puree.

4 tablespoons grapeseed or other neutral oil, divided

8 medium garlic cloves, minced

3 thin slices fresh ginger, plus 2 tablespoons ginger matchsticks (see headnote), reserved separately

1 cup red lentils

2 teaspoons ground turmeric

Kosher salt and ground black pepper

14-ounce can coconut milk

¾ cup chopped fresh cilantro

1 tablespoon cumin seeds

½ teaspoon red pepper flakes

In a large saucepan over medium, combine 1 tablespoon oil, half the garlic and the sliced ginger. When the mixture sizzles, cook, stirring, until the garlic begins to brown, 1 to 2 minutes. Stir in the lentils, turmeric, 2 teaspoons salt, ½ teaspoon black pepper and 3 cups water. Bring to a boil over medium-high, then reduce to medium and simmer, uncovered and stirring occasionally, for 10 minutes. Stir in the coconut milk and cook, whisking occasionally, until the lentils are tender and have broken down, about another 10 minutes.

Off heat, taste and season with salt and black pepper. Remove and discard the ginger slices, then transfer the dal to a serving bowl and sprinkle with about two-thirds of the cilantro.

To make the tarka, in a small saucepan over medium-high, combine the remaining 3 tablespoons oil and the cumin seeds. Cook, swirling the pan often, until the seeds begin to sizzle, 45 to 90 seconds. Add the remaining garlic, ginger matchsticks and pepper flakes; cook, swirling the pan often, until fragrant, about 1 minute. Pour the tarka over the lentils, then sprinkle with the remaining cilantro.

Optional garnish: Lemon wedges **OR** chopped roasted cashews **OR** both

Spanish-Style Lentil Stew with Garlic and Smoked Paprika

Start to finish: 1½ hours (20 minutes active)
Servings: 4 to 6

Warming lentil stews are common throughout Spain, where they're often enriched with chorizo, a spiced dry-cured sausage. In this recipe, we mimic chorizo's smoky, savory flavor with a combination of bacon and smoked paprika. We also simmer a whole head of garlic in the mix—it mellows and sweetens with long, slow cooking, infusing the stew with a subtle garlicky flavor that complements the earthy lentils. Round out the meal with a salad of bitter greens and a loaf of crusty bread.

4 ounces bacon, chopped

1 tablespoon extra-virgin olive oil

1 medium yellow onion, chopped

2 teaspoons smoked paprika, plus more to serve

Kosher salt and ground black pepper

14½-ounce can diced tomatoes, drained, juices reserved

1¼ cups brown OR green lentils, rinsed and drained

1 head garlic, outer papery skins removed, top third cut off and discarded

1 medium red OR orange bell pepper, stemmed, seeded and chopped OR 2 medium carrots, peeled and thinly sliced

1 cup lightly packed fresh flat-leaf parsley, chopped

In a large pot over medium-high, cook the bacon, stirring occasionally, until browned and crisp, 3 to 5 minutes. Using a slotted spoon, transfer to a paper towel–lined plate; set aside. Pour off and discard all but 1 tablespoon of the fat in the pot.

Return the pot to medium-high, add the oil and heat until shimmering. Add the onion, paprika, ½ teaspoon salt and ¼ teaspoon pepper. Cook, stirring often, until the onion begins to brown and soften, about 3 minutes. Add the tomato juices and scrape up the browned bits, then cook, stirring, until the juices are reduced and syrupy, about 2 minutes.

Stir in the lentils, the drained tomatoes, garlic and 6 cups water. Bring to a simmer, then reduce to medium and cook, uncovered and stirring occasionally, until the lentils are tender but not falling apart, about 25 minutes. Add the bell pepper and simmer, uncovered and stirring occasionally, until the lentils are fully softened and beginning to break down, 20 to 25 minutes.

Off heat, using tongs, squeeze the garlic cloves from the head into the lentil mixture; discard the empty skins. Stir the stew, mashing some of the garlic and lentils against the side of the pot to thicken slightly. Stir in half each of the parsley and bacon. Taste and season with salt and pepper. Serve sprinkled with the remaining parsley and bacon and additional paprika (if desired).

Braised Sausages and Lentils with Parsley-Caper Relish

Start to finish: 55 minutes (20 minutes active)
Servings: 4

The classic combination of sausages and lentils makes a satisfying meal on a cold winter day. There are many ways to prepare the dish; we use a skillet, start to finish. Dark-green French lentils du Puy, which hold their shape beautifully when fully cooked, take their time to soften compared to other types of lentils, so they need to simmer for 20 minutes before the browned sausages are added to the pan. A quick lemon, caper and parsley relish served alongside adds a welcome pop of tangy, herbal and citrusy flavor.

4 tablespoons extra-virgin olive oil, divided	1 cup lentils du Puy, rinsed and drained
1 pound sweet OR hot Italian sausages	1 teaspoon grated lemon zest, plus 1 tablespoon lemon juice
2 medium carrots, peeled and chopped	2 cups lightly packed fresh flat-leaf parsley, finely chopped
1 small red OR yellow onion, chopped	1 tablespoon drained capers, chopped
Kosher salt and ground black pepper	
4 medium garlic cloves, minced	

In a 12-inch skillet over medium-high, heat 1 tablespoon oil until shimmering. Add the sausages and cook, turning occasionally, until browned on all sides, 4 to 6 minutes. Transfer to a plate.

To the fat in the skillet, add the carrots, onion, and ½ teaspoon each salt and pepper. Reduce to medium and cook, stirring occasionally, until the vegetables begin to soften, 5 to 7 minutes. Stir in the garlic, lentils and 2 cups water, then bring to a simmer over medium-high. Cover, reduce to medium-low and simmer, stirring occasionally, for 20 minutes (the lentils will be only partially cooked).

Place the sausages on the lentils, re-cover and cook until the lentils are tender and the sausages reach 160°F, 23 to 25 minutes.

Meanwhile, in a small bowl, whisk together the lemon zest and juice and the remaining 3 tablespoons oil. Stir in the parsley and capers; set aside until ready to serve.

When the lentils and sausages are done, remove the pan from the heat. Transfer the sausages to a cutting board and cut them on the diagonal into pieces of the desired size. Taste the lentils and season with salt and pepper, then transfer to a serving dish. Place the sausages on top. Serve with the parsley-caper relish on the side.

Umbrian-Style Lentil Soup

Start to finish: 1 hour / Servings: 4 to 6

In her kitchen in Perugia, Italy, home cook Silvia Buitoni taught us how to make brothy but hearty Umbrian lentil soup, or zuppa di lenticchie, a fine example of rustic Italian cooking. She used Castelluccio lentils, grown in the Umbrian village of the same name, that have a taste that is richly nutty and earthy. Though they become tender and plump with cooking, the lentils retain their shape beautifully. For this adaptation of Umbrian lentil soup we use easier-to-source French lentils du Puy, which are green-gray and have similar texture and flavor characteristics.

3 tablespoons extra-virgin olive oil, plus more to serve

1 medium yellow onion, chopped

2 medium celery stalks, halved lengthwise and chopped

2 medium carrots, peeled, halved lengthwise and cut into ¼-inch pieces

Kosher salt and ground black pepper

2 medium garlic cloves, finely grated

3 tablespoons tomato paste

1¼ cups lentils du Puy, rinsed and drained

1 teaspoon dried rosemary

¼ to ½ teaspoon red pepper flakes

In a Dutch oven over medium-high, heat the oil until shimmering. Add the onion, celery, carrots and ½ teaspoon salt; cook, stirring occasionally, until the vegetables are lightly browned, about 5 minutes. Add the garlic and cook, stirring, until fragrant, about 30 seconds. Add the tomato paste and cook, stirring often, until the paste begins to brown and stick to the bottom of the pot, about 2 minutes.

Add 6 cups water and scrape up any browned bits. Stir in the lentils, rosemary and pepper flakes. Bring to a simmer, stirring often, then cover and reduce to medium-low and simmer, stirring occasionally, until the lentils are just shy of tender, 40 to 45 minutes.

Uncover, increase the heat to medium and cook, stirring occasionally, until the lentils are fully tender and the soup has thickened slightly, 8 to 10 minutes. Taste and season with salt and black pepper. Serve drizzled with additional oil.

Optional garnish: Finely grated Parmesan cheese

Broth BOOSTED

Roman-Style Egg Drop Soup / 98

Mexican Noodle Soup with Fire-Roasted Tomatoes / 99

Pasta e Ceci / 100

Curried Rice and Vegetable Soup / 101

Creamy Pinto Bean and Tomato Soup / 102

Spanish Garlic and Bread Soup / 104

Romanian-Style Cabbage and Potato Soup with Bacon and Paprika / 105

Miso, Shiitake Mushroom and Kimchi Soup / 106

Greek Egg-Lemon Soup (Avgolemono) / 109

Roman-Style Egg Drop Soup

Start to finish: 20 minutes / Servings: 4

Most cultures have a version of chicken soup. The one from Rome is known as stracciatella, which comes from the Italian word straccetti, or "little rags," and that's what the eggs resemble after they're stirred into the soup. It's made with just a handful of basic ingredients, including chicken broth, grated Parmesan and eggs. In our version, we also add small-shaped pasta and baby spinach (or arugula) to create a satisfying meal in a bowl.

4 large eggs

2 ounces Parmesan OR pecorino Romano cheese, finely grated (1 cup), plus more to serve

½ cup finely chopped fresh flat-leaf parsley

Kosher salt and ground black pepper

6 cups low-sodium chicken broth

¾ cup orzo OR ditalini pasta

3 ounces (4 cups lightly packed) baby spinach OR baby arugula

Extra-virgin olive oil, to serve

Lemon wedges, to serve

In a medium bowl, whisk together the eggs, cheese, half of the parsley and ½ teaspoon pepper; set aside.

In a large saucepan, bring the broth to a vigorous simmer. Add the pasta and cook, stirring occasionally, until al dente. With the broth still at a vigorous simmer, drizzle in the egg mixture, stirring with a fork as you pour; the eggs will rise to the surface and appear light and feathery.

Off heat, stir in the spinach until just wilted, then taste and season with salt and pepper. Serve drizzled with oil, sprinkled with additional cheese and the remaining parsley; offer lemon wedges on the side.

Mexican Noodle Soup with Fire-Roasted Tomatoes

Start to finish: 25 minutes / Servings: 4 to 6

Known as sopa de fideos, this much-loved Mexican soup is pure comfort food. Thin noodles (vermicelli or capellini pasta) are lightly browned in oil, then simmered in chicken broth seasoned with onion, garlic and jalapeño. Traditional recipes often call for roasting fresh tomatoes before adding them to the soup; to mimic those flavors, we opt for canned fire-roasted tomatoes. If you have only regular canned tomatoes (whole or diced) in the pantry, they'll work fine but will lack the smoky subtleties. To easily break the noodles before browning them, place in a zip-top plastic bag and seal, then snap them into 1- to 2-inch pieces. Garnishes will lend lovely color and texture, so choose from the suggestions below to enhance your soup.

½ **medium white OR yellow onion, halved**

3 **medium garlic cloves, smashed and peeled**

2 **jalapeño chilies, 1 stemmed, halved and seeded, 1 stemmed, seeded and thinly sliced**

14½-**ounce can diced fire-roasted tomatoes OR diced tomatoes**

Kosher salt and ground black pepper

3 **tablespoons extra-virgin olive oil**

8 **ounces vermicelli OR capellini, broken into 1- to 2-inch pieces**

6 **cups low-sodium chicken broth**

In a blender, combine the onion, garlic, the halved jalapeño, tomatoes with juices and ½ teaspoon each salt and pepper. Blend until smooth, about 1 minute, scraping the jar as needed; set aside.

In a large saucepan over medium-high, heat the oil until shimmering. Add the noodles and cook, tossing often with tongs, until golden brown, 3 to 4 minutes. Remove the pan from the heat. Carefully stir in the puree and the broth (the liquids may splatter). Bring to a simmer over medium-high and cook, uncovered and stirring occasionally, until the noodles are tender, 2 to 3 minutes.

Off heat, taste and season with salt and pepper. Serve garnished with the sliced jalapeño.

Optional garnish: Chopped fresh cilantro **OR** chopped red onion **OR** diced avocado **OR** crumbled tortilla chips **OR** crumbled queso fresco **OR** a combination

Pasta e Ceci

Start to finish: 35 minutes / Servings: 4 to 6

Classic Italian pasta e ceci, or pasta and chickpeas, is a soup-stew hybrid, and a satisfying meal in a bowl. Our version requires minimal knife work so it can be on the table in well under 45 minutes, and it includes some spinach (or kale) to boost color, freshness and nutrients. We cook a can's worth of chickpeas with the tomatoes and a little broth, then mash the mixture right in the pan as an easy way to thicken the broth; the rest of the chickpeas are added with the pasta and remain whole and chunky.

1 tablespoon extra-virgin olive oil, plus more to serve

3 medium garlic cloves, minced

¼ teaspoon red pepper flakes

½ teaspoon dried oregano

14½-ounce can whole tomatoes, crushed by hand OR 2 ripe medium tomatoes, cored and chopped

Two 15½-ounce cans chickpeas, rinsed and drained

4 cups low-sodium chicken OR vegetable broth, divided

½ cup elbow macaroni OR ditalini OR orzo pasta

3 cups (2 ounces) lightly packed baby spinach OR baby kale, roughly chopped

In a large saucepan, combine the oil, garlic and pepper flakes. Cook over medium, stirring occasionally, until fragrant, about 1 minute. Add the oregano and tomatoes with juices; cook, stirring occasionally, until the tomatoes begin to soften, 2 to 3 minutes. Add half of the chickpeas and 1 cup broth. Bring to a simmer over medium-high, then reduce to medium and simmer, uncovered and stirring occasionally, until the tomatoes have broken down and the liquid is reduced and saucy, 8 to 10 minutes.

Remove the pan from the heat. Using a potato masher, mash the chickpeas until mostly smooth. Add the remaining chickpeas, the pasta and the remaining 3 cups broth. Bring to a simmer over medium-high, then cook, uncovered and stirring occasionally and reducing the heat as needed to maintain a steady simmer (rather than a boil), until the pasta is al dente. Add the spinach and stir until wilted, about 1 minute.

Off heat, taste and season with salt and pepper. Serve drizzled with additional oil.

Optional garnish: Chopped fresh flat-leaf parsley **OR** fresh basil **OR** finely grated Parmesan cheese **OR** a combination

Curried Rice and Vegetable Soup

Start to finish: 40 minutes (20 minutes active)
Servings: 4

The inspiration for this simple, yet richly aromatic, flavorful—and colorful—soup comes from mulligatawny, the Anglo-Indian classic. If you wish to make the soup vegetarian, use vegetable broth in place of the chicken broth. Though this already is a substantial soup, you could stir in some shredded cooked chicken for an even heartier bowl.

2 tablespoons grapeseed or other neutral oil

1 medium yellow onion, halved and thinly sliced

1 jalapeño chili, stemmed, seeded and chopped

Kosher salt and ground black pepper

4 teaspoons curry powder

14½-ounce can diced tomatoes, drained OR 2 medium ripe tomatoes, cored and chopped

1 pound sweet potato, peeled and cut into ½-inch cubes OR 3 medium carrots, peeled, halved lengthwise and cut into ¼-inch pieces

6 cups low-sodium chicken broth

½ cup long-grain white rice

½ cup coconut milk

In a large saucepan over medium-high, heat the oil until shimmering. Stir in the onion, jalapeño and ¼ teaspoon salt. Cover and cook, stirring occasionally, until the onion is softened and beginning to brown, 10 to 12 minutes.

Add the curry powder and cook, stirring, until fragrant, about 1 minute. Add the tomatoes, sweet potato and broth. Cover and bring to a boil over medium-high, scraping up any browned bits. Stir in the rice, then reduce to medium, cover partially and simmer, stirring occasionally, until the rice and vegetables are tender, 18 to 20 minutes.

Add the coconut milk and cook, stirring, until heated through, about 3 minutes. Off heat, taste and season with salt and pepper.

Optional garnish: Chopped fresh cilantro OR lemon (or lime) wedges OR both

Creamy Pinto Bean and Tomato Soup

Start to finish: 35 minutes / Servings: 4 to 6

According to Mexican food authority Diana Kennedy, there are two types of sopa Tarasca, or Tarascan soup, from the state of Michoacán in central Mexico. One is tortilla-based, the other a bean puree. The latter inspired this satisfying pantry-centric soup that can be on the table in under 45 minutes. Fire-roasted tomatoes add a subtle smokiness and the lime juice stirred in at the end adds brightness. Finish the smooth, velvety soup with a garnish or two to add contrasting colors, flavors and textures; see below for suggestions.

½ medium white **OR** yellow onion, halved

3 medium garlic cloves, smashed and peeled

14½-ounce can diced fire-roasted tomatoes

1 tablespoon chili powder

Kosher salt and ground black pepper

2 tablespoons extra-virgin olive oil

Two 15½-ounce cans pinto beans, rinsed and drained

2 cups low-sodium chicken broth **OR** vegetable broth

1 teaspoon dried oregano, preferably Mexican oregano

2 tablespoons lime juice, plus lime wedges to serve

In a blender, combine the onion, garlic, tomatoes with juices, chili powder and ½ teaspoon each salt and pepper. Blend until smooth, about 1 minute, scraping the jar as needed.

In a large saucepan over medium, heat the oil and the tomato puree until it comes to a simmer; reserve the blender jar. Cook, stirring occasionally and reducing the heat if the mixture begins to spatter, until slightly thickened, 4 to 5 minutes. Meanwhile, add the beans and broth to the blender and blend until smooth, 1 minute.

Add the bean puree to the pan along with the oregano. Bring to a simmer over medium and cook, stirring occasionally, until the soup is lightly thickened, 5 to 6 minutes.

Off heat, stir in the lime juice. Taste and season with salt and pepper. Serve with lime wedges.

Optional garnish: Diced avocado **OR** chopped fresh cilantro **OR** sour cream (or Mexican crema) **OR** crumbled queso fresco **OR** crumbled tortilla chips **OR** a combination

Spanish Garlic and Bread Soup

Start to finish: 45 minutes / Servings: 4

José Andrés taught us this "end of month" recipe—the sort of meal to make quickly with whatever is on hand. His approach: garlic cooked in copious amounts of olive oil with thinly sliced stale bread and several tablespoons of smoked paprika. Add some water and simmer, then off heat whisk in four or five eggs. For our version, we realized the bread, garlic and smoked paprika we had in our cupboards weren't up to Andrés' standards. So we boosted the flavor by using chicken broth instead of water, and we sautéed both sweet and smoked paprika with garlic and scallions. And instead of using stale bread, we turned a loaf of rustic sourdough (a baguette or any crusty loaf will do) into delicious croutons.

6 tablespoons extra-virgin olive oil, divided, plus more to serve

1 bunch scallions, thinly sliced, whites and greens reserved separately

6 medium garlic cloves, thinly sliced

4 teaspoons sweet paprika

1½ teaspoons smoked paprika

6 ounces sourdough or other rustic bread, cut into ½-inch cubes (about 4 cups), divided

6 cups low-sodium chicken broth

Kosher salt and ground black pepper

4 large egg yolks

In a medium saucepan over medium-low, combine 3 tablespoons oil, the scallion whites and garlic; cook, stirring occasionally, until beginning to color, 8 to 10 minutes.

Add both paprikas and cook, stirring, until fragrant and darkened, 30 seconds. Add 1 cup of the bread cubes and stir well. Stir in the broth, then bring to a simmer over medium-high. Reduce to medium-low and cook, whisking occasionally to break up the bread, for 15 minutes. Whisk vigorously to ensure the bread has fully broken down.

While the broth mixture cooks, in a 12-inch skillet over medium, combine the remaining 3 tablespoons oil, the remaining bread, the scallion greens and ½ teaspoon each salt and pepper. Cook, stirring occasionally, until the bread is browned and crisp, 8 to 10 minutes. Remove from the heat and set aside.

When the broth mixture is done, in a medium bowl, whisk the egg yolks. Remove the pan from the heat. Gradually whisk 1 cup of the hot broth mixture into the yolks to temper them. With the pan still off the heat, vigorously whisk the egg yolk–mixture into the soup. Taste and season with salt and pepper.

Divide the toasted bread among individual bowls. Ladle the soup into the bowls and drizzle with additional oil.

Romanian-Style Cabbage and Potato Soup with Bacon and Paprika

Start to finish: 40 minutes / Servings: 4 to 6

A category of Romanian soup, ciorbă is characterized by a pleasant sourness that comes from vinegar, pickle brine or the juice of sour fruits. There are many types of ciorbă; here we took inspiration from ciorbă de varză acră, which derives its tang from sauerkraut. To mimic those classic flavors in our pantry version, we replace the sauerkraut with fresh green cabbage plus a dash of vinegar. Chunks of potatoes and a garnish of crisp bacon turn this soup into a hearty meal. Serve with crusty bread and a green salad for a satisfying supper.

In a large pot over medium, cook the bacon, stirring often, until crisp, 6 to 7 minutes. Using a slotted spoon, transfer to a paper towel–lined plate; set aside.

To the fat in the pot, add the cabbage and cook over medium-high, stirring often, until softened and beginning to brown, 6 to 7 minutes.

Add the paprika and ½ teaspoon pepper; cook, stirring, until fragrant, 30 to 60 seconds. Add the broth and scrape up any browned bits, then add the potatoes and bay and bring to a simmer over medium-high. Cover, reduce to medium and simmer, stirring occasionally, until the potatoes are tender, about 15 minutes

Off heat, remove and discard the bay. Stir in the vinegar and half of the parsley. Taste and season with salt and pepper. Serve sprinkled with the bacon and the remaining parsley.

8 ounces bacon, chopped

2-pound head green OR red cabbage, quartered lengthwise, cored and thinly sliced (about 8 cups)

2 teaspoons sweet paprika

Kosher salt and ground black pepper

6 cups low-sodium chicken broth

1 pound Yukon Gold potatoes, peeled and cut into ¾-inch chunks

2 bay leaves

2 tablespoons cider vinegar

½ cup lightly packed fresh flat-leaf parsley, roughly chopped OR ½ cup loosely packed dill leaves, chopped

Miso, Shiitake Mushroom and Kimchi Soup

Start to finish: 45 minutes (20 minutes active)
Servings: 4

Though it's made with just a handful of staple Asian ingredients, this soup is a satisfying flavor bomb because miso, kimchi and dried shiitake mushrooms all pack tons of umami. Be sure to use low-sodium broth, as miso can be quite salty. If you like, you can make the soup more substantial by stirring in cooked shredded chicken near the end of simmering. Serve with steamed rice.

1 ounce (12 to 14 medium) dried shiitake mushrooms

2 cups boiling water

2 tablespoons grapeseed or other neutral oil

1 medium garlic clove, minced

1 tablespoon minced fresh ginger

1 quart low-sodium chicken broth OR vegetable broth

¼ cup white miso

1 cup cabbage kimchi, roughly chopped

4 scallions, thinly sliced on the diagonal

Toasted sesame oil, to serve

In a small bowl, combine the mushrooms and boiling water. Cover and let stand until the mushrooms are fully hydrated, 20 to 30 minutes. Remove the mushrooms; reserve the water. Trim off and discard the mushroom stems and thinly slice the caps.

In a large saucepan over medium-high, heat the oil until shimmering. Add the mushrooms and cook, stirring occasionally, until lightly browned, 4 to 6 minutes. Add the garlic and ginger; cook, stirring, until fragrant, 30 to 60 seconds. Add the broth, the mushroom liquid and 1 cup water. Bring to a simmer, scraping up any browned bits, then cover, reduce to medium and simmer, stirring occasionally, until the mushrooms are tender, about 30 minutes.

In a small bowl, whisk together the miso and ¼ cup of the hot broth until the miso is dissolved. Stir the miso mixture and kimchi into the broth. Return the soup to a simmer over medium-high, stirring occasionally, then remove from the heat. Serve sprinkled with the scallions and drizzled with sesame oil.

Optional garnish: Soft- or hard-cooked eggs, halved OR toasted sesame seeds OR both

Greek Egg-Lemon Soup (Avgolemono)

Start to finish: 45 minutes (20 minutes active)
Servings: 4

This Greek soup gets its name, avgolemono, from the egg-lemon mixture used to thicken the broth. Some versions are simply broth that's thickened and seasoned, while others are more substantial and include rice and chicken, as we've done here. To boost the flavor of store-bought chicken broth, we poach bone-in chicken breasts in it, then shred the meat and add it to the soup just before serving. Grated carrots lend sweetness and color, while lemon zest deepens the citrus notes. To prevent the eggs from curdling, keep these tips in mind: Temper the eggs first by slowly adding a small amount of the hot broth to the bowl before whisking the mixture into the pan. And after adding the mixture, don't let the soup reach a boil or even a simmer.

1 quart low-sodium chicken broth

12-ounce bone-in, skin-on chicken breast, halved crosswise

Three 2-inch strips lemon zest, plus 3 tablespoons lemon juice

2 medium carrots, peeled and shredded on the large holes of a box grater

1 medium yellow onion, chopped

¾ cup long-grain white rice, rinsed and drained

Kosher salt and ground black pepper

3 large eggs

In a large saucepan, combine the broth, chicken, 2 cups water, the lemon zest strips, carrots and onion. Bring to a simmer over medium-high, then reduce to low, cover and cook until the thickest part of the chicken reaches 160°F, 15 to 18 minutes.

Using tongs, remove and discard the zest strips; transfer the chicken to a plate and set aside. Return the broth to a simmer over medium, then stir in the rice, ¾ teaspoon salt and ¼ teaspoon pepper. Reduce to low, cover and cook, stirring once halfway through, until the rice is tender, 12 to 15 minutes. Meanwhile, remove and discard the skin and bones from the chicken and shred the meat; set aside.

When the rice is done, remove the pan from the heat and uncover. In a medium bowl, whisk together the eggs and lemon juice. While whisking constantly, slowly ladle about 1 cup of the hot rice-broth mixture into the egg mixture, then slowly whisk this mixture into the pan. Stir in the shredded chicken.

Return the pan to low and cook, stirring constantly, until the soup is warm and lightly thickened, 2 to 4 minutes; do not allow the soup to simmer. Off heat, taste and season with salt and pepper

Optional garnish: Chopped fresh dill **OR** chives

Cold
STORAGE

Root
CELLAR

Baked Kibbeh with Sweet Potato / 115

Afghan-Style Braised Butternut Squash / 116

Spicy Kidney Bean and Sweet Potato Soup / 117

Barley, Bean and Butternut Stew / 119

Sweet Potato and Quinoa Stew / 120

Sweet Potatoes with Coriander, Orange and Olives / 121

Agrodolce Acorn Squash / 123

Sweet Potato Brown Rice with Soy and Scallions / 124

Bulgur and Winter Squash Pilaf / 125

Baked Kibbeh with Sweet Potato

Start to finish: 1½ hours (30 minutes active)
Servings: 4 to 6

A traditional Middle Eastern dish, kibbeh bil sanieh is a mixture of bulgur and ground lamb or beef that's baked then cut into pieces for serving. The warming spices used in kibbeh work exceptionally well with sweet potatoes, which we used in place of ground meat in this vegetarian version. Before combining with the potatoes, the bulgur is soaked in boiling water to hydrate the grain. Fine bulgur is key to the best texture. If you can't find it, process coarse bulgur in a spice grinder for 10 to 30 seconds. We serve the kibbeh with a tangy herbed yogurt sauce to brighten the flavors.

2 medium yellow onions, 1 peeled, 1 halved and thinly sliced

½ cup fine bulgur (see headnote)

Kosher salt and ground black pepper

1 cup boiling water

1 pound sweet potato (preferably orange-fleshed), peeled and cut into 1-inch chunks

¾ teaspoon ground cumin

½ teaspoon ground allspice OR ground cardamom

¼ teaspoon ground cinnamon

5 tablespoons extra-virgin olive oil, divided

¾ cup plain whole-milk yogurt

½ cup chopped fresh flat-leaf parsley OR mint

Heat the oven to 400°F with a rack in the middle position. Set a box grater in a large bowl. Grate the whole onion on the large holes down to the root end. Stir in the bulgur and ½ teaspoon salt, then stir in the boiling water. Cover and let stand until the bulgur is softened, about 20 minutes.

Meanwhile, in a medium microwave-safe bowl, stir together the sweet potato, 2 tablespoons water and ½ teaspoon salt. Cover and microwave on high until the potatoes are completely tender, 5 to 7 minutes, stirring once halfway through. Carefully uncover and cool slightly. Pour off and discard any water in the bowl, then mash the potato until smooth.

When the bulgur is softened, drain it in a fine-mesh sieve, pressing to remove excess liquid, then return it to the bowl. Add the sweet potato, cumin, allspice, cinnamon, ½ teaspoon salt and ¾ teaspoon pepper; stir well, then set aside.

In an oven-safe 12-inch skillet (preferably cast-iron) over medium-high, heat 2 tablespoons oil until shimmering. Add the sliced onion and ¼ teaspoon salt; cook, stirring occasionally, until golden brown, 3 to 5 minutes. Remove from the heat.

Spoon the bulgur mixture over the onion, then use a spatula to spread in an even layer. Using a paring knife, score a diamond pattern on the surface. Drizzle with the remaining 3 tablespoons oil. Bake until golden brown, 35 to 45 minutes. Cool on a wire rack for 10 minutes.

Meanwhile, in a small bowl, stir together the yogurt and parsley; taste and season with salt and pepper. Cut the kibbeh into slices and serve with the yogurt sauce.

Afghan-Style Braised Butternut Squash

Start to finish: 50 minutes (25 minutes active)
Servings: 4 to 6

This is our version of the Afghan pumpkin dish called borani kadoo. We use butternut squash, available year-round, and swap tomato paste for the fresh tomatoes called for in many versions. Keep an eye on the squash as it braises and make sure the pot moisture doesn't cook off. Add water 2 tablespoons at a time as needed to ensure the sauce remains loose, not thick.

4 tablespoons grapeseed or other neutral oil, divided

2-pound butternut squash, peeled, seeded and cut into 1½-inch chunks

1 medium yellow onion, chopped

Kosher salt and ground black pepper

1 medium garlic clove, minced

1¼ teaspoons ground coriander

½ teaspoon ground turmeric

½ teaspoon ground cinnamon

1 tablespoon tomato paste

1 tablespoon white sugar

In a large Dutch oven over medium-high, heat 2 tablespoons oil until shimmering. Add the squash and cook, stirring often, until golden brown, 6 to 8 minutes. Transfer to a medium bowl.

To the pot, add the remaining 2 tablespoons oil along with the onion and ½ teaspoon salt. Cook over medium-high, stirring often, until lightly browned, about 3 minutes. Add the garlic, coriander, turmeric and cinnamon; cook, stirring, until fragrant, about 30 seconds. Stir in the tomato paste and return the squash to the pot. Add the sugar and 1 cup water, then bring to a simmer. Cover, reduce to medium-low and cook, stirring occasionally and adding water 2 tablespoons at a time if the mixture looks dry, until the squash is tender and only a little lightly thickened liquid remains, 25 to 30 minutes. Off heat, taste and season with salt and pepper.

Optional garnish: Plain yogurt **OR** chopped fresh mint **OR** both

Spicy Kidney Bean and Sweet Potato Soup

Start to finish: 30 minutes / Servings: 4

Jamaican red peas soup was the inspiration for this recipe. Many traditional recipes call for cooking dumplings in the broth as well as meat. We opted for canned beans and skipped the meat, though you can stir in some cooked chicken or serve the soup with rice for a more substantial meal. If using a habanero or Scotch bonnet chili, remove seeds from the chili halves to tone down the soup's spiciness.

2 tablespoons grapeseed or other neutral oil

1 bunch scallions, thinly sliced, white and green parts reserved separately OR ½ medium yellow onion, finely chopped

6 medium garlic cloves, minced

3 serrano OR Fresno chilies, stemmed, seeded and chopped OR 1 habanero or Scotch bonnet chili, halved

1 teaspoon ground allspice

1 teaspoon dried thyme OR 4 fresh thyme sprigs

Two 15½-ounce cans red kidney beans, rinsed and drained

10 ounces sweet potato, peeled and cut into ½-inch pieces OR butternut squash, peeled, seeded and cut into ½-inch pieces

1 quart low-sodium chicken broth OR vegetable broth

Kosher salt and ground black pepper

In a large saucepan over medium, heat the oil until shimmering. Add the scallion whites and garlic, then cook, stirring often, until golden brown, 2 to 4 minutes. Add the chilies, allspice and thyme; cook, stirring, until fragrant, about 30 seconds. Add the beans, sweet potato, broth, 2 cups water, 1 teaspoon salt and ¼ teaspoon pepper. Bring to a simmer over medium-high, then reduce to medium and simmer, uncovered and stirring occasionally, until the sweet potato is tender, 15 to 20 minutes.

Off heat, remove and discard the thyme sprigs and habanero or Scotch bonnet chili (if used). Using the back of a spoon or a potato masher, lightly mash some of the beans and sweet potato to thicken; stir to combine. Stir in the scallion greens (if using), then taste and season with salt and pepper.

Optional garnish: Lime wedges **OR** hot sauce **OR** both

Barley, Bean and Butternut Stew

Start to finish: 1 hour 10 minutes (30 minutes active)
Servings: 4 to 6

To create this hearty stew, we took inspiration from cholent, a long-simmered Jewish dish traditionally made for the Sabbath. It usually includes beef along with barley and vegetables, but we opted for a lighter, fresher meat-free version with chunks of earthy-sweet butternut squash. Be sure to use pearled barley, which has been polished, or "pearled," to remove the outer husk and bran layers; this process shortens the cooking time. To enhance the barley's nutty flavor, we toast the grains for a few minutes before simmering them.

1 cup pearled barley

2 tablespoons extra-virgin olive oil

1 medium yellow onion, halved and sliced about ½ inch thick

Kosher salt and ground black pepper

3 tablespoons tomato paste

1 tablespoon sweet paprika

1 quart low-sodium vegetable broth OR chicken broth

1 pound butternut squash, peeled, seeded and cut into 1½-inch chunks (about 4 cups)

15½-ounce can kidney beans OR cannellini beans OR pinto beans, rinsed and drained

½ cup finely chopped fresh flat-leaf parsley OR dill

In a large pot over medium-high, toast the barley, stirring occasionally, until lightly browned, 4 to 5 minutes. Transfer to a small bowl; set aside.

In the same pot over medium, heat the oil until shimmering. Add the onion and ½ teaspoon salt, then cook, stirring occasionally, until the onion starts to soften and brown, 4 to 5 minutes. Add the tomato paste and cook over medium-high, stirring, until the paste browns and slightly sticks to the pot, about 2 minutes. Stir in the paprika and 1 teaspoon pepper.

Add the broth and 2 cups water and scrape up the browned bits. Stir in the barley, squash and beans. Bring to a boil, then reduce to medium-low, cover and simmer, stirring occasionally, until the barley and squash are tender, 40 to 45 minutes. Off heat, stir in the parsley. Taste and season with salt and pepper.

Optional garnish: Prepared horseradish OR sliced radishes

Sweet Potato and Quinoa Stew

Start to finish: 45 minutes / Servings: 4

This hearty stew of sweet potatoes and quinoa was inspired by the Peruvian dish called quinua atamalada. Use quinoa of any color, and be sure to cook it to a creamy, risotto-like consistency; it should not be dry and fluffy. While true atamalada uses Peruvian chilies, this recipe incorporates Mexican canned chipotle chilies in adobo sauce, which we always keep on hand because they're a terrific way to add chili heat along with smoky flavor and a touch of tanginess. Peruvian salsa criolla, a simple relish of lime-steeped sliced onion and chopped cilantro, is a perfect embellishment that brings sharp, fresh flavor and crisp texture to the stew; if you wish to try it, see the recipe below.

2 tablespoons extra-virgin olive oil

1 medium red onion, finely chopped

Kosher salt and ground black pepper

3 medium garlic cloves, minced

1 chipotle chili in adobo sauce, minced, plus 1 tablespoon adobo sauce

1½ pounds sweet potatoes, peeled and cut into ½-inch cubes

14½-ounce can whole peeled tomatoes, crushed by hand

1 quart low-sodium chicken broth **OR** vegetable broth

¾ cup quinoa, rinsed and drained (see headnote)

Lime wedges, to serve

In a Dutch oven over medium, heat the oil until shimmering. Add the onion and ¼ teaspoon salt; cook, stirring often, until softened, about 5 minutes. Add the garlic, chipotle and adobo sauce, then cook, stirring, until the mixture begins to stick to the pot, 2 to 3 minutes.

Stir in the sweet potatoes, followed by the tomatoes with juices, broth and ½ teaspoon salt. Bring to a simmer over medium high, then stir in the quinoa, cover and reduce to medium-low. Simmer, stirring occasionally, until both the sweet potatoes and quinoa are tender, about 30 minutes. The stew should be creamy and slightly saucy; if it is too thick, add hot water as needed to thin it. Taste and season with salt and pepper. Serve with lime wedges.

Optional garnish: Crumbled feta cheese (or queso fresco) **OR** chopped fresh cilantro **OR** both

Peruvian Salsa Criolla
Start to finish: 10 minutes / Makes about 1½ cups

In a small bowl, stir together ½ **medium red onion** (thinly sliced), ⅓ **cup lightly packed fresh cilantro** (chopped), **2 tablespoons lime juice** and ¼ **teaspoon kosher salt.**

Sweet Potatoes with Coriander, Orange and Olives

Start to finish: 45 minutes / Servings: 4

This colorful side dish features an unusual combination of flavors; the inspiration comes from a recipe in "365," a cookbook by German food blogger Meike Peters. Earthy sweet potatoes pair well with the subtle citrusy notes of coriander and the fruitiness of orange juice, while savory onion, spicy cayenne and salty olives balance the natural sugars. We love the texture and flavor pop of lightly crushed coriander seeds; a mortar and pestle are the best tools for the task but the bottom of a heavy skillet works, too. If you prefer, you can use 1 tablespoon ground coriander in place of the seeds, but it will require less than a minute to bloom in the oil.

3 tablespoons extra-virgin olive oil

2 teaspoons coriander seeds, lightly crushed

1 medium red onion, halved and thinly sliced

Kosher salt and ground black pepper

2 pounds orange-flesh sweet potatoes, peeled and cut into 1-inch chunks

⅔ cup orange juice

¼ teaspoon cayenne pepper

½ cup black or green pitted olives, or a mixture, chopped

In a Dutch oven over medium-high, cook the oil and coriander seeds, stirring, until fragrant and sizzling, 2 to 4 minutes. Add the onion and ¼ teaspoon salt, then cook, stirring occasionally, until the onion is softened and lightly browned, 3 to 5 minutes.

Add the sweet potatoes, orange juice, cayenne, ½ teaspoon salt, ¼ teaspoon pepper and ½ cup water. Bring to a simmer, cover and reduce to medium. Cook, stirring occasionally, until a skewer inserted into the potatoes meets no resistance, 8 to 11 minutes.

Uncover and cook, stirring constantly, until the liquid has almost fully reduced and the potatoes are glazed, about 2 minutes. Off heat, stir in the olives. Taste and season with salt and pepper.

Agrodolce Acorn Squash

Start to finish: 1 hour / Servings: 4 to 6

In Italian cooking, agrodolce translates as sweet-and-sour; the term also refers to a condiment of that flavor profile. Vinegar provides the "agro" and a sweetener the "dolce," and dried fruits and nuts are common. Often, chilies, alliums and spices add layers of complexity. We roast acorn squash and finish it with an agrodolce mixture that takes on a glaze-like luster in the oven. We add toasted almonds as a garnish so they retain their crispness and contrast the velvety squash. Butternut squash will also work in the recipe, but it will need to be peeled.

1½- to 2-pound acorn squash, halved lengthwise, seeded and sliced into 1-inch-thick half rings

4 tablespoons extra-virgin olive oil, divided

Kosher salt and ground black pepper

½ cup balsamic vinegar OR cider vinegar

2 tablespoons honey

2 tablespoons Dijon mustard

1 teaspoon dried rosemary OR dried thyme

½ teaspoon red pepper flakes

¼ cup raisins

¼ cup whole almonds, roughly chopped OR slivered almonds OR sliced almonds, toaste

Heat the oven to 475°F with a rack in the middle position. On a rimmed baking sheet, drizzle the squash with 1 tablespoon oil and sprinkle with ½ teaspoon salt and ¼ teaspoon black pepper. Toss until well coated, then distribute in an even layer. Roast until the squash is browned on both sides and a skewer inserted into a piece meets no resistance, 25 to 30 minutes.

Meanwhile, in a small bowl, whisk together the remaining 3 tablespoons oil, the vinegar, honey, mustard, rosemary and pepper flakes, then stir in the raisins.

When the squash is done, remove the baking sheet from the oven. Pour the vinegar-raisin mixture onto the squash, distributing the raisins evenly, then roast until the liquid is bubbling and syrupy, 5 to 7 minutes.

Using a wide metal spatula, transfer the squash to a platter. Drizzle with the glaze from the baking sheet and sprinkle with the almonds.

Optional garnish: Fresh flat-leaf parsley OR pomegranate seeds OR both

Sweet Potato Brown Rice with Soy and Scallions

Start to finish: 50 minutes (10 minutes active)
Servings: 4

Goguma-bap is a traditional Korean dish of sweet potatoes (goguma) and cooked rice (bap). Our take has a pure sweet potato flavor accented by chewy short-grain rice; we prefer the nuttiness of brown short-grain rice for added complexity. The sweet potatoes and rice usually are steamed together plain, then seasoned at the table with a mixture of soy sauce. We opt to season the sweet potatoes with just a little of this sauce before cooking to make them especially flavorful.

1 cup short-grain brown rice, rinsed and drained

1 bunch scallions, thinly sliced

¼ cup low-sodium soy sauce

1 tablespoon unseasoned rice vinegar

1 medium garlic clove, finely grated

1 teaspoon red pepper flakes

1 teaspoon honey **OR** white sugar

1 pound orange-flesh sweet potatoes, peeled and cut into ½-inch chunks

Kosher salt and ground black pepper

In a large saucepan, combine the rice and 1¾ cups water. Bring to a simmer over medium, then reduce to low, cover and cook without stirring for 15 minutes.

Meanwhile, in a small bowl, stir together the scallions, soy sauce, vinegar, garlic, pepper flakes, honey and 2 tablespoons water. In a medium bowl, toss the sweet potatoes with 2 tablespoons of the soy mixture and ½ teaspoon black pepper.

After the rice has cooked for 15 minutes, uncover the pot, scatter the sweet potato mixture over the surface of the rice (without disturbing the grains) and re-cover. Cook over low until both the potatoes and rice are tender, 20 to 25 minutes.

Remove from the heat and let stand, covered, for 10 minutes. Gently fluff with a fork, trying not to break up the potatoes. Serve with the remaining soy sauce mixture for drizzling.

Optional garnish: Toasted sesame seeds

124

Bulgur and Winter Squash Pilaf

Start to finish: 45 minutes / Servings: 4 to 6

Bulgar pilafs are popular throughout the Middle East, and this version, featuring hearty winter squash, combines the nuttiness of bulgur with the earthy sweetness of butternut squash. The grain and squash cook in about the same amount of time, so the dish comes together quickly in a single pot. A squeeze of lemon juice contrasts nicely with the sweet squash and raisins. If you like, garnish the pilaf with a handful of chopped mint to lend color and freshness. Be sure to use coarse bulgur, rather than finely ground; the hearty texture of coarse bulgur holds up well when cooked for a pilaf.

4 tablespoons extra-virgin olive oil, divided

1 pound butternut squash, peeled, seeded and cut into ½- to ¾-inch chunks (about 3½ cups)

1 medium yellow onion, chopped

Kosher salt and ground black pepper

1 cup coarse bulgur

½ cup raisins **OR** chopped dried apricots

¾ teaspoon ground cumin

½ teaspoon ground cinnamon

1¾ cups low-sodium chicken broth

2 tablespoons lemon juice

In a large pot over medium-high, heat 3 tablespoons oil until shimmering. Add the squash, onion, ½ teaspoon salt and ¼ teaspoon pepper. Cook, stirring occasionally, until the squash and onion begin to brown, 6 to 7 minutes.

Add the bulgur, raisins, cumin and cinnamon; cook, stirring, until fragrant, 1 to 2 minutes. Add the broth and bring to a simmer, then cover, reduce to medium-low and simmer until all of the liquid has been absorbed and the squash and bulgur are tender, 17 to 20 minutes. Remove from the heat, uncover, drape a kitchen towel across the pot and re-cover. Let stand for 5 minutes.

Using a fork, fluff the bulgur mixture. Stir in the lemon juice and the remaining 1 tablespoon oil. Taste and season with salt and pepper. Serve warm or at room temperature.

Optional garnish: Chopped fresh mint

Potato PRIMER

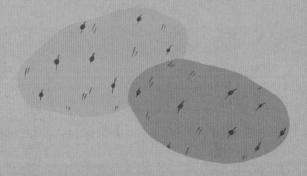

Gnocchi in an Instant

Start to finish: 30 minutes, plus cooling / Servings: 4

Using instant potato flakes to make gnocchi might make purists cringe, but it's a surefire way to make the softest, most pillowy dumplings. It's an easy and mess-free method, too, because it eliminates the need to boil a russet potato, then rice it or put it through a food mill. The gnocchi are delicious tossed with pesto or a simple tomato sauce or dressed with browned butter and finished with fresh herbs.

1 cup instant potato flakes

1 cup boiling water

1 large egg, lightly beaten

1 cup all-purpose flour, plus more for dusting

½ teaspoon kosher salt

In a large bowl, stir together the potato flakes and water. Let stand until cooled to room temperature. Add the egg, flour and salt, then mix with your hands until the ingredients are just incorporated. Lightly dust the counter with flour and turn the dough out onto it. Gently knead until the dough is smooth.

Using a rolling pin, roll the dough into a ½-inch-thick rectangle. Cut the dough into ½-inch strips, then, using your hands, roll each strip against the counter into a ½-inch diameter log. Cut each log into 1-inch pieces. If desired, dip the back of the tines of a fork into flour, then gently press into each piece to create a ridged surface.

In a large pot, bring 4 quarts salted water to a boil. Add half of the gnocchi, return to a boil and cook, stirring gently and occasionally, until the gnocchi float to the surface. Cook for 1 minute, then use a slotted spoon to transfer the gnocchi to a wire rack. Return the water to a boil and repeat with the remaining gnocchi. Let the gnocchi cool for at least 15 minutes before using.

Portuguese-Style Soup with Potatoes, Kale and Sausage

Start to finish: 50 minutes (20 minutes active)
Servings: 4

Known as caldo verde in Portugal, this hearty soup traditionally is made with linguiça or chouriço, but just about any type of smoked, spiced sausage, including kielbasa or Cajun andouille, yields a flavorful potful. Often, water is used as the base for the soup, though chicken broth, which we call for here, deepens the flavor. Some versions are brothy, with the potatoes left in chunks, while others are pureed and thick. We chose to puree, including some of the sausage, which yields a rich, well-seasoned soup. Then the kale is added at the end and cooked briefly so it offers textural contrast and vibrant color.

3 tablespoons extra-virgin olive oil, plus more to serve

8 ounces kielbasa OR linguiça sausage, quartered lengthwise and sliced ½ inch thick

1 medium yellow onion, chopped

4 medium garlic cloves, smashed and peeled

1 pound russet OR Yukon Gold potatoes, peeled and cut into 1-inch chunks

1 quart low-sodium chicken broth

3 bay leaves

1 small bunch lacinato kale OR curly kale, stemmed and finely chopped (about 6 cups)

1 tablespoon white wine vinegar

Kosher salt and ground black pepper

In a large pot over medium, combine the oil and sausage. Cook, stirring occasionally, until lightly browned, 3 to 4 minutes. Using a slotted spoon, transfer to a plate; set aside.

To the fat in the pot, add the onion and garlic, then cook over medium, stirring occasionally, until golden brown, 4 to 6 minutes. Add the potatoes, stirring to coat with the fat, then add half of the sausage, the broth, bay and 3 cups water. Bring to a simmer over medium-high, then reduce to medium-low and simmer, uncovered and stirring occasionally, until the potatoes are tender, 10 to 15 minutes. Remove the pot from the heat and let the soup cool for about 5 minutes. Remove and discard the bay.

Using a blender and working in batches so the jar is never more than half full, puree the soup until smooth, 1 to 2 minutes, then return the soup to the pot. Add the kale and the remaining sausage; cook, uncovered, over medium-high, stirring often and scraping along the bottom to prevent scorching, until the soup has thickened slightly and the kale is just tender, 3 to 5 minutes.

Off heat, stir in the vinegar, then taste and season with salt. Serve with a generous grinding of pepper and a drizzle of additional oil.

Cairo-Style Potatoes with Cumin, Coriander and Cilantro

Start to finish: 20 minutes (10 minutes active)
Servings: 4 to 6

In Cairo, patates mekhalel are served by street vendors as a side to liver sandwiches, their acidity and spices balancing the richness of the liver. For our version, we peel, cut and cook the potatoes in water seasoned with both salt and vinegar, then dress the hot, just-drained potatoes with additional vinegar. To lightly crush the cumin and coriander seeds, use a mortar and pestle or the back of a heavy pan, or pulse them several times in a spice grinder.

2½ pounds Yukon Gold potatoes, peeled and cut into 1-inch chunks

½ cup white vinegar, divided

Kosher salt and ground black pepper

¼ cup grapeseed or other neutral oil

4 teaspoons cumin seeds, lightly crushed

4 teaspoons coriander seeds, lightly crushed

4 medium garlic cloves, minced

2 teaspoons hot paprika OR 2 teaspoons sweet paprika plus ¼ teaspoon cayenne pepper

2 teaspoons honey

1½ cups lightly packed fresh cilantro, roughly chopped

In a large saucepan over high, combine the potatoes, ¼ cup vinegar, 1 tablespoon salt and 6 cups water. Bring to a boil and cook, stirring occasionally, until a skewer inserted into the potatoes meets no resistance, 6 to 8 minutes. Drain, then transfer to a large bowl. Drizzle with the remaining ¼ cup vinegar and toss; set aside.

In a small saucepan over medium-high, combine the oil, cumin and coriander, then cook, swirling, until sizzling, 45 to 90 seconds. Add the garlic and cook, stirring, until it just begins to turn golden, about 30 seconds.

Off heat, stir in the paprika and honey, then pour over the potatoes. Add the cilantro and ½ teaspoon each salt and pepper; toss to combine. Let stand at room temperature for at least 10 minutes or up to 45 minutes. Serve warm or at room temperature.

Wine-Braised Potatoes with Garlic and Bay

Start to finish: 1 hour (25 minutes active) / Servings: 4

The traditional way of cooking potatoes with these classic Portuguese flavors is to slow-roast them in the oven or long-braise them on the stovetop alongside meat. But in "Authentic Portuguese Cooking," author Ana Patuleia Ortins includes a quicker, meat-free version that yields a wonderfully delicious side.

2 pounds Yukon Gold OR red potatoes, peeled and cut into 1- to 1½-inch chunks

2 medium garlic cloves, minced

1 bay leaf

½ teaspoon red pepper flakes

1¼ teaspoons smoked paprika

Kosher salt and ground black pepper

¼ cup extra-virgin olive oil

1 small yellow onion, finely chopped

¾ cup dry white wine

¾ cup low-sodium chicken broth OR vegetable broth

¼ cup lightly packed fresh flat-leaf parsley, chopped

In a medium bowl, toss the potatoes with the garlic, bay, pepper flakes, paprika, ¼ teaspoon salt and ½ teaspoon black pepper.

In a large saucepan over medium, heat the oil until shimmering. Add the onion and ½ teaspoon salt, then cook, stirring occasionally, until fully softened, 7 to 10 minutes. Stir in the potato mixture, then add the wine and broth. Bring to a boil over medium-high, then cover, reduce to medium and simmer, stirring occasionally, until a skewer inserted into the potatoes meets no resistance, about 30 minutes.

Uncover and cook over medium, now stirring more often and adjusting the heat to maintain a gentle simmer, until the liquid has thickened and lightly coats the potatoes, about 7 minutes. Remove from the heat, cover and let stand for about 5 minutes. Remove and discard the bay and stir in the parsley. Taste and season with salt and black pepper.

Potato Soup with Almonds, Garlic and Lemon

Start to finish: 50 minutes / Servings: 4 to 6

The Greek dip called skordalia is a puree of potatoes and garlic that's enriched with a generous amount of olive oil. Occasionally nuts are added, and oftentimes lemon juice or vinegar, to lift the flavors. This pantry-friendly recipe takes those ingredients and turns them into a simple, flavorful soup. For safer pureeing—that is, to avoid hot liquid spouting out the top of the blender jar—allow the soup base to cool for about 5 minutes before blending, and process it in batches. You can use an immersion blender, if you own one, to puree the soup directly in the pot but the texture won't be quite as silky-smooth.

2 tablespoons extra-virgin olive oil, plus more to serve

¼ cup slivered OR sliced almonds

1 pound russet potatoes, peeled and cut into ¾-inch chunks

1 medium yellow onion, finely chopped

8 medium garlic cloves, smashed and peeled

Kosher salt and ground black pepper

1 quart low-sodium chicken broth OR vegetable broth

½ cup fresh flat-leaf parsley, roughly chopped, plus more to serve

⅓ cup lemon juice

In a medium saucepan, combine 2 tablespoons oil and the almonds. Place the pan over medium and cook, stirring occasionally, until lightly browned, about 3 minutes. Using a slotted spoon, transfer the almonds to a small bowl; set aside.

To the oil remaining in the pan, stir in the potatoes, onion, garlic, and ½ teaspoon each salt and pepper. Cover and cook over medium, stirring occasionally, until the potatoes begin to soften, about 10 minutes.

Add half of the almonds, the broth and 1 cup water; bring to a simmer over medium-high. Cover, reduce to medium and cook, stirring occasionally, until a skewer inserted into the potatoes meets no resistance, about 20 minutes. Remove from the heat and cool, uncovered, for about 5 minutes.

Stir the parsley into the soup base. Using a blender and working in 2 or 3 batches to avoid overfilling the jar, puree the mixture until smooth. Return the soup to the pot and warm over low, stirring, until heated through. Stir in the lemon juice, then taste and season with salt and pepper. Serve sprinkled with additional parsley and the remaining almonds and drizzled with additional oil.

Smashed Potatoes with Red Chimichurri

Start to finish: 1¼ hours (35 minutes active)
Servings: 4

To make smashed potatoes with creamy-dense interiors that contrast perfectly against craggy, well-browned exteriors, we first simmer the potatoes in heavily salted water until tender. We then drain them, put them on an oiled baking sheet, crush them with a flat-bottomed object such as a ramekin, then roast them in a hot oven. It's a multi-step process that's well worth the effort. A pantry-friendly red chimichurri sauce is a perfect spicy, tangy-sweet accompaniment to the potatoes. Leftover chimichurri, if you have any, will keep for up to a week in the refrigerator; bring to room temperature before serving.

1½ pounds small (1- to 1½-inch) Yukon Gold OR fingerling potatoes, unpeeled

Kosher salt

9 tablespoons grapeseed or other neutral oil, divided

2 tablespoons sweet paprika

2 tablespoons red pepper flakes

2 tablespoons dried oregano

1 medium garlic clove, finely grated

¼ cup balsamic vinegar

Chopped fresh flat-leaf parsley OR cilantro, to serve

Heat the oven to 500°F with a rack in the middle position. Add the potatoes and ¼ cup salt to a large saucepan, then add 1 quart water. Bring to a boil over high and cook, uncovered and stirring occasionally, until a skewer inserted into the largest potato meets no resistance, about 25 minutes.

Meanwhile, to make the chimichurri, in a small saucepan over low, combine 6 tablespoons oil, the paprika, pepper flakes and oregano. Cook, stirring occasionally, until the mixture begins to bubble, 5 to 7 minutes. Remove from the heat and stir in the garlic, then cool to room temperature.

When the potatoes are done, drain them in a colander and let cool for about 10 minutes. Coat a rimmed baking sheet with 2 tablespoons of the remaining oil. Distribute the potatoes in an even layer on the baking sheet and, using the bottom of a dry measuring cup or ramekin, press down on each potato so it is slightly flattened and splits open but remains intact. Brush the tops of the potatoes with the remaining 1 tablespoon oil. Roast the potatoes without turning them until browned and crisp, 35 to 40 minutes.

Meanwhile, whisk the vinegar and ½ teaspoon salt into the infused oil. When the potatoes are done, use a wide metal spatula to transfer them to a platter. Drizzle with some of the chimichurri and sprinkle with parsley. Serve the remaining chimichurri on the side.

Optional garnish: Flaky sea salt

Potatoes Boulangère

Start to finish: 2 hours (30 minutes active), plus cooling
Servings: 6 to 8

Pommes à la boulangère is a humble French potato gratin that turns a few basic ingredients into a satisfying side dish. We embellish our version with smoky, salty bacon and a few cloves of garlic. To prevent the potatoes from oxidizing, prep them while the onions cook, so the slices don't wait around long enough to discolor. A mandoline or a food processor fitted with the thin slicing disk makes quick work of the potato prep. This recipe can be halved and baked in an 8-inch square baking dish; bake covered for 45 minutes, then uncovered for 30 minutes.

3 tablespoons salted butter, cut into 1-tablespoon pieces, divided	**3 medium garlic cloves, minced**
4 ounces bacon, chopped	**½ cup low-sodium beef broth OR chicken broth**
3 medium yellow onions, halved and thinly sliced	**1 teaspoon dried rosemary OR dried thyme**
Kosher salt and ground black pepper	**3 pounds Yukon Gold potatoes**

Heat the oven to 375°F with a rack in the middle position. Coat a 9-by-13-inch baking dish with 1 tablespoon butter. In a 12-inch skillet over medium, cook the bacon, stirring occasionally, until crisp, about 5 minutes. Using a slotted spoon, transfer to a paper towel–lined plate, then pour off and discard all but 1 tablespoon bacon fat.

Return the pan to medium and add the remaining 2 tablespoons butter, followed by the onions and ¼ teaspoon each salt and pepper. Cover and cook, stirring occasionally, until the onions are softened and lightly golden, about 12 minutes. Off heat, stir in the garlic, followed by the broth and half of the cooked bacon.

While the onions cook, in a large bowl, stir together the rosemary, 1 teaspoon salt and ½ teaspoon pepper. Peel and slice the potatoes into rounds about ¹⁄₁₆ inch thick. Add the potatoes to the bowl and toss.

Distribute about a quarter of the potatoes in an even layer in the prepared baking dish, then evenly spoon on about a third of the onion mixture. Repeat the layering, dividing the remaining potatoes into thirds and the remaining onion mixture in half, for a total of 4 potato layers separated by 3 onion layers. Press down on the top to compress. Sprinkle with the remaining cooked bacon, cover tightly with foil and bake for 50 minutes.

Carefully remove the foil and bake until the surface of the gratin is browned and a skewer inserted into the potatoes meets no resistance, about another 40 minutes. Cool for about 10 minutes before serving.

Optional garnish: Flaky sea salt **OR** chopped fresh flat-leaf parsley

Butter-Browned Potatoes with Onion and Mustard

Start to finish: 40 minutes / Servings: 4

Potatoes and onions are a ho-hum combination, but in this recipe, inspired by classic French pommes de terre à la Lyonnaise, the humble ingredients become a fantastic dish. The secret: brown the potatoes and onions in butter so they take on a wonderful nutty flavor. This rustic side pairs deliciously with everything from seafood to meat, or simply serve them with eggs. To jump-start the cooking process, we partially cook the potatoes in the microwave, then finish them in the skillet. Be sure to rinse them well before microwaving; this removes some of the excess starch that will cause the slices to stick together.

3 tablespoons salted butter, cut into 1-tablespoon pieces, divided

2 tablespoons extra-virgin olive oil, divided

1 large yellow onion, halved and thinly sliced

Kosher salt and ground black pepper

1 tablespoon whole-grain mustard **OR** Dijon mustard, plus more if needed

1½ pounds Yukon Gold potatoes, unpeeled, cut crosswise into ¼-inch-thick slices

2 tablespoons chopped fresh flat-leaf parsley

In a 12-inch nonstick skillet over medium, melt 1 table-spoon butter with 1 tablespoon oil. Add the onion and ½ teaspoon salt. Cover and cook, stirring occasionally, until the onion is soft and lightly browned, about 12 minutes, adjusting the heat as needed so the onion cooks evenly. Transfer to a bowl, then stir in the mustard and ¼ teaspoon pepper; set aside. Reserve the skillet.

While the onion cooks, put the potatoes in a colander and rinse under cold running water, using your hands to separate slices. Transfer the potatoes to a medium microwave-safe bowl. Add the remaining 1 tablespoon oil and 3 tablespoons water; toss to combine. Cover and microwave on high until a skewer inserted into a potato slice meets no resistance, 6 to 7 minutes, stirring once about halfway through. Drain the potatoes.

In the same skillet over medium, melt the remaining 2 tablespoons butter. Add the potatoes and ½ teaspoon salt; stir to combine. Cook, turning the potatoes often with a spatula, until lightly browned, about 10 minutes.

Add the onion and stir gently to combine. Cook, stirring once or twice, until the onion is heated through, about 2 minutes.

Off heat, stir in the parsley. Taste and season with salt and pepper and additional mustard, if desired.

Turmeric Potatoes with Cumin Seeds and Ginger

Start to finish: 30 minutes / Servings: 4

This is our take on jeera aloo, a simple Indian dish of potatoes ("aloo") seasoned with cumin ("jeera") and other spices. Because the dish isn't saucy, it's sometimes referred to as a "dry curry." Traditional recipes call for amchoor, a tart, fruity-tasting powder made by pulverizing dried green mangoes. For ease, we swap in lemon juice. Cilantro stirred in at the last minute adds freshness and a pop of color. Serve the potatoes with steamed rice, warm naan and/or dal if you like.

1½ pounds small Yukon Gold potatoes (1 to 1½ inches in diameter), unpeeled, halved or quartered if larger

3 tablespoons grapeseed or other neutral oil

1 tablespoon minced fresh ginger

2 teaspoons cumin seeds

½ teaspoon ground turmeric

½ teaspoon ground coriander

¼ teaspoon cayenne pepper

Kosher salt

2 tablespoons chopped fresh cilantro

Lemon wedges, to serve

In a medium microwave-safe bowl, toss the potatoes with ¼ cup water. Cover and microwave on high until a skewer inserted into a potato meets no resistance, 6 to 7 minutes, stirring halfway through. Drain the potatoes; set aside.

In a 12-inch nonstick skillet over medium, combine the oil, ginger and cumin seeds; cook, stirring, until just sizzling, about 30 seconds. Add the turmeric, coriander and cayenne; cook, stirring, until fragrant, about 30 seconds. Add the potatoes and ½ teaspoon salt, then cook, stirring occasionally, until the potatoes are browned and crisp, about 10 minutes.

Off heat, stir in the cilantro, then taste and season with salt. Serve with lemon wedges.

Optional garnish: Plain yogurt

Potato and Pasta Soup

Start to finish: 45 minutes / Servings: 4 to 6

Known as pasta e patate, this rustic Italian carb-on-carb soup is hearty and satisfying, and it comes together easily with ingredients you likely already have in the pantry. It's also a great way to use up those odds and ends of pasta lingering in your cupboard, so feel free to mix whatever small shapes you have on hand. To boost the flavor, add some simple garnishes; see suggestions below.

2 tablespoons extra-virgin olive oil, plus more to serve

1 medium yellow onion, chopped

2 medium carrots, peeled, halved lengthwise and cut into ¼-inch pieces

Kosher salt and ground black pepper

3 medium garlic cloves, minced

3 tablespoons tomato paste

12 ounces Yukon Gold potatoes, peeled and cut into ¾-inch cubes

2 quarts low-sodium chicken broth **OR** vegetable broth

1 cup ditalini **OR** elbow macaroni **OR** other small pasta **OR** a combination

In a large saucepan over medium-high, heat the oil until shimmering. Stir in the onion, carrots and ½ teaspoon salt. Cover partially and cook, stirring occasionally, until the onion is softened and the carrots are slightly softened, 8 to 10 minutes.

Add the garlic and tomato paste, then cook, stirring, until the paste begins to brown and slightly sticks to the pan, about 1 minute. Add the potatoes and broth, then bring to a simmer. Stir in the pasta and ½ teaspoon salt. Cook, uncovered and stirring occasionally to keep the pasta from sticking, until the vegetables are tender and the pasta is al dente, about 15 minutes; adjust the heat as needed to maintain a brisk simmer.

Off heat, taste and season with salt and pepper. Serve drizzled with additional oil.

Optional garnish: Grated pecorino Romano (or Parmesan) cheese **OR** basil pesto **OR** chopped fresh flat-leaf parsley (or basil) **OR** a combination

Bold
BRASSICAS

Orecchiette with Broccolini / 143

Creamy, Garlicky Cauliflower and Cheddar Soup / 144

Cabbage, Apples and Kielbasa / 145

Stir-Fried Broccoli and Noodles / 146

Kale and Cheddar Melts with Caramelized Onion / 148

Pasta with Kale Pesto and Sun-Dried Tomatoes / 150

Roasted Broccolini and Chickpea Salad with Tahini-Lemon Dressing / 151

Greek-Style Braised Greens with Tomatoes and Paprika / 153

Kale and Miso Soup with Tofu and Ginger / 155

Pasta with Cauliflower, Olives and Sun-Dried Tomatoes / 156

Braised Cauliflower with Garlic, Bacon and Scallions / 157

Greens and Beans with Pecorino Crostini / 159

Orecchiette with Broccolini

Start to finish: 40 minutes / Servings: 4

Orecchiette with broccoli rabe (orecchiette con cime di rapa) is a signature pasta dish from the Puglia region of southern Italy. We were taught how to make it by Nunzia da Scalo, a cook in Bari, Italy. The bitterness of rabe is challenging for some palates, so we use sweeter, milder Broccolini. However, if you like the assertiveness of rabe, it can easily be used in place of the Broccolini, though rabe will cook a little more quickly. We boil the pasta in a minimal amount of water, then the starchy liquid that remains becomes the base for the sauce that marries the orecchiette and Broccolini. A finishing sprinkle of toasted seasoned breadcrumbs adds a crisp texture.

6 tablespoons extra-virgin olive oil, divided

8 medium garlic cloves, 4 minced, 4 thinly sliced

8 oil-packed anchovy fillets, minced

¾ cup panko breadcrumbs

1½ pounds Broccolini, trimmed and cut crosswise into ¼-inch pieces

½ to 1 teaspoon red pepper flakes

Kosher salt and ground black pepper

12 ounces orecchiette pasta

In a large Dutch oven over medium-high, heat 2 tablespoons of oil until shimmering. Add the minced garlic and half the anchovies, then cook, stirring, until fragrant, about 45 seconds. Add the panko and cook, stirring, until golden brown, about 3 minutes. Transfer to a bowl and set aside; wipe out the pot.

In the same pot over medium-high, heat 2 tablespoons of the remaining oil until shimmering. Add the Broccolini, pepper flakes, sliced garlic, ¾ teaspoon salt and ½ teaspoon black pepper. Cook, stirring occasionally, until the Broccolini is crisp-tender and the garlic is golden brown, 6 to 7 minutes. Add ½ cup water and continue to cook, stirring, until most of the moisture has evaporated and the Broccolini is fully tender, about 2 minutes. Transfer to a medium bowl and set aside.

In the same pot over medium-high, boil 5 cups water. Add 1 teaspoon salt and the pasta, then cook, stirring occasionally, until the pasta is al dente. Stir in the Broccolini mixture, the remaining 2 tablespoons oil and the remaining anchovies. Continue to cook over medium-high, stirring constantly, until the liquid has thickened enough to cling lightly to the pasta and Broccolini, about 1 minute. Remove from the heat, then taste and season with salt and pepper. Transfer to a serving bowl and sprinkle with the breadcrumbs.

Creamy, Garlicky Cauliflower and Cheddar Soup

Start to finish: 45 minutes (20 minutes active)
Servings: 4 to 6

Cauliflower simmered until completely tender then pureed yields a luxe, velvety soup without any cream. A good dose of garlic and sharp cheddar cheese adds big flavor to the mild, subtly sweet vegetable. If you own an immersion blender and would like to puree the soup directly in the pot, do so after the cauliflower mixture has cooled for five minutes. Add all of the cheese to the pot, then blend; the texture will be a little less smooth than when processed in a conventional blender but the flavor still will be great.

2 tablespoons extra-virgin olive oil, plus more to serve

1 large yellow onion, halved and thinly sliced

10 medium garlic cloves, smashed and peeled

Kosher salt and ground black pepper

½ teaspoon smoked paprika

3-pound head cauliflower, trimmed and cut into 1-inch florets

1 quart low-sodium chicken OR vegetable broth

8 ounces sharp white cheddar cheese, shredded (2 cups)

In a large pot over medium, heat the oil until shimmering. Stir in the onion, garlic and ½ teaspoon salt, then cover and cook, stirring occasionally, until the onion is softened but not browned, 6 to 8 minutes. Stir in the paprika and the cauliflower, then add the broth and 1 cup water. Bring to a simmer, then cover and cook until the cauliflower is fully tender, 15 to 20 minutes. Cool, uncovered, for about 5 minutes.

Using a blender and working in 2 or 3 batches to avoid overfilling the jar, puree the mixture with the cheddar until smooth. Return the soup to the pot and heat over low, stirring, until heated through; do not simmer. Taste and season with salt and pepper. Serve drizzled with oil and sprinkled with pepper.

Optional garnish: Thinly sliced scallions **OR** hot sauce **OR** a combination

Cabbage, Apples and Kielbasa

Start to finish: 40 minutes / Servings: 4

Cabbage, apples and sausage are a classic combination. We use kielbasa, a smoked sausage, but feel free to use whatever you have on hand, such as andouille or bratwurst. The sausages are sliced and combined with the other ingredients in the skillet, allowing their meaty flavor to permeate the dish. Any variety of apple will be delicious, though firm, crisp ones like Granny Smith or Fuji work best, as they hold their shape well when cooked.

2 tablespoons extra-virgin olive oil

1 medium yellow onion, chopped

2 medium apples, quartered, cored and sliced ¼ inch thick

2 medium garlic cloves, thinly sliced

1 teaspoon dried thyme OR caraway seeds, lightly crushed

1 pound green cabbage, cored and roughly chopped (about 8 cups)

Kosher salt and ground black pepper

14 to 16 ounces kielbasa OR other smoked sausage, cut on the diagonal into ½-inch slices

2 tablespoons cider vinegar

⅓ cup chopped fresh flat-leaf parsley

In a 12-inch skillet over medium, heat the oil until shimmering. Add the onion, half of the apple slices and the garlic. Cover and cook, stirring occasionally, until the onion and apple start to soften without browning, 5 to 7 minutes. Add the thyme and cook, stirring, until fragrant, about 30 seconds.

Add the cabbage, ½ teaspoon pepper and ½ cup water. Cover and cook over medium, stirring occasionally, until the cabbage is just tender, 10 to 12 minutes. Stir in the sausage, the remaining apple slices and the vinegar. Cover and cook without stirring until the sausage and apples are warmed through, another 3 to 5 minutes.

Off heat, stir in the parsley. Taste and season with salt and pepper.

Optional garnish: Mustard (Dijon, whole-grain or spicy brown)

Stir-Fried Broccoli and Noodles

Start to finish: 30 minutes / Servings: 4

This stir-fry pairs broccoli and onion (or bell pepper) with satisfyingly starchy noodles. To mimic the flavoring-building char of high-heat wok cooking, we sear the broccoli in a hot skillet before adding the sauce ingredients. With saltiness, sweetness and umami, either oyster sauce or hoisin offers big flavor and lots of complexity. We think both are handy, must-have ingredients to keep in the refrigerator. A couple tablespoons of rice vinegar and fresh ginger brighten up the flavors.

¼ **cup oyster sauce OR hoisin sauce**

2 **tablespoons unseasoned rice vinegar**

2 **tablespoons soy sauce**

Ground black pepper

8 **ounces linguine OR spaghetti OR dried lo mein**

2 **tablespoons grapeseed or other neutral oil**

1 **pound broccoli, stems peeled and thinly sliced, florets cut into ½- to 1-inch pieces**

½ **medium red onion, halved and thinly sliced OR 1 small bell pepper, stemmed, seeded and thinly sliced**

⅓ **cup roasted peanuts OR cashews, chopped**

1 **tablespoon minced fresh ginger**

In a large pot, bring 2 quarts water to a boil. Meanwhile, in a small bowl, whisk together the oyster sauce, vinegar, soy sauce and ½ teaspoon pepper.

When the water reaches a boil, stir in the pasta, then cook, stirring occasionally, until the noodles are tender. Reserve ½ cup of the cooking water, then drain in a colander. Whisk the reserved cooking water into the hoisin mixture. Set both the noodles and sauce mixture aside.

In a 12-inch skillet over medium-high, heat the oil until barely smoking. Add the broccoli and cook, stirring occasionally, until well browned in spots, 2 to 4 minutes. Reduce to medium and add the onion, peanuts and ginger; cook, stirring often, until the onion is browned, about 2 minutes.

Stir in the sauce mixture and simmer, uncovered, until the broccoli is bright green and the stem pieces are tender, 3 to 5 minutes; the sauce should be lightly syrupy. Add the noodles and cook, stirring and tossing, until the sauce coats the vegetables and noodles, about 2 minutes.

Optional garnish: Chopped fresh cilantro **OR** chili oil **OR** Sriracha

Kale and Cheddar Melts with Caramelized Onion

Start to finish: 40 minutes / Servings: 4

This recipe gives basic grilled cheese a tasty—and healthful!—update. We combine earthy wilted kale with sweet caramelized onions and melty cheese, plus a slathering of mustard for tangy contrast. To add a salty-smoky note, tuck crisp bacon slices inside the sandwiches before cooking them. Be sure to use a hearty sandwich bread that's sturdy enough to contain all of the fillings.

2 tablespoons
extra-virgin olive oil

1 medium yellow onion,
halved and thinly sliced

Kosher salt and ground
black pepper

1 large bunch lacinato
kale OR curly kale,
stemmed and chopped
into rough 1-inch pieces
(about 12 cups)

2 tablespoons salted
butter, room temperature

8 slices hearty white

OR whole-wheat OR
rye sandwich bread

4 teaspoons whole-
grain mustard OR Dijon
mustard

8 slices cheddar OR
provolone OR whole-milk
mozzarella OR pepper
jack cheese

4 slices cooked bacon
(optional)

In a 12-inch nonstick skillet over medium-high, heat the oil until shimmering. Add the onion, ¾ teaspoon salt and ½ teaspoon pepper. Cook, stirring occasionally, until the onion is soft and golden brown, about 10 minutes. Add the kale a large handful at a time, stirring to slightly wilt after each addition. Add ¼ cup water, then reduce to medium, cover and cook, stirring occasionally, until the kale is tender, 10 to 12 minutes. Transfer the kale mixture to a medium bowl; set aside. Wipe out the skillet.

Meanwhile, spread butter over 1 side of each slice of bread, evenly dividing the butter. Flip the slices buttered side down, then spread about ½ teaspoon mustard on each slice. Top each of 4 bread slices with 1 slice of cheese, a quarter of the kale mixture and 1 slice of bacon (if using), torn to fit. Top each with a slice of the remaining cheese, then with another slice of bread, buttered side up. Press on the sandwiches to compact the fillings.

Heat the skillet over medium until droplets of water flicked onto the surface quickly sizzle and evaporate. Add 2 of the sandwiches and cook until golden brown on the bottoms, 2 to 3 minutes. Using a wide spatula, flip the sandwiches and cook, pressing down lightly and adjusting the heat as needed, until golden brown on the second sides and the cheese is melted, 2 to 3 minutes. Transfer to a cutting board. Cook the remaining sandwiches in the same way (the second batch may cook faster). Cut each sandwich in half.

Pasta with Kale Pesto and Sun-Dried Tomatoes

Start to finish: 30 minutes / Servings: 4 to 6

We blend earthy, pleasantly bitter lacinato kale (also called Tuscan or dinosaur kale) with roasted almonds (or cashews) and Parmesan for richness and umami in this Italian-inspired dish. Just whirl everything in a food processor, then toss with cooked pasta and chopped oil-packed sun-dried tomatoes.

1 pound penne OR ziti OR farfalle pasta

Kosher salt and ground black pepper

1 cup whole roasted almonds OR cashews, plus more, chopped, to serve

2 ounces (without rind) Parmesan OR pecorino Romano cheese, cut into rough 1-inch pieces, plus more, finely grated, to serve

1 medium garlic clove, smashed and peeled

½ teaspoon red pepper flakes

1 small bunch lacinato kale, stemmed and roughly chopped OR 5-ounce container baby kale

½ cup extra-virgin olive oil

¼ cup oil-packed drained sun-dried tomatoes, chopped, plus 1 tablespoon sun-dried tomato oil

In a large pot, bring 4 quarts water to a boil. Add the pasta and 1 tablespoon salt, then cook, stirring occasionally, until al dente. Reserve 1 cup of the cooking water, then drain and return to the pot.

While the pasta cooks, in a food processor, combine the almonds, Parmesan, garlic, pepper flakes and ½ teaspoon each salt and black pepper. Process until the mixture resembles coarse sand. Add the kale and olive oil; process, scraping the bowl as needed, until almost completely smooth, about another 20 seconds.

Add the pesto to the pasta in the pot along with the sun-dried tomatoes, their oil and ½ cup of the reserved cooking water, then toss; add more cooking water as needed so the pesto coats the noodles. Taste and season with salt and black pepper. Serve sprinkled with chopped almonds and grated Parmesan.

Optional garnish: Lemon wedges

Roasted Broccolini and Chickpea Salad with Tahini-Lemon Dressing

Start to finish: 40 minutes / Servings: 4 to 6

Roasting brings out nutty notes in Broccolini (or broccoli) and accentuates the vegetable's natural sweetness. For this salad, we roast chickpeas alongside the vegetable, which gives the legumes a denser texture and a more concentrated earthy flavor. To pull all the elements together, we toss in a tahini-lemon dressing that adds a creamy, tangy richness, as well as a garlicky kick. This dish is hearty enough to be a vegetarian main, and it's great warm or at room temperature.

1 pound Broccolini, stems chopped into ¼-inch pieces, florets cut into 2-inch pieces OR 1 pound broccoli, stems halved and chopped into ¼-inch pieces, florets cut into 2-inch pieces

Two 15½-ounce cans chickpeas, rinsed and drained

4 tablespoons extra-virgin olive oil, divided

Kosher salt and ground black pepper

¼ cup tahini

2 teaspoons grated lemon zest, plus 3 tablespoons lemon juice

2 teaspoons honey

1 medium garlic clove, minced

¼ cup chopped drained roasted red peppers OR chopped drained oil-packed sun-dried tomatoes

Heat the oven to 425°F with the rack in the upper-middle position. In a large bowl, toss together the Broccolini, the chickpeas, 2 tablespoons oil, 2 teaspoons salt and 1 teaspoon pepper. Distribute in an even layer on a rimmed baking sheet; reserve the bowl. Roast until the florets are charred and tender-crisp and the chickpeas begin to brown, 20 to 25 minutes; stir once about halfway through.

Meanwhile, in the same bowl, whisk together the remaining 2 tablespoons oil, the tahini, lemon zest and juice, honey, garlic, ¼ cup water and ¼ teaspoon each salt and pepper; set aside.

When the Broccolini-chickpea mixture is done, immediately add it to the tahini mixture along with the roasted peppers. Toss, then taste and season with salt and pepper. Serve warm or at room temperature.

Optional garnish: Toasted sliced almonds OR roughly chopped roasted pistachios

Greek-Style Braised Greens with Tomatoes and Paprika

Start to finish: 35 minutes / Servings: 4

The Greek dish called tsigarelli served as inspiration for this flavorful way with greens. Wild edible plants are used in traditional tsigarelli, but we opt for kale (either curly or lacinato—also called Tuscan or dinosaur—kale) or Swiss chard. In most recipes, kale stems are discarded, but for this, we chop them and sauté them with a sliced onion to give the dish more substance. Tomatoes, garlic, paprika, lemon and extra-virgin olive oil bring bold Mediterranean flavor to the mix. Serve as a side dish or make it a vegetarian main with orzo or polenta alongside.

2 tablespoons extra-virgin olive oil, plus more to serve

1 large yellow onion, halved and thinly sliced

1 large bunch (about 1 pound) lacinato kale OR curly kale OR Swiss chard, stems chopped, leaves roughly chopped, reserved separately

Kosher salt and ground black pepper

2 medium garlic cloves, minced

1 tablespoon sweet paprika

¼ to ½ teaspoon cayenne pepper

14½-ounce can whole tomatoes, crushed by hand OR 2 ripe tomatoes, cored and chopped

1 cup lightly packed fresh flat-leaf parsley OR mint OR dill OR a combination

2 tablespoons lemon juice, plus lemon wedges, to serve

In a large Dutch oven over medium, heat the oil until shimmering. Add the onion, kale stems and ½ teaspoon salt, then cook, stirring occasionally, until the onion is softened, 6 to 8 minutes. Add the garlic, paprika and cayenne; cook, stirring, until fragrant, about 30 seconds.

Stir in the tomatoes with juices, ½ cup water and ½ teaspoon each salt and black pepper. Bring to a simmer, then reduce to medium-low and simmer, uncovered and stirring occasionally, until the tomatoes have broken down and formed a thick sauce, 6 to 8 minutes.

Stir in the kale leaves. Cook, uncovered and stirring occasionally, until the leaves are tender, 5 to 6 minutes. Stir in the parsley and lemon juice, then taste and season with salt and pepper. Serve with lemon wedges.

Optional garnish: Crumbled feta cheese

Kale and Miso Soup with Tofu and Ginger

Start to finish: 45 minutes / Servings: 4

This soup is clean and light yet packed with flavor thanks to umami-rich miso. Sriracha (or chili-garlic sauce) adds garlicky notes as well as spiciness and a little tang; use the smaller amount for mild palates or the larger amount (or even more) for those who like a little burn. We prefer lacinato kale (also called Tuscan kale or dinosaur kale) over curly kale in the soup, as lacinato's texture is silkier and more tender, but either type works. You also can use tofu of any firmness, from silken to extra-firm, but if using the softer types, be sure to stir gently to avoid breaking up the pieces.

3 tablespoons
white miso OR red miso

1 to 2 tablespoons
Sriracha OR chili-garlic
sauce

2 tablespoons grapeseed
or other neutral oil

1 bunch scallions,
white and green parts
thinly sliced, reserved
separately

2 medium carrots, peeled,
quartered lengthwise and
thinly sliced

2 tablespoons
minced fresh ginger

1 quart low-sodium
chicken broth OR
vegetable broth

1 bunch lacinato
OR curly kale, stemmed
and roughly chopped

14-ounce container tofu
(see headnote), drained,
cut into ½-inch cubes

Kosher salt and ground
black pepper

In a medium bowl, whisk together the miso, Sriracha and 3 tablespoons water.

In a large pot over medium, heat the oil until shimmering. Add the scallion whites and carrots; cook, stirring occasionally, until the vegetables are softened, about 2 minutes. Add the ginger and cook, stirring, until fragrant, about 30 seconds. Stir in the broth and 2 cups water, then bring to a boil over medium-high. Reduce to medium-low and simmer, uncovered and stirring occasionally, until the carrots are tender, 5 to 8 minutes.

Stir in the kale, return to a simmer and cook, stirring occasionally, until the kale is tender, about 10 minutes. Stir in the miso mixture and return to a simmer. Remove the pot from the heat, add the scallion greens and the tofu, then gently stir. Let stand until the tofu is heated through, 2 to 3 minutes. Taste and season with salt and pepper.

Optional garnish: Toasted sesame seeds OR crumbled seaweed snacks OR both

Pasta with Cauliflower, Olives and Sun-Dried Tomatoes

Start to finish: 40 minutes / Servings: 4 to 6

Naturally sweet and mild in flavor, cauliflower pairs well with bold ingredients. In this recipe, we create a plant-based pasta dish that packs a punch thanks to briny olives, tangy-sweet sun-dried tomatoes and lots of garlic. A toasty breadcrumb topping spiked with red pepper flakes adds crisp texture. We like to use Japanese-style panko because it's light and airy and crisps beautifully when toasted. Finish the dish with chopped fresh herbs or grated cheese, if you like; see the suggestions below.

4 tablespoons extra-virgin olive oil, divided

½ cup panko breadcrumbs

3 medium garlic cloves, minced

½ teaspoon red pepper flakes, divided

Kosher salt and ground black pepper

2-pound head cauliflower, trimmed and chopped into ½-inch pieces

½ cup pitted black OR green olives OR a combination, chopped

¼ cup drained oil-packed sun-dried tomatoes, chopped

2 tablespoons red wine vinegar

8 ounces shells OR ziti

In a 12-inch nonstick skillet over medium, combine 1 tablespoon oil, the panko, half of the garlic, ¼ teaspoon pepper flakes and ¼ teaspoon each salt and black pepper. Cook, stirring often, until the panko is golden brown, about 3 minutes. Transfer to a small bowl; set aside. Wipe out the skillet.

In the same skillet over medium, heat the remaining 3 tablespoons oil until shimmering. Add the cauliflower and ½ teaspoon each salt and black pepper. Cook, uncovered and stirring occasionally, until the cauliflower is well browned and tender, 12 to 15 minutes. Add the remaining garlic and cook, stirring often, until fragrant, about 1 minute. Transfer the cauliflower to a large bowl, then stir in the olives, sun-dried tomatoes, vinegar and the remaining ¼ teaspoon pepper flakes.

In a large saucepan, bring 2 quarts water to a boil. Add the pasta and 2 teaspoons salt, then cook, stirring occasionally, until al dente. Drain the pasta, add to the bowl with the cauliflower mixture and toss. Taste and season with salt and black pepper. Serve sprinkled with the breadcrumbs.

Optional garnish: Chopped fresh flat-leaf parsley (or basil) **OR** finely grated Parmesan (or pecorino Romano) cheese **OR** both

Braised Cauliflower with Garlic, Bacon and Scallions

Start to finish: 30 minutes / Servings: 4 to 6

Salty, smoky bacon and lightly toasted garlic bring loads of flavor to cauliflower simmered in chicken broth. At the end of cooking, we thicken the broth with a cornstarch slurry to create a velvety sauce. A full bunch of scallions, thinly sliced and stirred in to finish, adds punchy allium flavor.

4 to 6 ounces thick-cut bacon, cut crosswise into ½-inch pieces

3 medium garlic cloves, thinly sliced

2- to 2½-pound head cauliflower, trimmed and cut into 1-inch florets

2 cups low-sodium chicken broth

2 tablespoons cornstarch

Kosher salt and ground black pepper

1 bunch scallions, thinly sliced on the diagonal

In a 12-inch skillet, cook the bacon, stirring occasionally, until browned and crisp. Add the garlic and cook, stirring, until lightly browned. Stir in the cauliflower and broth. Cover, bring to a simmer and cook until the florets are tender. In a small bowl, whisk together the cornstarch and 2 tablespoons water. Stir the cornstarch slurry into the cauliflower mixture and cook, stirring, until the sauce returns to a simmer and has thickened. Season with salt and pepper, then stir in the scallions.

Optional garnish: Chili oil **OR** hot sauce

Greens and Beans with Pecorino Crostini

Start to finish: 40 minutes / Servings: 4

Greens and beans are great companions. In this take, hearty kale and creamy white beans are a perfect match especially when accented by the high-impact flavors of garlic, rosemary and pepper flakes. We use the liquid from one can of beans to create a cooking liquid that's full-bodied, and when the kale is tender, we mash a small portion of the beans to create creaminess. Toasty, cheesy crostini are an ideal accompaniment, but if you like, simply serve hunks of warm, crusty bread alongside.

Two 15½-ounce cans cannellini OR great northern beans

Twelve ½-inch-thick baguette slices

3 tablespoons extra-virgin olive oil, divided, plus more to serve

2 ounces (1 cup) pecorino Romano OR Parmesan cheese, finely grated, plus more to serve

3 medium garlic cloves, minced

½ teaspoon dried rosemary OR 1 sprig fresh rosemary

¼ teaspoon red pepper flakes

2 bunches lacinato OR curly kale, stemmed and chopped (about 6 cups)

Kosher salt and ground black pepper

Heat the oven to 400°F with a rack in the upper-middle position. Drain and discard the liquid from 1 can of beans. Drain the liquid from the second can into a 2-cup liquid measuring cup, then add enough water to equal 2 cups.

Brush both sides of the baguette slices with 2 tablespoons oil. Place the bread in a single layer on a rimmed baking sheet and bake until browned and crisped on both sides, 6 to 8 minutes, flipping the slices about halfway through. Remove from the oven and sprinkle evenly with half of the cheese. Bake until the cheese is melted, about 2 minutes; set aside.

In a 12-inch skillet over medium, cook the remaining 1 tablespoon oil, the garlic, rosemary and pepper flakes, stirring occasionally, until fragrant, about 1 minute. Add about half of the kale, ½ each teaspoon salt and black pepper, and half of the bean liquid; toss with tongs until the greens are wilted, 1 to 2 minutes. Add the remaining kale and the remaining bean liquid, tossing until the greens are wilted. Stir in the beans and bring to a simmer over medium-high; cover, reduce to medium-low and simmer, stirring occasionally, until the kale is tender, 8 to 10 minutes.

Off heat, remove and discard the rosemary sprig (if used). Using a fork, mash some of the beans for a little creaminess. Stir in the remaining cheese, then taste and season with salt and black pepper. Serve drizzled with additional oil and sprinkled with additional cheese; offer the crostini on the side.

Good
EGGS

Eggs Fried in Parmesan Breadcrumbs with Wilted Spinach

Start to finish: 20 minutes / Servings: 2 or 4

Eggs fried in breadcrumbs were the creation of the late Judy Rodgers, the longtime chef of Zuni Cafe, San Francisco's landmark restaurant. The iconic dish consists of crisp, toasted breadcrumbs as a textural underlay for eggs that are cooked on top, the whites seeping slightly into the crumbs before they set and the yolks on the surface remaining sunny and runny. For our version, we use panko instead of stale bread torn into pieces, as Rodgers did, and before toasting, we mix in a little Parmesan (or manchego) cheese to add umami, plus a touch of vinegar to sharpen the flavors. Baby spinach scattered over the eggs as they fry in the covered pan offers insulation so they cook gently. If you prefer your yolks medium- or hard-set, add 1 to 3 minutes to the cooking time. Only four eggs fit comfortably in a 12-inch skillet; if you need more for serving, it's best to make another batch or use a second 12-inch nonstick skillet.

¾ cup panko breadcrumbs

1 ounce finely grated (½ cup) Parmesan cheese, plus more to serve

¾ teaspoon dried thyme

½ teaspoon smoked sweet paprika

2 teaspoons sherry vinegar

Kosher salt and ground black pepper

5 tablespoons extra-virgin olive oil, divided, plus more to serve

4 large eggs

2½ ounces (about 3½ cups) baby spinach

In a 12-inch nonstick skillet, combine the panko, Parmesan, thyme, paprika, vinegar, ½ teaspoon pepper and 3 tablespoons oil. Stir until well combined.

Set the skillet over medium-high and toast the mixture, stirring often, until light golden brown, 2 to 3 minutes. Working quickly, use the back of a spoon to create 4 evenly spaced clearings in the mixture. Pour the remaining 2 tablespoons oil into the clearings, dividing it evenly, then crack an egg into each; it should sizzle on contact.

Sprinkle the eggs with salt, then cover them with the spinach. Reduce to medium-low, cover the skillet and cook, occasionally rotating the pan to help ensure even browning, until the whites are set but the yolks are still runny, 5 to 7 minutes. Remove the pan from the heat. Using a thin, wide spatula, transfer the eggs to individual plates. Drizzle with additional oil and sprinkle with additional cheese.

Cheesy Tex-Mex Migas

Start to finish: 20 minutes / Servings: 4 to 6

Migas is a Tex-Mex favorite of tortilla chips mixed into scrambled eggs that are flavored with sautéed aromatic vegetables. The chips soften slightly, taking on a satisfying crunchy-chewy texture. This version includes melty cheese folded in at the end to give the migas rich flavor and gooeyness. If you can, finish the dish with at least one of the optional garnishes listed below, and serve it with warmed tortillas. Refried beans also are great alongside.

8 large eggs

Kosher salt and ground black pepper

2 tablespoons extra-virgin olive oil

1 medium green OR red bell pepper, stemmed, seeded and chopped

1 large ripe tomato, cored and chopped OR 1 cup cherry or grape tomatoes, halved

1 medium yellow onion, chopped

1 teaspoon chili powder OR ground cumin

3 ounces tortilla chips (4 cups), roughly crushed

2 ounces cheddar OR Monterey jack cheese, shredded (½ cup)

In a large bowl, whisk together the eggs and ½ teaspoon salt; set aside. In a 12-inch nonstick skillet over medium-high, heat the oil until shimmering. Add the bell pepper, tomato, onion, chili powder and ¼ teaspoon salt; cook, stirring occasionally, until the vegetables are softened and lightly browned, 7 to 9 minutes.

Reduce to medium and add about ½ cup of the crushed tortilla chips. Cook, stirring, until any moisture from the vegetables is absorbed, about 30 seconds. Pour the egg mixture into the center of the skillet and cook, using a silicone spatula to stir continuously, pushing the egg mixture toward the middle as the edges begin to set, until the eggs are partially set but still a bit runny, about 2 minutes.

Scatter on the cheese and cook, stirring, until the cheese melts and the eggs are mostly set, about 30 seconds. Remove the pan from the heat, add the remaining tortilla chips and fold just until combined. Taste and season with salt and pepper.

Optional garnish: Chopped fresh cilantro OR diced or sliced avocado OR salsa OR pickled jalapeños OR hot sauce OR a combination

Spanish Tortilla with Potato Chips

Start to finish: 35 minutes / Servings: 4 to 6

Spanish chef Ferran Adrià, father of the molecular gastronomy movement, came up with a genius shortcut for making tortilla española, using potato chips instead of slowly cooking sliced raw potatoes in olive oil. Borrowing his time-saving technique, we keep our version of this egg and potato tortilla simple, adding some softened onions and a dash of smoked paprika.

10 large eggs

Kosher salt and ground black pepper

3½ ounces (5 cups) kettle-style potato chips, lightly crushed

3 tablespoons extra-virgin olive oil

2 medium yellow onions, halved and thinly sliced

1 teaspoon smoked paprika, plus more to serve

⅓ cup lightly packed fresh flat-leaf parsley, chopped

Heat the oven to 350°F with a rack in the middle position. In a large bowl, whisk together the eggs and ½ teaspoon salt. Add the potato chips and stir to coat; set aside.

In a 10-inch oven-safe nonstick skillet over medium-high, heat the oil until shimmering. Add the onions, paprika and ¼ teaspoon each salt and pepper. Cover and cook, stirring often, until the onions are softened and lightly browned, 12 to 15 minutes. Reduce to medium-low, then add the egg mixture and quickly stir to combine with the onions. Cook undisturbed until the eggs are set and opaque at the edges, 1 to 2 minutes.

Place the skillet in the oven and bake until the eggs are just set on the surface, about 12 minutes. Remove the skillet from the oven (the handle will be hot). Run the spatula around the edges of the tortilla and underneath it to loosen, then carefully slide onto a cutting board. Serve warm or at room temperature, garnished with the parsley, sprinkled with additional paprika and cut into wedges.

Optional garnish: Chopped fresh chives **OR** flaky salt **OR** both

164

Chinese Stir-Fried Eggs with Tomatoes

Start to finish: 20 minutes / Servings: 4

Stir-fried eggs with tomatoes is quick, pantry-friendly Chinese comfort food, and there are endless variations. In our version, we don't add sugar (a classic ingredient), but we do add a dollop of sweet tomato flavor via a tablespoon of ketchup. We cook the eggs and tomatoes separately, starting with the eggs. We then add tomatoes to the empty skillet, cook them until just beginning to blister, then arrange them on the eggs. Finally, our sauce goes into the skillet to heat and thicken. Serve the eggs with rice for a quick dinner.

3 ripe plum tomatoes (about 12 ounces total), cored, halved and seeded

4 tablespoons unseasoned rice vinegar, divided

Kosher salt and ground white pepper

1 tablespoon ketchup

2 teaspoons finely grated fresh ginger **OR** 1 medium garlic clove, finely grated **OR** both

½ teaspoon red pepper flakes

1 teaspoon toasted sesame oil

3 teaspoons soy sauce, divided

8 large eggs

3 tablespoons grapeseed or other neutral oil, divided

Cut each tomato half into thirds. In a medium bowl, toss the tomatoes with 1 tablespoon vinegar and ½ teaspoon white pepper. In a small bowl, stir together ¼ cup water, the remaining 3 tablespoons vinegar, the ketchup, ginger, pepper flakes, sesame oil, 2 teaspoons soy sauce and ½ teaspoon white pepper; set aside. In a second medium bowl, whisk together the eggs, remaining 1 teaspoon soy sauce and ½ teaspoon white pepper.

Drain the tomatoes and set aside. In a 12-inch nonstick skillet over medium-high, heat 2 tablespoons grapeseed oil until barely smoking. Pour the eggs into the center of the pan, letting the eggs puff up at the edges. Use a spatula to stir the eggs, pushing them toward the middle as they begin to set at the edges and folding the cooked egg onto itself. Cook until just set, 45 to 60 seconds; transfer to a plate.

In the empty skillet, heat the remaining 1 tablespoon oil over medium-high until beginning to smoke. Add the drained tomatoes and cook, undisturbed, until just beginning to blister, 30 to 60 seconds. Arrange the tomatoes on top of the eggs.

Return the skillet to high heat and pour the sauce mixture into the skillet. Cook, stirring constantly, until thickened, about 30 seconds. Taste and season with salt and white pepper. Pour over the tomatoes.

Optional garnish: Thinly sliced scallions **OR** toasted sesame seeds **OR** chili oil **OR** a combination

Egg Salad with Harissa, Olives and Almonds

Start to finish: 30 minutes / Makes about 2 cups

Egg salad is an excellent way to create a satisfying meal with ingredients that probably already are in your kitchen. It can take on any number of flavor profiles, from North African to East Asian. We prefer to hard-cook our eggs by steaming them, then shock them in ice water to stop the cooking and quickly cool them. The eggs never crack during cooking, the yolks are perfectly done every time and the shells peel off easily. This egg salad and any of the variations below are great sandwiched between slices of pillowy bread or served in crisp lettuce leaves.

8 large eggs

2 tablespoons mayonnaise

2 tablespoons harissa paste

1 tablespoon lemon juice

Kosher salt and ground black pepper

2 tablespoons chopped pitted green olives

2 tablespoons slivered almonds, toasted and chopped

1 tablespoon finely chopped fresh flat-leaf parsley OR cilantro

Fill a large saucepan with about 1 inch of water. Place a steamer basket in the pan, cover and bring the water to a boil over medium-high. Add the eggs to the steamer basket, cover and cook for 11 minutes. Meanwhile, fill a medium bowl with ice water. Using tongs, transfer the eggs to the ice water and let stand until cool, 10 to 15 minutes. Peel and roughly chop the eggs.

In a medium bowl, whisk together the mayonnaise, harissa, lemon juice, ½ teaspoon salt and ¼ teaspoon pepper. Add the eggs, olives, almonds and parsley. Using a silicone spatula, fold until just combined. Taste and season with salt and pepper. Serve at room temperature or chilled.

Curried Egg Salad with Raisins and Cashews

Prepare the eggs as directed. In a large bowl, whisk together **2 tablespoons mayonnaise, 4 teaspoons curry powder, 1 teaspoon grated lime OR lemon zest plus 2 teaspoons lime OR lemon juice, ¼ teaspoon cayenne pepper, ½ teaspoon kosher salt and ¼ teaspoon ground black pepper.** Add the chopped eggs, **¼ cup raisins** (soaked in hot water to cover until softened, then drained), **¼ cup roasted cashews** (chopped), **1 medium carrot** (peeled and shredded on the large holes of a box grater). Using a silicone spatula, fold until just combined. Taste and season with salt and black pepper. Serve at room temperature or chilled.

Chipotle and Cumin Egg Salad

Prepare the eggs as directed. In a medium bowl, whisk together **2 tablespoons mayonnaise, 2 chipotle chilies in adobo sauce** (minced), **1 tablespoon lime juice, 1 teaspoon ground cumin, ½ teaspoon dried oregano, ½ teaspoon kosher salt and ¼ teaspoon ground black pepper.** Add the chopped eggs and **1 tablespoon chopped fresh cilantro.** Using a silicone spatula, fold until just combined. Taste and season with salt and black pepper. Serve at room temperature or chilled.

Egg Salad with Gochujang, Sesame and Scallions

Prepare the eggs as directed. In a medium bowl, whisk together **2 tablespoons mayonnaise, 2 tablespoons gochujang, 1 teaspoon toasted sesame oil, ½ teaspoon kosher salt and ¼ teaspoon ground black pepper.** Add the chopped eggs, **¼ cup thawed frozen peas** (patted dry), **1 tablespoon sesame seeds** (toasted) and **3 scallions** (thinly sliced). Using a silicone spatula, fold until just combined. Taste and season with salt and black pepper. Serve at room temperature or chilled.

Chinese-Style Vegetable Omelets

Start to finish: 40 minutes (30 minutes active)
Servings: 2 to 4

These vegetable-packed omelets are inspired by egg foo young, minus the deep-frying and gloppy brown gravy. They're a great way to use up leftover vegetables. We call for cabbage, onion and bell pepper, but bean sprouts, mushrooms and scallions also are good choices; you'll need a total of about 4 cups raw vegetables. To boost the protein, stir in some chopped cooked shrimp, pork or chicken. And for a fun twist, make St. Paul sandwiches, which actually come from St. Louis. Slather the Sriracha mayo on white bread, then tuck the omelet, lettuce, tomato and pickles inside.

¼ cup mayonnaise

1 tablespoon Sriracha OR chili-garlic sauce

6 large eggs

1 tablespoon soy sauce

1 tablespoon cornstarch

Kosher salt and ground white OR black pepper

3½ tablespoons grapeseed or other neutral oil, divided

2 cups thinly sliced green cabbage

1 small yellow onion, halved and thinly sliced

½ medium red bell pepper, stemmed, seeded and thinly sliced

In a small bowl, stir together the mayonnaise and Sriracha; set aside. In a medium bowl, whisk together the eggs, soy sauce, cornstarch, ½ teaspoon salt and ¼ teaspoon pepper; set aside.

In a 12-inch nonstick skillet over medium-high, heat 1½ tablespoons oil until shimmering. Add the cabbage, onion, bell pepper, ½ teaspoon salt and ¼ teaspoon pepper; cook, stirring occasionally, until the vegetables are lightly browned, 6 to 8 minutes. Remove from the heat. Whisk the egg mixture to recombine, then add the hot vegetables and, using a silicone spatula, stir until well combined. Wipe out the skillet.

In the same skillet over medium-high, heat 1 tablespoon of the remaining oil until shimmering. Drop 2 heaping ½-cup portions of the egg-vegetable mixture into the skillet, spacing them on opposite sides of the pan. Using the spatula, spread each portion into a 4- to 5-inch round; if they spread into an oval shape, don't worry, just keep them separated. Cook until the edges start to brown and puff and the omelets are nicely browned on the bottoms, about 3 minutes. Using a wide spatula, flip the omelets and cook, reducing the heat as needed if the omelets are cooking too quickly, until golden brown on the second sides, about another 2 minutes. Transfer to a large plate.

Cook the remaining two omelets in the same way using the remaining 1 tablespoon oil. Serve with the Sriracha mayo.

Optional garnish: Toasted sesame oil **OR** thinly sliced scallions **OR** both

Oven-Baked Eggs in a Hole with Toasted Parmesan

Start to finish: 20 minutes / Servings: 4

The childhood favorite, egg in a hole, gets a boost in flavor from the garlic clove that's rubbed onto the bread before toasting and the Parmesan cheese that browns and crisps during cooking. For ease, we use a baking sheet in the oven rather than a skillet on the stovetop, so four servings can be made simultaneously. Be sure to choose large, sturdy sandwich bread that's sliced about ¾ inch thick. Thinner slices won't be deep enough to hold the cracked egg in the center cutouts. This recipe can easily be increased by half to make six servings.

4 slices hearty white sandwich bread (see headnote)

1 medium garlic clove, halved lengthwise

2 tablespoons salted butter, melted

2 tablespoons extra-virgin olive oil

4 large eggs

Kosher salt and ground black pepper

1 ounce Parmesan cheese, finely grated (½ cup)

Heat the oven to 475°F with a rack in the middle position. Mist a rimmed baking sheet with cooking spray. Rub each slice of bread on both sides with the cut side of the garlic, then place the slices in a single layer on the prepared baking sheet; discard the garlic. In a small bowl, stir together the butter and oil. Brush both sides of each slice with the butter-oil mixture.

Using a 2½- to 3-inch round biscuit cutter, stamp out the center of each slice of bread and place the cutouts on the baking sheet. Crack 1 egg into the hole of each slice of bread. Sprinkle salt and pepper onto the eggs and the bread, including the cutouts, followed by the Parmesan. Bake until the bread is toasted and the eggs are just set, 3 to 4 minutes for runny yolks or 5 minutes for fully set eggs.

Using a wide metal spatula, transfer each egg in a hole and its cutout to an individual plate.

Optional garnish: Chopped fresh flat-leaf parsley **OR** thinly sliced scallions **OR** hot sauce **OR** a combination

Turkish-Style Eggs and Spinach

Start to finish: 30 minutes / Servings: 4 to 6

The Turkish spinach and egg dish known as ispanakli yumurta resembles Middle Eastern shakshuka, but spinach takes the place of a tomato-based sauce. Prepackaged baby spinach makes the recipe quick to prepare—the key is to cook it very briefly so it doesn't become watery. Frozen spinach also works well; just thaw it, drain it in a colander and, if it's still very wet, pat it dry with paper towels. This dish often is served with yogurt. We stir some in with the spinach to create a rich, creamy sauce that won't break under moderate heat. Serve flatbread alongside.

2 tablespoons salted butter

1 tablespoon extra-virgin olive oil, plus more to serve

1 medium yellow OR red onion, finely chopped

Kosher salt and ground black pepper

2 medium garlic cloves, minced

½ teaspoon ground cumin

¼ teaspoon red pepper flakes OR ½ teaspoon Aleppo pepper

1-pound container baby spinach OR 1-pound bag frozen chopped spinach, thawed, drained in a colander and patted dry (see headnote)

½ cup plain whole-milk Greek yogurt

6 large eggs

In a large Dutch oven over medium-high, heat the butter and oil until the butter melts. Add the onion and ½ teaspoon each salt and black pepper. Cook, stirring often, until softened but not brown, 5 to 7 minutes. Add the garlic, cumin and pepper flakes; cook, stirring, until fragrant, about 30 seconds.

If using fresh spinach, add it a large handful at a time, stirring to slightly wilt before each addition. Add the yogurt and ½ teaspoon salt. Cook until the spinach is just wilted and deep green and the yogurt is mostly incorporated, about 2 minutes. If using frozen spinach, add it to the pot, along with the yogurt and salt, and stir until combined.

Reduce to medium and use the back of a spoon to form 6 evenly spaced wells in the spinach, each about 2 inches wide and deep enough that the bottom of the pot is visible. Crack 1 egg into each, then sprinkle with salt and black pepper. Cover and cook until the egg whites are set but the yolks are still runny, 3 to 5 minutes, rotating the pot about halfway through for even cooking. Serve drizzled with additional oil.

Optional garnish: Crumbled feta cheese **OR** hot sauce **OR** both

Throw-it-Together TOFU

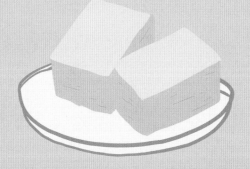

Tofu and Sweet Pepper Scramble with Smoked Paprika

Start to finish: 35 minutes / Servings: 4 to 6

This easy, speedy tofu scramble takes on a Spanish accent thanks to red bell pepper, smoked paprika, cumin and garlic. To prevent the dish from becoming watery, we pat the tofu dry before and after crumbling it in order to wick away some of the moisture. Then the crumbles get a quick toss with olive oil and spices to boost their otherwise mild flavor. The bell pepper and onion are cooked low and slow until they're silky and softened before the tofu is added to the skillet.

14-ounce container extra-firm **OR** firm tofu, drained and patted dry

4 tablespoons extra-virgin olive oil, divided, plus more to serve

1 teaspoon smoked paprika, divided

1 teaspoon ground cumin, divided

Kosher salt and ground black pepper

1 medium red bell pepper, stemmed, seeded and chopped

1 medium red **OR** yellow onion, chopped

2 medium garlic cloves, thinly sliced

3 tablespoons finely chopped fresh flat-leaf parsley

Line a large plate with a double layer of paper towels. Using your hands or a fork, crumble the tofu into small pieces. Cover with another double layer of paper towels and gently press to remove excess moisture, then transfer to a medium bowl. Add 1 tablespoon oil, ½ teaspoon paprika, ½ teaspoon cumin and ¾ teaspoon each salt and pepper; toss, then set aside.

In a 12-inch nonstick skillet over medium, heat the remaining 3 tablespoons oil until shimmering. Add the bell pepper, onion and ¼ teaspoon salt, then cook, stirring occasionally, until the vegetables soften and start to brown, 13 to 16 minutes. Add the garlic and remaining ½ teaspoon each paprika and cumin; cook, stirring occasionally, until the garlic softens, about 2 minutes.

Add the tofu and cook over medium-high, stirring occasionally, until the tofu is warmed through, 2 to 3 minutes. Off heat, stir in the parsley, then taste and season with salt and pepper. Serve drizzled with additional oil.

Tofu and Kimchi Soup

Start to finish: 40 minutes / Servings: 4

This flavorful soup is a much-simplified version of
Korean kimchi jjigae. Bacon takes the place of the pork
that's commonly used in kimchi jjigae; its smokiness
works perfectly with the spiciness and fermented notes
of both kimchi and gochujang, and its fat lends the
soup just enough richness. Be sure to reserve the juices
that drain from the kimchi, as they're great for adding
salty tang to the soup at the very end, if needed. Serve
with steamed rice on the side.

**2 slices bacon, finely
chopped**

**1 bunch scallions, white
parts thinly sliced,
green parts cut into
1-inch pieces, reserved
separately**

**6 cups low-sodium
chicken broth**

**1½ tablespoons soy sauce,
plus more if needed**

**3 to 4 tablespoons
gochujang**

2 tablespoons mirin

**14-ounce container
firm OR extra-firm tofu,
drained, patted dry and
cut into ½-inch cubes**

**2 cups cabbage kimchi,
drained (juices reserved)
and roughly chopped**

In a large saucepan over medium, cook the bacon,
stirring, until lightly browned, about 2 minutes. Pour
off and discard all but 1 tablespoon of the fat. Add the
scallion whites and cook, stirring, until softened, about
1 minute. Add the broth and bring to a simmer, scraping
up any browned bits. Whisk in the soy sauce, gochujang
and mirin. Bring to a simmer and cook uncovered for
15 minutes.

Pour off and discard any water released by the tofu,
then add the tofu and kimchi to the saucepan; stir to
combine. Return to a simmer and cook, stirring
occasionally, until heated through, about 10 minutes.
Off heat, stir in the scallion greens; let stand for about
5 minutes. Taste and, if desired, stir in additional soy
sauce and some or all of the reserved kimchi juices.

Optional garnish: Toasted sesame oil **OR** toasted
sesame seeds **OR** halved soft-cooked eggs **OR** a
combination

Salt and Pepper Tofu

Start to finish: 30 minutes / Servings: 4 to 6

Instead of deep-frying, a common cooking technique to make Chinese salt and pepper tofu, we coat the pieces of tofu with seasoned cornstarch, then pan-fry them in batches to brown and crisp the exteriors. In the empty skillet, a punchy mix of garlic, fresh chili and scallions is quickly cooked, and the tofu is tossed back in. The finished dish is sauceless but incredibly flavorful from the savory bits that cling to the tofu's crisped surfaces.

Kosher salt and ground black pepper

¼ teaspoon Chinese five-spice powder (optional)

⅓ cup cornstarch

Two 14-ounce containers firm OR extra-firm tofu, drained, halved lengthwise, cut crosswise into ½-inch-thick pieces and pressed dry with paper towels

4 tablespoons plus 1 teaspoon grapeseed or other neutral oil

4 medium garlic cloves, finely chopped

1 serrano OR Fresno chili, stemmed and finely chopped

4 scallions, thinly sliced on the diagonal, whites and greens reserved separately

In a pie plate, whisk together 2 teaspoons salt, 1 tablespoon pepper, the five-spice (if using) and cornstarch. Working a few pieces at a time, coat the tofu on all sides with the cornstarch mixture, then transfer to a large plate.

In a 12-inch nonstick skillet over medium-high, heat 2 tablespoons oil until shimmering. Add half of the tofu in a single layer and cook until browned on the bottom, 3 to 5 minutes. Using tongs, flip the pieces and cook until the second sides are browned, 3 to 5 minutes; transfer to a paper towel–lined plate. Using 2 tablespoons of the remaining oil, cook the remaining tofu in the same way and transfer to the plate.

In the same skillet, combine the remaining 1 teaspoon oil, the garlic, chili and scallion whites; cook over medium, stirring, until the garlic is fragrant and lightly browned, about 1 minute. Stir in the scallion greens, then return the tofu to the skillet and gently toss to combine. Transfer to a platter, scraping the bits from the pan onto the tofu.

Stir-Fried Tofu with Ginger Green Beans

Start to finish: 40 minutes / Servings: 4 to 6

Seasoned with fish and soy sauces, sugar and ginger, this simple stir-fry features a Southeast Asian flavor profile. We prefer the more yielding texture of firm tofu to extra-firm, but either works. Whichever you use, be sure to salt the tofu cubes and let them drain in a colander for five to 10 minutes as the recipe instructs. Salted tofu better absorbs the flavorings during cooking.

14-ounce container firm tofu, drained, patted dry and cut into ½- to ¾-inch cubes

Kosher salt and ground black pepper

2 tablespoons fish sauce

2 tablespoons soy sauce

1 tablespoon packed brown sugar

3 tablespoons grapeseed or other neutral oil, divided

1 pound green beans, trimmed and halved on the diagonal

1 tablespoon finely grated fresh ginger

½ teaspoon red pepper flakes

2 tablespoons unseasoned rice vinegar

In a colander set over a medium bowl, toss the tofu with ¼ teaspoon salt and let stand for 5 to 10 minutes. In a small bowl, stir together the fish sauce, soy sauce and sugar until the sugar dissolves; set aside.

Transfer the tofu to paper towels and pat dry. In a 12-inch nonstick skillet over medium-high, heat 1 tablespoon of oil until shimmering. Add the tofu in an even layer and cook, stirring occasionally, until golden brown, 6 to 7 minutes. Add 2 tablespoons of the fish sauce-soy mixture and cook, stirring occasionally, until the liquid thickens and coats the tofu, about 1 minute. Transfer to a plate and wipe out the skillet.

In the same skillet over medium-high, heat the remaining 2 tablespoons oil until shimmering. Add the green beans and cook, stirring occasionally, until charred and tender-crisp, 6 to 7 minutes. Add the ginger and pepper flakes, then cook, stirring, until fragrant, about 30 seconds. Add the remaining fish sauce-soy sauce mixture and cook, stirring occasionally, until the liquid thickens and coats the beans, about 1 minute. Off heat, stir in the tofu and vinegar. Taste and season with black pepper.

Spicy Seared Tofu with Sweet Pepper

Start to finish: 40 minutes / Servings: 4

This vegetarian dish is full of contrasting flavors and textures. The inspiration comes from classic Sichuan home-style tofu, which is deep-fried and finished with an umami-rich sauce. For our adaptation, we sear the tofu instead of fry it, and we make a deeply flavored sauce with a few kitchen staples. Korean gochujang or chili-garlic sauce stands in for toban djan, the chili-bean paste used in traditional home-style tofu; if you happen to have toban djan, use an equal amount. Dry sherry imitates the flavor of Shaoxing wine, whereas balsamic vinegar mimics the malty sweetness of Chinese black vinegar. Use whichever is in the cupboard. Serve with steamed rice; brown rice is an especially tasty pairing.

14-ounce container firm OR extra-firm tofu, drained

Kosher salt and ground black pepper

2 tablespoons gochujang OR chili-garlic sauce (see headnote)

1 tablespoon soy sauce

1 tablespoon dry sherry OR balsamic vinegar (see headnote)

1 tablespoon cornstarch

3 tablespoons grapeseed or other neutral oil, divided

2-inch piece fresh ginger, peeled and cut into matchsticks

¼ cup minced fresh cilantro stems plus 1 cup lightly packed leaves OR 4 scallions, white parts thinly sliced, greens cut into 1-inch lengths

1 medium red OR orange bell pepper, stemmed, seeded and cut into 1-inch pieces OR 4 ounces snow peas, trimmed

Cut the tofu block in half lengthwise, then cut each half crosswise into ½-inch-thick squares or rectangles. Stack 2 or 3 pieces, then cut into quarters diagonally, creating triangles. Pat the triangles dry, then season all over with ¾ teaspoon each salt and pepper. Let stand at room temperature for 10 minutes. Meanwhile, in a small bowl, whisk together 1 cup water, the gochujang, soy sauce, sherry and cornstarch; set aside.

Pat the tofu dry once again. In a 12-inch nonstick skillet over medium-high, heat 2 tablespoons oil until barely smoking. Add the tofu in a single layer and cook, undisturbed, until lightly browned on the bottoms, 3 to 5 minutes. Using a spatula, flip each piece and cook until lightly browned on the second sides, 3 to 4 minutes. Transfer to a paper towel–lined plate.

In the now-empty skillet over medium, heat the remaining 1 tablespoon oil until shimmering. Add the ginger and cilantro stems (or scallion whites); cook, stirring, until the ginger is lightly browned, about 2 minutes. Add the bell pepper and cook, stirring occasionally, until crisp-tender, about 3 minutes.

Return the tofu to the skillet. Re-whisk the sauce mixture and add to the skillet. Cook, stirring constantly, until the sauce is thickened, about 3 minutes. Stir in the cilantro leaves (or scallion greens). Off heat, taste and season with salt and pepper.

Optional garnish: Chili oil

180

Jamaican-Style Tofu Curry

Start to finish: 30 minutes / Servings: 4

In our vegetarian version of Jamaican chicken curry, we turn to pantry basics to mirror the flavors of the classic dish: curry powder, along with allspice or thyme, two ubiquitous seasonings in Jamaican cooking. For the best-tasting curry, include them both if you have them in the cupboard. Coconut milk creates a silky sauce that brings richness to the mild-tasting tofu; be sure to use regular coconut milk, not the light version. For a more substantial curry, add 2 medium carrots, peeled and thinly sliced, or 8 ounces green beans, cut into 1-inch pieces—or a little of both—along with the onion.

2 teaspoons curry powder

¼ teaspoon ground allspice OR ½ teaspoon dried thyme OR both

Kosher salt and ground black pepper

14-ounce container medium OR firm OR extra-firm tofu, drained, patted dry and cut into ½-inch cubes

2 tablespoons grapeseed or other neutral oil

1 small yellow onion, halved and thinly sliced

1 tablespoon minced fresh ginger

1 jalapeño OR serrano chili, stemmed, seeded and minced OR 1 habanero chili, halved

1 cup coconut milk

2 tablespoons lime juice

In a small bowl, stir together the curry powder, allspice and 1 teaspoon each salt and pepper. In a medium bowl, toss the tofu with 2 teaspoons of the spice mix; set aside. Reserve the remaining spice mix for cooking the curry.

In a 12-inch skillet over medium-high, heat the oil until shimmering. Add the onion and cook, stirring occasionally, until golden brown, 5 to 6 minutes. Stir in the ginger, the remaining spice mix and the chili; cook, stirring occasionally, until fragrant, about 1 minute. Add 1 cup water and scrape up any browned bits. Add the coconut milk and bring to a simmer, then reduce to medium-low and simmer, uncovered and stirring occasionally, until the mixture starts to thicken, 4 to 5 minutes.

Stir in the tofu and bring to a simmer over medium-high; reduce to medium-low and simmer, uncovered and stirring occasionally, until the sauce has thickened and the tofu is heated through, about 5 minutes. Off heat, remove and discard the habanero (if used). Stir in the lime juice, then taste and season with salt and pepper.

Optional garnish: Chopped fresh cilantro **OR** thinly sliced scallions

Vietnamese-Style Tofu with Gingery Tomato Sauce

Start to finish: 45 minutes / Servings: 6

Vietnamese đậu hũ sốt cà chua pairs tofu with tomato sauce, an unlikely, but delicious combination. The tofu sometimes is deep-fried, but we opted to pan-fry it; it's sometimes stuffed with pork or pork may be simmered into the sauce, but here we make a meat-free version. Pressing the tofu releases excess water so the texture is drier and the surface browns better. Fresh tomatoes make the best sauce, but canned whole tomatoes also work. Serve with steamed jasmine rice.

Two 14-ounce containers firm OR extra-firm tofu, drained, cut into ¾- to 1-inch cubes

2 tablespoons cornstarch

Kosher salt and ground black pepper

4 tablespoons grapeseed or other neutral oil, divided

2 tablespoons minced fresh ginger

2 medium garlic cloves, minced

1 bunch scallions, thinly sliced, whites and greens reserved separately

1¼ pounds ripe tomatoes, cored and chopped OR 28-ounce can peeled whole tomatoes, drained, ½ cup juices reserved, tomatoes crushed by hand

2 tablespoons fish sauce, plus more if needed

Line a rimmed baking sheet with a double layer of paper towels. Distribute the tofu cubes in a single layer on top and cover with additional paper towels. Place another rimmed baking sheet on top, then set a few cans or jars on top as weights; let stand for about 15 minutes. Meanwhile, in a large bowl, stir together the cornstarch and ¼ teaspoon each salt and pepper.

Remove the weights and baking sheet from the tofu. Pat the tofu dry with fresh paper towels, then add the cubes to the cornstarch mixture. Gently toss until evenly coated.

In a 12-inch nonstick skillet over medium-high, heat 1½ tablespoons oil until shimmering. Add half of the tofu in an even layer and cook, stirring occasionally, until golden brown on all sides, 6 to 7 minutes; transfer to a paper towel–lined plate. Using 1½ tablespoons of the remaining oil, brown the remaining tofu in the same way; wipe out the skillet.

In the same skillet over medium-high, heat the remaining 1 tablespoon oil until shimmering. Add the ginger, garlic and scallion whites, then cook, stirring, until fragrant, 30 to 60 seconds. Stir in the tomatoes (and ½ cup juices, if using canned tomatoes) and ¼ teaspoon pepper; cook, stirring often, until the tomatoes begin to release their liquid, 1 to 2 minutes (if using canned tomatoes, simply bring to a simmer). Cover, reduce to medium and simmer, stirring occasionally, until the tomatoes have broken down and the sauce has thickened, 10 to 12 minutes.

Stir in the fish sauce, followed by the tofu. Cook, stirring, until the tofu is heated through, 1 to 2 minutes. Off heat, taste and season with pepper and additional fish sauce, if needed. Transfer to a serving dish and sprinkle with the scallion greens.

Stir-Fried Cumin Tofu

Start to finish: 30 minutes, plus marinating
Servings: 4

Xinjiang cumin lamb, a classic stir-fry that originated in the Xinjiang region of northwestern China, pairs lamb or sometimes beef with whole cumin seeds and chilies. We swap the meat for protein-rich tofu, marinating it with soy sauce and vinegar before searing it in a hot pan. Chinese black vinegar makes a great addition to the marinade, though easier-to-find balsamic makes a good substitute, as it mimics the sweet-tart, lightly syrupy character of Chinese black vinegar.

3 tablespoons
soy sauce, divided

2 tablespoons balsamic
vinegar, divided

Kosher salt and
ground black pepper

14-ounce container
firm **OR** extra-firm tofu,
drained, patted dry,
halved lengthwise,
then cut crosswise into
½-inch-thick planks

¼ cup cornstarch

3 tablespoons
grapeseed or other
neutral oil, divided

1 medium yellow onion,
halved and thinly sliced

4 teaspoons cumin
seeds, lightly crushed
OR 2 teaspoons ground
cumin

4 medium garlic cloves,
minced

½ teaspoon
red pepper flakes

In a pie plate or shallow bowl, stir together 1 tablespoon soy sauce, 1 tablespoon vinegar and ½ teaspoon each salt and black pepper. Add the tofu and toss to coat. Let stand at room temperature for at least 15 minutes or up to 1 hour. Pat the tofu dry in the pie plate. Sprinkle with the cornstarch and toss to coat, gently pressing to adhere.

In a 12-inch nonstick skillet over medium-high, heat 2 tablespoons oil until shimmering. Add the tofu, distributing it in an even layer, and cook until golden brown and crisp on the bottom, 3 to 4 minutes. Turn the tofu and cook until golden brown on the second sides, another 3 to 4 minutes. Transfer to a paper towel–lined plate; set aside. Wipe out the skillet.

In the same skillet over medium-high, heat the remaining 1 tablespoon oil until barely smoking. Add the onion and cumin; cook, stirring occasionally, until the onion is charred in spots and slightly softened, 3 to 5 minutes. Add the garlic and pepper flakes, then cook, stirring, until fragrant, 30 to 60 seconds. Add the tofu, the remaining 2 tablespoons soy sauce, the remaining 1 tablespoon vinegar and 2 tablespoons water. Cook, stirring often, until the liquid has evaporated, about 1 minute. Off heat, taste and season with salt and black pepper.

Optional garnish: Scallions, thinly sliced on the diagonal **OR** chili oil **OR** both

Tofu Katsu

Start to finish: 50 minutes / Servings: 2 to 4

To make classic Japanese tonkatsu, pork cutlets are breaded with panko, fried until perfectly browned and served with a savory-sweet dipping sauce. For this vegetarian version, we use tofu, cut horizontally into cutlet-like planks. The crisp breading is a delicious contrast to the tender tofu, and the umami-packed sauce is perfect for supplying loads of flavor. It's essential, however, to press the tofu planks for 30 minutes before breading. This forces out some of the moisture so the "cutlets" crisp well. Serve with Japanese-style rice and, if you like, a shredded cabbage salad.

14-ounce container firm **OR** extra-firm tofu, drained and cut lengthwise into 4 planks of equal thickness

¼ cup ketchup

¼ cup Worcestershire sauce

1 tablespoon soy sauce

⅓ cup all-purpose flour

Kosher salt and ground black pepper

2 large eggs

1½ cups panko breadcrumbs

¾ cup grapeseed or other neutral oil, divided

Line a rimmed baking sheet with a doubled layer of paper towels. Lay the tofu planks in a single layer and cover with additional paper towels. Place another rimmed baking sheet on top, then set a few cans or jars on top as weights; let stand for about 30 minutes.

Meanwhile, in a small bowl, stir together the ketchup, Worcestershire and soy sauce; set aside. In a pie plate, stir together the flour and ¼ teaspoon each salt and pepper. In a second similar dish, whisk the eggs. To a third dish, add the panko.

Uncover the tofu; reserve the top baking sheet. Pat the tofu slabs dry with fresh paper towels and sprinkle both sides with salt and pepper. One at a time, dredge the planks in the flour mixture, turning to coat and shaking off any excess. Coat both sides with egg, then coat on all sides with panko, pressing firmly so the crumbs adhere. Set aside on the reserved baking sheet.

In a 12-inch nonstick skillet over medium, heat the oil until shimmering. Add the tofu and cook until the bottoms are golden brown, 2 to 3 minutes. Using a spatula and tongs, carefully flip the tofu and cook until the second sides are golden brown, about 3 minutes. Transfer to a large paper towel–lined plate and sprinkle with salt. If desired, on a cutting board, cut the "cutlets" into strips about ¾ inch wide. Transfer to a platter and serve with the sauce.

Chicken WINNERS

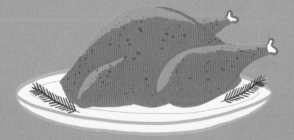

Plov with Chicken

Start to finish: 1 hour 20 minutes (30 minutes active)
Servings: 4

Considered the national dish of Uzbekistan, plov is a robust blend of rice, meat, onions, carrots and spices. It's served as a dish for everyday meals, as well as at celebratory gatherings. In our simplified, pantry-centric version featuring chicken thighs (lamb or beef are traditional), both the meat and the cumin—a key seasoning for plov—are first browned to develop deep, rich flavor. Be sure to soak and rinse the rice before adding it to the pot; this ensures that the grains will cook up light and separate.

1 cup basmati rice

Kosher salt and ground black pepper

1½ tablespoons grapeseed or other neutral oil

1 pound boneless, skinless chicken thighs, trimmed and cut into 2-inch pieces

2 medium carrots, peeled, halved lengthwise and thinly sliced on the diagonal

1 medium yellow onion, halved and sliced ½ inch thick

2 teaspoons cumin seeds OR ground cumin

6 medium garlic cloves, peeled

¼ cup raisins OR golden raisins OR dried currants

In a medium bowl, combine the rice and 1½ teaspoons salt. Add water to cover by 1 inch, then stir; set aside.

In a large pot over medium-high, heat the oil until shimmering. Add the chicken and cook, turning as needed, until browned all over, 6 to 8 minutes. Add the carrots, onion, cumin, 1 teaspoon salt and ½ teaspoon pepper. Cook, stirring occasionally, until the vegetables start to soften, 3 to 5 minutes.

Add 2 cups water and bring to a simmer, scraping up the browned bits. Add the garlic, then reduce to medium-low. Cover and cook, stirring occasionally, until the carrots are tender, about 12 minutes. Remove from the heat and stir in the raisins.

Drain the rice in a fine-mesh strainer, then rinse under cool running water and drain again. Sprinkle the rice in an even layer over the chicken mixture. Bring to a boil over medium-high, then cover, reduce to low and cook without stirring until all of the water has been absorbed, 30 to 35 minutes.

Remove from the heat and let stand, covered, for 10 minutes. Using a fork, fluff the rice, then stir to incorporate the chicken mixture. Taste and season with salt and pepper.

Optional garnish: Pomegranate seeds **OR** chopped fresh flat-leaf parsley **OR** both

Chicken and Chickpea Tagine

Start to finish: 1 hour (25 minutes active)
Servings: 4 to 6

This recipe calls for fast-cooking boneless chicken thighs and a handful of fragrant spices, yielding the deep, rich flavors that are the hallmark of Moroccan tagines. Raisins (or dried apricots) add pops of sweetness to balance the savoriness and spice. Some of the cooking time is hands-off; while the stew simmers, you may wish to prepare some couscous or heat up flatbreads to serve alongside.

1 tablespoon
ground cumin

2 teaspoons
ground coriander

½ teaspoon
ground cinnamon

Kosher salt and
ground black pepper

2 pounds boneless,
skinless chicken thighs,
trimmed

2 tablespoons grapeseed
or other neutral oil

1 large yellow onion,
halved and thinly sliced

2 medium carrots,
peeled and cut into
¼-inch rounds

Two 15½-ounce cans
chickpeas, rinsed and
drained

½ cup raisins OR golden
raisins OR chopped dried
apricots

In a small bowl, stir together the cumin, coriander, cinnamon and 1 teaspoon each salt and pepper. In a large bowl, toss the chicken with 4 teaspoons of the spice mix; set aside. Reserve the remaining spice mix for cooking the tagine.

In a large Dutch oven over medium-high, heat the oil until shimmering. Add the onion and ½ teaspoon salt, then cook, stirring occasionally, until beginning to brown, 4 to 6 minutes.

Stir in the remaining spice mix, the carrots, chicken and 2½ cups water. Bring to a simmer, then reduce to medium-low and cook, uncovered and stirring occasionally, until a skewer inserted into the largest thigh meets no resistance, about 30 minutes.

Stir in the chickpeas and raisins. Bring to a simmer over medium-high, then reduce to medium and simmer, uncovered and stirring occasionally, until the sauce is thickened, about 15 minutes. Off heat, taste and season with salt and pepper.

Optional garnish: Chopped fresh cilantro OR lemon wedges OR both

Red Stew with Chicken

Start to finish: 1 hour 25 minutes (30 minutes active)
Servings: 4

With a tomato–red pepper puree as its base and aromatic flavorings such as ginger, chilies and curry powder, Nigerian red stew can include almost any type of meat or fish. For our simplified version of the braise, we chose bone-in chicken parts and included sweet potatoes to lend a bit more substance (the sweet potatoes are, however, optional). A couple pantry items—canned tomatoes and jarred roasted peppers—supply the "red" in our red stew. We seed the fresh chilies to tame their spiciness, but if you're seeking a little heat, leave in some or all of the seeds.

1 teaspoon curry powder **OR** dried thyme **OR** 1 teaspoon each

Kosher salt and ground black pepper

2 pounds bone-in, skin-on chicken thighs **OR** drumsticks **OR** breasts (halved crosswise) **OR** a combination, trimmed

28-ounce can whole peeled tomatoes

1 cup roasted red peppers, drained and patted dry

4 or 5 jalapeño **OR** Fresno chilies **OR** 2 habanero chilies, stemmed and seeded

1-inch piece fresh ginger, peeled and roughly chopped **OR** 1½ teaspoons ground ginger

2 tablespoons grapeseed or other neutral oil

1 medium yellow onion, chopped

1½ pounds sweet potatoes, peeled and cut into 1-inch chunks (optional)

In a small bowl, stir together the curry powder, 2 teaspoons salt and ½ teaspoon pepper. Sprinkle the chicken all over with the spice mix, rubbing it into the meat; set aside.

In a blender, combine the tomatoes with juices, roasted red peppers, chilies and ginger. Puree until smooth, scraping the jar as needed, about 1 minute; set aside.

In a large Dutch oven over medium-high, heat the oil until shimmering. Add the chicken, skin side down, and cook until browned on the bottom, 3 to 4 minutes. Flip the pieces and cook until browned on the second sides, 2 to 3 minutes, then transfer to a large plate and set aside.

Return the Dutch oven to medium; add the onion and ¼ teaspoon each salt and pepper. Cook, stirring occasionally, until the onion is softened and golden brown, about 5 minutes. Add the tomato-pepper puree; simmer, uncovered and stirring occasionally, until a spatula leaves a trail when drawn through the mixture, 16 to 20 minutes.

Stir in the sweet potatoes (if using), then nestle in the chicken and pour in the accumulated juices. Bring to a simmer over medium-high, then cover, reduce to medium-low and cook, stirring and turning the chicken occasionally, until a skewer inserted into the largest chicken piece meets no resistance and the sweet potatoes are tender (if used), 35 to 40 minutes. Off heat, taste and season with salt and pepper.

Optional garnish: Chopped fresh cilantro **OR** chopped scallions

Stir-Fried Hoisin Chicken and Bell Peppers

Start to finish: 25 minutes / Servings: 4 to 6

Thick, savory-sweet, umami-rich hoisin sauce drives the flavor in this stir-fry that pairs snappy bell peppers with tender chicken breast. Be sure to slice the chicken crosswise, or against the grain, so the muscle fibers are short rather than stringy. The cooking here goes quickly, so be sure the ingredients are prepped and at the ready before you head to the stove. Serve with steamed rice.

¼ cup hoisin sauce

2 tablespoons dry sherry OR sake

1 tablespoon soy sauce, plus more if needed

3 tablespoons grapeseed or other neutral oil

2 medium green OR red OR orange OR yellow bell peppers OR a combination, stemmed, seeded and sliced about ¼ inch thick

2 medium garlic cloves, minced

1 tablespoon finely grated fresh ginger

½ teaspoon red pepper flakes

1½ pounds boneless, skinless chicken breasts, sliced crosswise ¼ inch thick

In a small bowl, stir together the hoisin, sherry and soy sauce; set aside. In a 12-inch skillet over medium-high, heat the oil until shimmering. Add the bell peppers and cook, stirring occasionally, until softened and beginning to brown, 4 to 5 minutes. Add the garlic, ginger and pepper flakes, then cook, stirring, until fragrant, 30 to 60 seconds.

Add the chicken and cook, stirring occasionally, until lightly browned and opaque throughout, 7 to 8 minutes. Add the hoisin mixture and cook, stirring, until the sauce slightly thickens, 1 to 2 minutes. Off heat, taste and season with additional soy sauce, if needed.

Optional garnish: Thinly sliced scallions

194

Chicken Braised with Sweet Peppers and Tomatoes

Start to finish: 45 minutes / Servings: 4

Pollo con i peperoni is a classic Italian braise of chicken with sweet peppers and tomatoes. Savory and sweet with a velvety sauce that's rich yet bright, the dish is comfort food that comes together quickly and easily. In our version, we add a sliced onion for sweetness and stir in minced garlic at the end for a little pungency. Serve the braise over pasta or polenta, or with warm, crusty bread on the side.

2 tablespoons
extra-virgin olive oil

1½ pounds boneless,
skinless chicken thighs,
trimmed and cut in half

1 medium yellow onion,
thinly sliced

2 medium red **OR** orange
OR yellow bell peppers,
stemmed, seeded and
sliced about ¼ inch thick

2½ teaspoons dried
oregano **OR** 3 tablespoons
chopped fresh oregano,
divided

¼ to ½ teaspoon
red pepper flakes

Kosher salt and
ground black pepper

¼ cup dry white wine

28-ounce can whole
peeled tomatoes,
crushed by hand

1 medium garlic clove,
minced

In a large Dutch oven over medium-high, heat the oil until shimmering. Add the chicken and cook, undisturbed, until browned on the bottom, about 5 minutes. Add the onion, peppers, 2 teaspoons dried oregano (or 2 tablespoons fresh oregano), red pepper flakes and ¾ teaspoon salt; cook, stirring occasionally, until the vegetables are wilted, 3 to 5 minutes.

Add the wine, bring to a simmer and cook for about 2 minutes, scraping up any browned bits. Add the tomatoes with juices and bring to a simmer. Cover partially, reduce to medium and cook, stirring occasionally, until the sauce is thickened and a skewer inserted into the chicken meets no resistance, 13 to 16 minutes.

Uncover and cook over medium, stirring occasionally, until the sauce has reduced and thickened, about 10 minutes. Off heat, stir in the remaining ½ teaspoon dried oregano (or the remaining 1 tablespoon fresh oregano), the garlic and ½ teaspoon black pepper. Taste and season with salt.

Optional garnish: Torn fresh basil **OR** shaved Parmesan cheese

Chicken Paprikash

Start to finish: 1 hour 10 minutes (30 minutes active)
Servings: 4 to 6

Paprikash is one of the most famous dishes from Hungary. In our version, chicken is cooked in a bold paprika-infused sauce, then finished with sour cream to create a tangy, creamy stew. Sweet paprika is a key ingredient, so make sure yours is fresh and fragrant. And for the richest flavor and a full-bodied consistency, opt for full-fat sour cream. Don't be concerned if the sauce looks broken when you add the sour cream. As the sauce simmers and reduces, the cornstarch helps the sour cream emulsify into the sauce. Buttered egg noodles are the perfect accompaniment to this homey dish.

3 pounds bone-in, skin-on chicken thighs, trimmed

Kosher salt and ground black pepper

1 tablespoon grapeseed or other neutral oil

1 large yellow onion, finely chopped

2 tablespoons sweet paprika, plus more to serve

2 tablespoons tomato paste

¾ cup sour cream

1 tablespoon cornstarch

Season the chicken all over with salt and pepper. In a large Dutch oven over medium-high, heat the oil until shimmering. Add the chicken skin side down and cook until browned on the bottom, 3 to 4 minutes. Flip the pieces and cook until browned on the second sides, 2 to 3 minutes, then transfer to a large plate and set aside. Pour off and discard all but 1 tablespoon of the fat in the pot.

Return the Dutch oven to medium and add the onion, ½ teaspoon salt and ¼ teaspoon pepper. Cook, stirring occasionally, until the onion is golden brown, about 6 minutes. Add the paprika and tomato paste; cook, stirring, until fragrant, about 1 minute. Add 2 cups water and scrape up the browned bits, then nestle in the chicken and pour in the accumulated juices.

Bring to a simmer over medium-high, then cover, reduce to medium-low and cook, stirring and turning the chicken occasionally, until a skewer inserted into the largest thigh meets no resistance, 35 to 40 minutes. Remove the pot from the heat and, using tongs, transfer the chicken to a wide, shallow serving bowl; set aside.

In a small bowl, whisk together the sour cream and cornstarch, then whisk this mixture into the braising liquid in the pot. Bring to a simmer over medium-high and cook, whisking often, until the sauce is creamy and slightly thicker than heavy cream, 5 to 7 minutes. Return the chicken and accumulated juices to the pot, turning to coat in the sauce. Off heat, taste and season with salt and pepper. Transfer the chicken and sauce to the serving bowl and sprinkle with additional paprika.

Optional garnish: Chopped fresh dill **OR** chopped fresh chives

Bulgur and Chicken Salad with Pomegranate Molasses

Start to finish: 35 minutes / Servings: 4

Made with the meat from a store-bought rotisserie chicken, this salad is deliciously loaded with nutty, fruity and herbal elements but doesn't require any cooking aside from boiling water to hydrate the bulgur. What's more, it can be on the table in under 45 minutes. Pomegranate molasses, much-used in Middle Eastern cooking, is a powerhouse ingredient that we like to keep on hand. Look for pomegranate molasses sold in bottles in the international aisle of the supermarket or in Middle Eastern grocery stores.

1 cup fine bulgur

⅓ cup dried cranberries, roughly chopped

2 medium garlic cloves, minced

Kosher salt and ground black pepper

1 cup boiling water

2 cups shredded cooked chicken

1 cup lightly packed fresh flat-leaf parsley OR

mint OR a combination, roughly chopped

2 serrano OR jalapeño chilies, stemmed, seeded and minced

3 tablespoons pomegranate molasses

2 tablespoons extra-virgin olive oil, plus more to serve

⅓ cup sliced almonds, toasted, OR roasted pistachios, chopped

In a large bowl, combine the bulgur, cranberries, garlic, ½ teaspoon salt and ¼ teaspoon pepper. Stir in the boiling water, then cover and let stand for 10 minutes.

Using a fork, fluff the bulgur mixture. Add the chicken, parsley, chilies, pomegranate molasses and oil, then fold with a silicone spatula until well combined. Stir in half of the almonds, then taste and season with salt and pepper. Transfer to a serving dish, sprinkle with the remaining almonds and drizzle with additional oil.

Optional garnish: Pomegranate seeds

Chicken and Potato Traybake with Garlic, Lemon and Parsley

Start to finish: 45 minutes (15 minutes active)
Servings: 4 to 6

For this easy, one-pan meal, we took a cue from chicken Vesuvio, an Italian-American classic that combines chicken and potatoes with lots of garlic, lemon and oregano. The dish typically is a saucy stovetop braise, but we've turned it into a traybake by roasting everything together in the oven. The high heat helps the chicken brown, leaving concentrated bits of flavor stuck to the pan. Those tasty bits are combined with lemon juice, mashed garlic and parsley to make a simple and delicious pan sauce.

3 tablespoons extra-virgin olive oil

2 teaspoons dried oregano

Kosher salt and ground black pepper

3 pounds bone-in, skin-on chicken thighs OR breasts OR both, trimmed and patted dry

1½ pounds medium Yukon Gold OR red potatoes, unpeeled, cut into 1-inch-thick wedges

10 medium garlic cloves, peeled

2 lemons, halved crosswise

3 tablespoons chopped fresh flat-leaf parsley

Heat the oven to 475°F with a rack in the middle position. In a large bowl, stir together the oil, oregano, 1¼ teaspoons salt and ½ teaspoon pepper. Add the chicken and potatoes; toss, then rub the seasoning mixture into the chicken and potatoes.

Place the garlic in the center of a rimmed baking sheet, then arrange the chicken, skin side up, around the garlic; this placement helps prevent the garlic from scorching during roasting. Arrange the lemons, cut sides up, and the potatoes, cut sides down, in an even layer around the chicken. Drizzle any oil mixture remaining in the bowl over the ingredients. Roast until the chicken is golden brown and the thickest part of the breasts (if using) reaches 160°F and the thickest part of the largest thigh (if using) reaches 175°F, about 30 minutes.

Transfer the chicken, potatoes and lemon halves to a serving platter, leaving the garlic in the center. Using a fork, mash the garlic to a rough paste. Squeeze 2 of the lemon halves onto the baking sheet, then add 3 tablespoons water and the parsley. Stir to combine, scraping up any browned bits, then taste and season with salt and pepper. Pour the sauce over and around the chicken and potatoes.

Cabbage and Chicken Salad with Gochujang and Sesame

Start to finish: 30 minutes / Servings: 4 to 6

Gochujang, ginger, scallions and sesame—core ingredients in the Korean kitchen—inject loads of flavor to a simple cabbage and shredded chicken salad. Gochujang, one of our pantry go-tos, is a fermented chili paste that packs spiciness, subtle sweetness, lots of umami and rich color in a single spoonful. Look for it in the international aisle of the supermarket or in Asian grocery stores. For convenience, use the meat from a rotisserie chicken; an average-size bird yields about 3 cups, the amount needed for this recipe.

3 tablespoons gochujang

2 tablespoons grapeseed or other neutral oil

1 tablespoon white sugar

1 tablespoon finely grated fresh ginger

2 teaspoons toasted sesame oil, plus more to serve

¼ cup unseasoned rice vinegar **OR** cider vinegar

Kosher salt and ground black pepper

1 pound green cabbage, cored and thinly sliced (about 4 cups)

3 cups shredded cooked chicken

1 bunch scallions, thinly sliced on the diagonal **OR** 1 large grated carrot **OR** both

In a large bowl, whisk together the gochujang, neutral oil, sugar, ginger, sesame oil, vinegar, ¼ teaspoon salt and ½ teaspoon pepper. Add the cabbage, chicken and half of the scallions; toss. Taste and season with salt and pepper.

Transfer to a serving dish, drizzle with additional sesame oil and sprinkle with the remaining scallions.

Optional garnish: Toasted sesame seeds **OR** toasted walnuts (or pine nuts)

Miso-Garlic Slashed Chicken

**Start to finish: 40 minutes (15 minutes active),
plus marinating / Servings: 4**

This recipe delivers big flavor and a delicious main with
minimal work. Umami-packed white miso does the
heavy lifting and gets an assist from soy sauce, rice
vinegar, sugar, ginger and garlic, each ingredient
holding its own. Slashes cut into bone-in chicken parts
allows the seasonings to really get into the meat instead
of just sitting on the surface. With more of the interior
exposed, the chicken cooks a bit more quickly, too.

¼ **cup white miso**

¼ **cup soy sauce**

¼ **cup unseasoned rice
vinegar**

2 **tablespoons white sugar**

1 **tablespoon finely grated
fresh ginger**

4 **medium garlic cloves,
finely grated**

3 **pounds bone-in skin-on
chicken leg quarters OR
bone-in skin-on chicken
thighs, trimmed**

In a large bowl, whisk together the miso, soy sauce,
vinegar, sugar, ginger and garlic. Using a sharp knife,
cut parallel slashes, spaced about 1 inch apart, in the
skin side of each piece of chicken, cutting all the way
to the bone. Add the chicken to the bowl and, using
your hands, rub the marinade onto the chicken and into
the slashes. Cover and refrigerate for at least 1 hour or
for up to 2 hours.

Heat the oven to 450°F with a rack in the middle
position. Line a rimmed baking sheet with foil and set
a wire rack in the baking sheet. Mist the rack with
cooking spray.

Arrange the chicken skin side up on the prepared rack.
Roast until well browned and the thickest part of the
thigh registers 175°F, 20 to 25 minutes. Using tongs,
transfer the chicken to a platter. Let rest for about
10 minutes before serving.

Optional garnish: Toasted sesame seeds **OR** sliced
scallions **OR** both

Chicken with Apples and Cider Vinegar Sauce

Start to finish: 45 minutes / Servings: 4

This easy, pantry-friendly sauté was inspired by poulet à la Normande, a classic braise from Normandy, the apple region of France. The recipe pairs boneless chicken breasts with crisp apples, tangy cider vinegar and rich butter that rounds out the flavors. Chicken breasts run the gamut in terms of sizing. The timing here is based on 6-ounce portions. If yours are larger, add a few minutes of cooking time to get them to the proper temperature.

Four 6-ounce boneless, skinless chicken breasts, patted dry

Kosher salt and ground black pepper

1 tablespoon extra-virgin olive oil

3 tablespoons salted butter, cut into 1-tablespoon pieces, divided

1 small yellow onion, halved and thinly sliced

2 medium firm-textured apples, such as Fuji OR Honeycrisp, quartered, cored and sliced ¼ inch thick

½ teaspoon dried thyme OR 4 fresh thyme sprigs

⅓ cup cider vinegar

⅓ cup low-sodium chicken broth

⅓ cup chopped fresh flat-leaf parsley

Season the chicken on all sides with salt and pepper. In a 12-inch skillet over medium-high, heat the oil and 1 tablespoon butter. When the butter begins to foam, add the chicken and cook until golden brown on the bottom, about 3 minutes. Flip, reduce to medium and cook until lightly browned on the second sides, 2 to 3 minutes. Using tongs, transfer to a large plate.

Return the skillet to medium. Add the onion and ½ teaspoon salt; cook, stirring often, until golden brown, 3 to 5 minutes. Add the apples and thyme, then cook, stirring occasionally and gently, until the apples are golden brown and beginning to soften, about 3 minutes. Add the vinegar and broth; bring to a simmer, scraping up any browned bits. Return the chicken to the skillet, nestling the breasts in the apple mixture, and add any accumulated juices. Cover and cook, turning the chicken two or three times, until the thickest part of the breasts reaches 160°F, 5 to 7 minutes.

Remove the pan from the heat. Using tongs, transfer the chicken to a cutting board and let rest. Meanwhile, bring the apple mixture to a simmer over medium-high, then add the remaining 2 tablespoons butter. Cook, stirring, until the butter is incorporated and the sauce is lightly thickened, about 2 minutes. Off heat, remove and discard the thyme sprigs, if used. Stir in the parsley, then taste and season with salt and pepper.

Using a slotted spoon, transfer the apples to a platter. Slice the chicken about ½ inch thick against the grain, place it on the apples and spoon on the sauce.

Tandoori-Inspired Chicken Kebabs

Start to finish: 30 minutes, plus marinating
Servings: 4 to 6

Tandoori chicken traditionally is marinated for hours in yogurt and fragrant spices before it is cooked in a tandoor oven. Our weeknight-friendly, tandoori-inspired kebabs feature an easy marinade of yogurt, paprika, garam masala, cayenne and a few other aromatics. Just whirl everything in a blender, then combine with chunks of chicken. If you have time, marinate the chicken overnight, though even 30 minutes will go a long way to boost flavor and tenderize the meat. The marinade also helps the kebabs brown beautifully under the broiler. Serve with warm naan or basmati rice.

1 cup plain whole-milk yogurt **OR** ¾ cup plain whole-milk Greek yogurt thinned with 3 tablespoons water

4 medium garlic cloves, smashed and peeled

1 medium red **OR** yellow onion, half roughly chopped, half thinly sliced, reserved separately

1-inch piece fresh ginger, peeled and roughly chopped

2 tablespoons grapeseed or other neutral oil

1 tablespoon sweet paprika

1½ teaspoons garam masala

½ teaspoon cayenne pepper **OR** ¼ teaspoon ground turmeric **OR** both

Kosher salt and ground black pepper

2 pounds boneless, skinless chicken breasts **OR** thighs, trimmed and cut into 1½-inch pieces

In a blender, combine half the yogurt, the garlic, chopped onion, ginger, oil, paprika, garam masala, cayenne, 1¼ teaspoons salt and 1 teaspoon black pepper. Puree until smooth, about 1 minute, scraping the jar as needed. Transfer 2 tablespoons of the puree to a small bowl and stir in the remaining yogurt. Cover and refrigerate until ready to serve. Scrape the remaining puree into a medium bowl, add the chicken and stir to coat. Cover and refrigerate for at least 30 minutes or up to 4 hours.

Heat the broiler with a rack about 4 inches from the element. Line a rimmed baking sheet with foil, set a wire rack in the baking sheet and mist it with cooking spray. Thread the chicken onto 4 to 6 metal skewers, scraping off excess marinade, and place on the prepared rack.

Broil until charred on the surface, 4 to 5 minutes. Remove the baking sheet from the oven, flip the skewers and continue to broil until well charred on the second sides and the chicken is just cooked through, 6 to 7 minutes. Serve the skewers with the yogurt sauce and sliced onion.

Optional garnish: Chopped fresh cilantro **OR** chutney **OR** sliced tomatoes **OR** lemon wedges **OR** a combination

Sausage
SOLUTIONS

Tomato and Sausage Ragù over Polenta

Start to finish: 40 minutes / Servings: 4 to 6

This recipe combines a few flavor-packed ingredients to create a hearty, meaty ragù that's ready to serve in less than 45 minutes. Either sweet or hot Italian sausage works here; use as much or as little red pepper flakes as you like to give the ragù a spicy kick. Serve it in bowls over creamy Parmesan-enriched polenta. Be sure to use fast-cooking instant polenta, not regular polenta, which requires longer cooking. Feel free to thin the polenta to your desired consistency with hot water.

4 tablespoons extra-virgin olive oil, divided

1 pound Italian sausage, casing removed, OR 1 pound bulk Italian sausage (see headnote)

3 medium garlic cloves, minced

¼ to ½ teaspoon red pepper flakes

Kosher salt and ground black pepper

28-ounce can whole peeled tomatoes, crushed by hand

1 cup instant polenta

1 cup fresh flat-leaf parsley OR basil, chopped

2 ounces Parmesan OR pecorino Romano cheese, finely grated (1 cup)

In a 12-inch skillet over medium, heat 2 tablespoons oil until shimmering. Add the sausage and cook, breaking it into small pieces, until no longer pink and starting to brown, 5 to 6 minutes. Stir in the garlic, pepper flakes, ½ teaspoon black pepper and the tomatoes with juices. Bring to a simmer over medium-high, then reduce to medium-low and simmer, uncovered and stirring occasionally, until a spatula leaves a trail when drawn through the mixture, 25 to 30 minutes. Remove from the heat, cover and set aside.

In a large saucepan, cook the polenta according to the package instructions. Remove from the heat, cover and let stand for 2 to 3 minutes. Stir in the remaining 2 tablespoons oil and half the cheese; add hot water to thin, if needed (the polenta should have the consistency of thin mashed potatoes). Taste and season with salt and black pepper.

Return the sauce to a simmer over medium-high. Off heat, stir in the parsley. Spoon the polenta into individual shallow bowls and top with the sauce. Sprinkle with the remaining cheese.

Harissa-Spiced Beef with Couscous and Scallions

Start to finish: 30 minutes / Servings: 4

In this recipe, we use harissa, a North African spice paste, as the flavor base for a simple skillet-cooked meat sauce, as well as to season the couscous that's served alongside. Scallion whites are caramelized to lend depth of flavor to the sauce and the greens are sprinkled on as a garnish. Dried fruit adds sweetness that plays off the spicy, savory notes.

1¼ cups couscous

Kosher salt and ground black pepper

3 tablespoons extra-virgin olive oil, divided

3 tablespoons harissa paste, divided, plus more to serve

1¼ cups boiling water

1 bunch scallions, thinly sliced, whites and greens reserved separately

2 teaspoons ground cumin

1 pound 80 percent lean ground beef OR ground lamb

¾ cup pitted dates, roughly chopped OR golden raisins

Chopped pitted green olives, to serve

In a large bowl, stir together the couscous, ½ teaspoon salt and 1½ tablespoons each oil and harissa. Stir in the boiling water; cover and let stand while you prepare the beef.

In a 12-inch nonstick skillet over medium-high, cook the remaining 1½ tablespoons oil, the scallion whites and cumin, stirring, until the scallions brown, about 3 minutes. Add the beef, the remaining 1½ tablespoons harissa, the dates, ¾ cup water and a pinch each of salt and pepper. Bring to a simmer and cook, uncovered and stirring occasionally while breaking up the beef, until the mixture is saucy and the meat is cooked through, 5 to 7 minutes.

Off heat, stir in the scallion greens. Taste and season with salt and pepper. Serve the beef mixture over the couscous, sprinkled with green olives.

Optional garnish: Chopped fresh cilantro **OR** chopped pistachios **OR** lemon wedges **OR** a combination

Risotto with Sausage and Sun-Dried Tomatoes

Start to finish: 40 minutes / Servings: 4

Contrary to popular belief, risotto does not require vigilance and uninterrupted stirring. Our method adds half the liquid early and depends on brisk intermittent stirring to agitate the rice grains and release their starch, thickening the cooking liquid and producing the creamy consistency that's the hallmark of great risotto. This version is rich with bits of sausage—use sweet or hot, depending on your preference. Sun-dried tomatoes are added at the end for a splash of color and tangy sweetness, while Parmesan cheese lends umami.

1 quart low-sodium chicken broth

2 tablespoons extra-virgin olive oil, divided

8 ounces sweet OR hot Italian sausage, casing removed

1 small yellow onion, finely chopped

Kosher salt and ground black pepper

1 cup Arborio rice

¼ cup drained oil-packed sun-dried tomatoes, chopped

⅓ cup finely chopped fresh flat-leaf parsley OR basil

1 ounce Parmesan cheese, finely grated (½ cup), plus more to serve

In a medium saucepan over medium, bring the broth and 2 cups water, covered, to a simmer. Reduce to low to keep warm.

In a large saucepan over medium, heat 1 tablespoon oil until shimmering. Add the sausage and cook, breaking it into small pieces, until no longer pink and starting to brown, 5 to 6 minutes. Using a slotted spoon, transfer the sausage to a small bowl; set aside.

To the same large saucepan over medium, add the remaining 1 tablespoon oil and heat until shimmering. Add the onion and ¼ teaspoon salt; cook, stirring occasionally, until softened, about 5 minutes. Add the rice and cook, stirring constantly, until the grains are translucent at the edges, 1 to 2 minutes. Add 3 cups of the hot broth mixture and bring to a boil over medium-high. Reduce to medium and cook, stirring often and briskly, until most of the liquid is absorbed, 10 to 12 minutes; adjust the heat as needed to maintain a vigorous simmer.

Cook, adding ¼ cup of the broth at a time, until the rice is al dente and loose but not soupy, another 8 to 10 minutes. You may not need all of the broth. Stir in the sausage and accumulated juices along with the sun-dried tomatoes; cook, stirring occasionally, until heated through, about 1 minute.

Off heat, stir in the parsley and Parmesan, then taste and season with salt and pepper. Serve sprinkled with additional Parmesan.

Italian Sausages with Grapes and Wine Vinegar

Start to finish: 40 minutes / Servings: 4 to 6

Sausages and grapes are a common pairing on the Italian table. In this easy one-skillet dish, the grapes burst as they cook, adding pops of sweetness, while wine vinegar forms a light, tangy glaze—a wonderful complement to the rich sausages. If you have both red and green grapes on hand, combine them for a colorful presentation. Serve with thick slices of crusty bread or creamy polenta to soak up the savory-sweet pan juices.

2 tablespoons extra-virgin olive oil

1½ pounds sweet OR hot Italian sausages

1 large yellow OR red onion, halved and thinly sliced

1 pound seedless red OR green grapes OR a combination (3 cups)

¼ cup red wine vinegar OR white wine vinegar OR balsamic vinegar

½ cup lightly packed fresh flat-leaf parsley, roughly chopped

Kosher salt and ground black pepper

In a 12-inch nonstick skillet over medium, heat the oil until barely smoking. Add the sausages, cover and cook, turning occasionally, until the centers reach 160°F, 8 to 10 minutes. Transfer to a cutting board.

In the same skillet over medium, combine the onion and ¼ cup water. Cook, stirring occasionally, until the onion begins to soften, 5 to 7 minutes. Stir in the grapes, then cover and cook, stirring occasionally, until the grapes begin to soften and some have burst, 7 to 8 minutes; press on the grapes with a silicone spatula to help release the juices. Add the vinegar and cook, uncovered and stirring occasionally, until reduced to a light glaze, 3 to 4 minutes. Remove the pan from the heat.

Cut the sausages on the diagonal into 1- to 2-inch pieces and add to the skillet. Cook over medium, stirring occasionally, until heated through, about 2 minutes. Off heat, stir in the parsley. Taste and season with salt and pepper.

Weeknight Lahmajoun

Start to finish: 30 minutes
Makes four 8-inch flatbreads

The meat-topped flatbread known as lahmajoun is popular in Turkey and Armenia. We've created an easy weeknight version by swapping the usual homemade flatbread dough for store-bought pita breads. Simply combine the meat mixture in a food processor and spread onto pita, then bake in a hot oven. When processing the mixture, don't overdo it or the meat may become tough. Pulse a few times, just until combined. If you like, finish the dish with a sprinkling of fresh herbs and a drizzle of cooling yogurt to complement the spiced meat.

Four 8-inch pita breads

1 small red OR yellow onion, roughly chopped

¼ cup roasted red peppers, drained and patted dry

2 tablespoons tomato paste

2 teaspoons smoked paprika

1½ teaspoons ground cumin

¾ teaspoon red pepper flakes

Kosher salt and ground black pepper

8 ounces ground beef OR ground lamb

Heat the oven to 500°F with racks in the upper- and lower-middle positions. Arrange the pita breads on 2 rimmed baking sheets; set aside.

In a food processor, pulse the onion until finely chopped, about 5 pulses. Add the roasted peppers, tomato paste, paprika, cumin, pepper flakes, ½ teaspoon salt and 1 teaspoon black pepper. Process until smooth, about 10 seconds, scraping the bowl as needed. Add the beef and pulse just until incorporated, 3 or 4 pulses.

Divide the beef mixture evenly among the pitas (about a scant ½ cup each) and spread over the rounds, leaving a ½-inch border around the edge. Bake until the pitas are golden brown on the edges and the meat is sizzling, switching and rotating the baking sheets halfway through, 8 to 10 minutes. Cool for a few minutes, then transfer to a cutting board and cut into wedges.

Optional garnish: Chopped fresh flat-leaf parsley OR whole-milk yogurt OR lemon wedges OR fresh mint OR a combination

Pinto Beans with Sausage, Kale and Eggs

Start to finish: 30 minutes / Servings: 4 to 6

During the era of Portuguese colonization of Brazil, feijão tropeiro, or cattlemen's beans, was born out of a need to create sustenance from ingredients that didn't require refrigeration, such as dried meats, dried beans and cassava flour. Modern versions, however, typically are made with vegetables and sometimes eggs, and they inspired this hearty one-pan meal that's a terrific option for breakfast, lunch or dinner. Any type of smoked sausage—kielbasa, linguiça or even andouille—works well in this dish.

3 large eggs

3 tablespoons extra-virgin olive oil

6 ounces kielbasa OR linguiça sausage, halved lengthwise, then sliced ¼ inch thick

½ medium yellow onion, chopped

½ medium red bell pepper, stemmed, seeded and chopped

2 medium garlic cloves, finely chopped

1 bunch lacinato OR curly kale, stemmed and sliced ¼ inch thick

15½-ounce can pinto beans, rinsed and drained

Kosher salt and ground black pepper

In a small bowl, whisk the eggs until well combined; set aside. In a 12-inch nonstick skillet over medium-high, heat the oil until shimmering. Add the kielbasa and cook, stirring occasionally, until beginning to brown, 2 to 3 minutes. Add the onion and bell pepper; cook, stirring occasionally, until the vegetables are softened and beginning to brown, 3 to 4 minutes. Add the garlic and cook, stirring, until fragrant, 30 to 60 seconds.

Using a silicone spatula, push the sausage-vegetable mixture to one side of the skillet. Pour the eggs into the other side of the pan and cook, stirring constantly, until just set, 1 to 2 minutes. Stir the eggs into the sausage-vegetable mixture, breaking apart any large curds.

Add the kale and cook, stirring, until the leaves are wilted and tender-crisp, 2 to 3 minutes. Add the beans and cook, stirring occasionally, until heated through, 3 to 4 minutes. Off heat, taste and season with salt and pepper.

Optional garnish: Thinly sliced scallions

Spicy Pork and Oyster Sauce Noodles

Start to finish: 30 minutes / Servings: 4 to 6

This recipe blends the meatiness of Sichuan dan dan mian with the simplicity of peanut noodles. We rely on a few heavy-hitting pantry staples to create a flavorful dish that comes together easily. Peanut butter, soy sauce and oyster sauce (or hoisin) provide saltiness, sweetness and umami along with a creamy texture. A touch of vinegar balances the richness. Balsamic, with its sweet-tart flavor, makes a good stand-in for the more traditional Chinese black vinegar. The noodles also are delicious topped with a fried egg.

1 pound spaghetti OR linguine OR dried udon noodles

3 tablespoons creamy OR crunchy peanut butter

3 tablespoons soy sauce, plus more if needed

3 tablespoons oyster sauce OR hoisin sauce

Ground black pepper

3 tablespoons grapeseed or other neutral oil

8 ounces ground pork OR turkey OR beef

2 medium garlic cloves, minced OR 1-inch piece fresh ginger, peeled and finely grated OR both

2 tablespoons balsamic vinegar

1 tablespoon chili-garlic sauce OR 1½ tablespoons Sriracha sauce OR ½ teaspoon red pepper flakes

In a large pot, bring 4 quarts water to a boil. Reserve ½ cup of the hot water. Add the pasta to the pot, then cook, stirring occasionally, until al dente. When the pasta is done, drain; set aside.

While the pasta is cooking, in a small bowl, whisk together the peanut butter, soy sauce, oyster sauce, ½ teaspoon pepper and the reserved water.

In a 12-inch skillet over medium-high, heat the oil until shimmering. Add the pork and cook, breaking the meat into little bits, until no longer pink, 1 to 1½ minutes. Add the garlic, vinegar and chili-garlic sauce. Cook, stirring constantly, until the pork is browned, about 1 minute. Stir in the peanut butter mixture, followed by the pasta. Cook, stirring and tossing with tongs, until the pasta is shiny and the sauce clings, 2 to 4 minutes.

Off heat, taste and season with additional soy sauce and black pepper.

Optional garnish: Chopped roasted peanuts **OR** chili oil **OR** cucumber matchsticks **OR** toasted sesame oil **OR** thinly sliced scallions **OR** a combination

Sausage, Potato and Sweet Pepper Traybake

Start to finish: 1 hour (20 minutes active)
Servings: 4 to 6

Traybakes are a great solution when you want to put dinner on the table but can't or don't want to spend time at the stovetop. With this mostly hands-off technique, the ingredients are combined on a single baking sheet, then roasted in the oven. In this recipe, we cook savory Italian sausages on top of potatoes, onion and bell pepper so that the rendered meaty juices flavor the vegetables. To finish the dish, a mixture of vinegar and honey is poured over the hot vegetables, forming a delicious tangy-sweet glaze.

1 pound Yukon Gold OR russet OR red potatoes, cut into ½-inch wedges

1 medium red OR yellow onion, halved and sliced about ½ inch thick

1 medium red OR orange OR yellow bell pepper, stemmed, seeded and sliced about ½ inch thick

3 tablespoons extra-virgin olive oil

1 tablespoon dried oregano OR dried rosemary

Kosher salt and ground black pepper

1½ pounds sweet OR hot Italian sausages OR other fresh sausages, poked in several places with a paring knife

¼ cup white wine vinegar OR red wine vinegar

1 tablespoon honey

3 tablespoons rinsed and drained capers OR ¼ cup pitted green OR black olives, roughly chopped

Heat the oven to 450°F with a rack in the middle position. On a rimmed baking sheet, toss together the potatoes, onion, bell pepper, oil, oregano and 1 teaspoon each salt and pepper, then distribute in an even layer. Roast until the vegetables begin to soften and brown, 18 to 20 minutes, stirring once halfway through.

Remove from the oven and stir the vegetables again, then arrange the sausages on top. Continue to roast until the centers of the sausages reach 160°F and the vegetables are tender and lightly browned, another 20 to 25 minutes. Meanwhile, in a small bowl, stir together the vinegar and honey.

When the sausages are done, transfer them to a cutting board, leaving the vegetables in the pan. Pour the vinegar mixture over the vegetables and stir, scraping up any browned bits. Add the capers and toss, then taste and season with salt and pepper. Transfer to a serving dish.

Cut the sausages on the diagonal into 1-inch pieces, then add to the vegetables and toss. Alternatively, serve the sausages whole with the vegetables alongside.

Optional garnish: Chopped fresh flat-leaf parsley

Lebanese-Style Beef and Spinach Stew

Start to finish: 40 minutes / Servings: 4

Inspired by the Lebanese dish yakhnet sabanekh, this hearty, homey stew of ground beef and spinach, plus a few alliums and spices for flavoring, comes together quickly and easily. Toasted nuts (almonds are great, pine nuts even better) sprinkled on just before serving add rich flavor and textural contrast. We prefer to use fresh baby spinach for its silky texture, but frozen spinach works well, too (you'll need two 1-pound bags). Just thaw it, drain it in a colander and, if it's still very wet, pat it dry with paper towels. This stew is great with rice and vermicelli pilaf, with a salad of cucumbers and tomatoes alongside.

1 pound ground beef

2 teaspoons ground coriander

¼ teaspoon ground allspice OR 1 teaspoon ground cumin OR both

Kosher salt and ground black pepper

2 tablespoons extra-virgin olive oil, plus more to serve

2 tablespoons slivered almonds OR pine nuts

1 medium yellow onion, finely chopped

6 medium garlic cloves, minced

1-pound container baby spinach OR two 1-pound bags frozen chopped spinach, thawed, drained in a colander and patted dry (see headnote)

1 teaspoon grated lemon zest, plus 1 tablespoon lemon juice

In a medium bowl, combine the beef, coriander, allspice and ½ teaspoon pepper. Add ⅓ cup water and mix with your hands until well combined; set aside.

In a large Dutch oven over medium-high, combine the oil and almonds. Cook, stirring often, until golden, 3 to 5 minutes. Using a slotted spoon, transfer the almonds to a small bowl; set aside.

To the pot over medium, add the onion, garlic and ½ teaspoon salt. Cook, stirring occasionally, until the onion is lightly browned, 5 to 7 minutes. Increase to medium-high, add the beef mixture and cook, breaking

the beef into small pieces, until the meat is no longer pink, about 5 minutes.

If using fresh spinach, add it a large handful at a time, stirring to slightly wilt before each addition. Cook until the spinach is just wilted and deep green, 2 to 3 minutes. If using frozen spinach, add it to the pot, and cook, stirring, until warmed through, about 3 minutes.

Off heat, stir in the lemon zest and juice. Taste and season with salt and pepper. Serve sprinkled with the almonds and drizzled with additional oil.

Optional garnish: Jalapeño chili, stemmed, seeded and chopped **OR** chopped fresh flat-leaf parsley **OR** both

Eight-Ingredient Beef and Bean Chili

Start to finish: 40 minutes / Servings: 4 to 6

To create a flavor-packed weeknight chili using just eight ingredients, we're not shy about the seasonings. We add ¼ cup of chili powder and two tablespoons of cumin, plus a surprising addition: cocoa powder. It imparts amazing depth and complexity without tasting like chocolate. We also include a generous amount of tomato paste and cook it until deeply browned, a trick that develops rich, concentrated flavor. Chili loves garnishes; see the list below for our favorites.

¼ cup chili powder

2 tablespoons ground cumin

Kosher salt and ground black pepper

1 pound ground beef OR pork OR turkey

Two 15½-ounce cans pinto beans OR red kidney beans, drained but not rinsed

28-ounce can whole peeled tomatoes

¼ cup grapeseed or other neutral oil

1 large yellow onion, chopped, plus more, finely chopped, to serve

¼ cup tomato paste

1 tablespoon unsweetened cocoa powder

In a small bowl, stir together the chili powder, cumin and ½ teaspoon each salt and pepper. In a medium bowl, combine the beef, 1 tablespoon of the spice mixture and ¼ cup plus 2 tablespoons water. Using your hands, mix well; set aside.

In a large bowl, using a potato masher, mash half of the beans to a coarse paste. Add the tomatoes with juices and mash until they are broken down. Stir in the remaining whole beans; set aside.

In a large Dutch oven over medium, heat the oil until shimmering. Add the onion and ½ teaspoon salt; cover and cook, stirring occasionally, until the onion begins to soften and brown, about 7 minutes. Add the tomato paste and cook, stirring often, until well browned, 2 to 3 minutes. Add the remaining spice mixture and cook, stirring, until fragrant, about 30 seconds.

Add 2 cups water and bring to a simmer over medium-high, scraping up any browned bits. Add the meat mixture and cook, breaking it into small bits, until the meat is no longer pink, about 1 minute. Add the bean-tomato mixture and cocoa, then return to a simmer. Reduce to medium and simmer gently, uncovered and stirring occasionally, until the chili has thickened, about 30 minutes. Off heat, taste and season with salt and pepper. Serve with finely chopped onion for sprinkling.

Optional garnish: Sour cream **OR** chopped fresh cilantro **OR** pickled jalapeños **OR** shredded cheddar cheese **OR** hot sauce **OR** tortilla chips **OR** a combination

Vietnamese Pork and Scallion Omelet

Start to finish: 20 minutes / Servings: 4 to 6

The Vietnamese omelet called chả trứng chiên is a great way to get a simple and speedy flavor-packed dinner on the table using just five ingredients (not including black pepper and neutral oil). Pork is the classic choice of ground meat for the dish, but ground turkey also works well. You will need an oven-safe 12-inch skillet for this recipe. Serve with steamed jasmine rice and, if you like, a simple salad.

6 large eggs

1 bunch scallions, thinly sliced

8 ounces ground pork OR turkey

3 medium garlic cloves, minced

4 teaspoons fish sauce

Ground black pepper

2 tablespoons grapeseed or other neutral oil

Heat the oven to 425°F with a rack in the middle position. In a medium bowl, whisk the eggs. Reserve a couple tablespoons of the scallions for garnish.

In a large bowl, use your hands to thoroughly mix the pork, the remaining scallions, garlic, fish sauce and ¼ teaspoon pepper. Add the eggs and mix with a silicone spatula, breaking the pork mixture into bits, until the ingredients are well combined and no large clumps of meat remain.

In a 12-inch nonstick oven-safe skillet over medium-high, heat the oil until barely smoking. Add the pork-egg mixture; using the silicone spatula, break up any large bits of pork and evenly distribute the meat. Cook until the bottom is browned and set enough that you can lift an edge of the omelet with the spatula, about 3 minutes. Transfer the skillet to the oven and cook until the omelet is set in the center, 3 to 4 minutes.

Remove the skillet from the oven (the handle will be hot). Run the spatula around the edges of the omelet and underneath it to loosen, then carefully slide onto a platter. Alternatively, to serve the omelet browned side up, carefully invert it onto a platter. Serve warm or at room temperature, sprinkled with the reserved scallions and cut into wedges.

Optional garnish: Chopped fresh cilantro **OR** Sriracha **OR** lime wedges **OR** a combination

Syrian-Style Meatball Soup with Rice and Tomatoes

Start to finish: 40 minutes / Servings: 4

This rustic meatball and rice soup is pure comfort food. The recipe is our adaptation of one from "Aromas of Aleppo" by Poopa Dweck. Made with canned tomatoes, rice and boxed broth, plus a few warming spices, onion and garlic, the soup requires only one refrigerated ingredient: ground beef (ground turkey works well, too). The prep is easy, too. We grate both the onion and garlic so no knifework is required. What's more, there's no need to pre-shape or brown the meatballs. As you form them, simply drop them into the simmering broth.

1 pound ground beef OR turkey	¼ teaspoon red pepper flakes OR ground cinnamon OR both
4 tablespoons extra-virgin olive oil, divided	Kosher salt and ground black pepper
1 large yellow onion, grated on the large holes of a box grater, divided	28-ounce can diced tomatoes
5 medium garlic cloves, finely grated	1 quart low-sodium beef OR chicken broth
2 teaspoons ground allspice OR ground cumin, divided	½ cup long-grain white rice OR basmati rice, rinsed and drained

In a medium bowl, combine the beef, 2 tablespoons oil, ¼ cup of the grated onion, half of the garlic, 1½ teaspoons of the allspice, the red pepper flakes, 1 teaspoon salt and ½ teaspoon black pepper. Mix with your hands until well combined; set aside.

In a large pot, combine the remaining 2 tablespoons oil, the remaining onion, the remaining garlic, the remaining ½ teaspoon allspice and ½ teaspoon salt. Cook over medium-high, stirring occasionally, until the mixture is browned and sticks to the pot, about 5 minutes.

Add the tomatoes with juices, the broth and 2 cups water. Bring to a simmer, scraping up any browned bits, then stir in the rice. Reduce to medium and cook, uncovered and stirring occasionally, for 8 minutes; the rice will not be fully cooked.

Using dampened hands, pinch off a 1-tablespoon portion of the meat mixture, form it into a ball and drop it into the broth. Shape the remaining meat mixture and add to the pot in the same way; it's fine if the meatballs are not completely uniform. Simmer, uncovered and stirring occasionally, until the soup is slightly thickened and the center of the meatballs reach 160°F, 10 to 15 minutes. Off heat, taste and season with salt and black pepper.

Optional garnish: Chopped fresh flat-leaf parsley **OR** chopped fresh cilantro **OR** pomegranate molasses **OR** a combination

From the
FREEZER

Frozen VEGETABLES

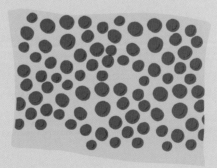

Japanese-Style Rice with Corn, Butter and Soy Sauce

Start to finish: 50 minutes (10 minutes active)
Servings: 4 to 6

Frozen corn kernels add color and sweetness to Japanese-style short-grain rice, with a little butter bringing richness and soy sauce adding umami. If you want to up the nutrition, substitute ¼ cup rinsed and drained quinoa or pearled barley for an equal amount of the rice. Whether you use only rice or mix your grains, be sure not to skip the soak or rest before or after steaming, respectively, as they are essential for even cooking.

1½ cups Japanese-style short-grain white rice, rinsed and drained

1 tablespoon soy sauce

Kosher salt and ground black **OR** white pepper

1½ cups frozen corn kernels, thawed and patted dry

2 tablespoons salted butter, cut into 6 pieces

4 scallion greens, cut on the diagonal into ¼-inch slices (about ¼ cup)

In a large saucepan, stir together the rice, 2 cups water, the soy sauce and ½ teaspoon salt. Scatter the corn evenly over the top; do not stir. Cover and let stand for 30 minutes.

Set the pan over medium-high and bring to a boil. Reduce to low and cook, covered and without stirring, until the rice has absorbed the water, about 18 minutes. Remove the pan from the heat and let stand, covered, for 10 minutes.

Uncover, scatter the butter on top, then fluff the rice with a fork, combining the rice and corn, until the butter is melted. Transfer to a serving dish and top with the scallions and a few grindings of pepper.

Optional garnish: Toasted sesame seeds **OR** lemon wedges **OR** both

Lemon and Green Pea Risotto

Start to finish: 35 minutes / Servings: 4

This simple recipe transforms a few basic ingredients into a risotto full of bright, bracing flavors. When cooked, the grains of Arborio rice should be tender but retain a slight chew at the center; they should not be evenly soft throughout. Chopped fresh parsley, basil or mint sprinkled on top just before serving offers vibrant color, flavor and fragrance; use whichever you have.

1 quart low-sodium chicken broth OR vegetable broth

3 tablespoons salted butter, cut into 1-tablespoon pieces, divided

1 small yellow onion, finely chopped

Kosher salt and ground black pepper

1 cup Arborio rice

1½ cups frozen peas, thawed and patted dry

2 teaspoons grated lemon zest, plus 2 tablespoons lemon juice

1 ounce Parmesan cheese, finely grated (½ cup), plus more to serve

Finely chopped fresh flat-leaf parsley OR basil OR mint, to serve

In a medium saucepan over medium, bring the broth and 2 cups water, covered, to a simmer; reduce to low to keep warm.

In a large saucepan over medium, melt 2 tablespoons butter. Add the onion and ¼ teaspoon salt; cook, stirring occasionally, until softened, about 5 minutes. Add the rice and cook, stirring constantly, until the grains are translucent at the edges, 1 to 2 minutes. Add 3 cups of the hot broth mixture and bring to a boil over medium-high. Reduce to medium and cook, stirring often and briskly, until most of the liquid is absorbed, 10 to 12 minutes; adjust the heat as needed to maintain a vigorous simmer.

Cook, adding ¼ cup of the broth at a time, until the rice is al dente and loose but not soupy, another 8 to 10 minutes. You may not need all of the broth. Off heat, stir in the remaining 1 tablespoon butter, the peas, lemon zest and juice, and Parmesan. Taste and season with salt and pepper. Serve sprinkled with parsley and additional Parmesan.

Spaghetti with Broccoli-Miso Sauce and Toasted Walnuts

Start to finish: 30 minutes / Servings: 4 to 6

Frozen broccoli, simmered until tender and pureed until smooth with blanched garlic and miso—yes, miso—becomes a creamy, elegant sauce for al dente pasta. Parmesan (or pecorino) cheese and toasted walnuts bring additional umami to the dish, for rich, full, complex flavor, while fresh, bright lemon zest and juice brighten up the flavors. Frozen broccoli is sold as either florets or "cuts" (a mix of florets and stalks); either works in this recipe.

Kosher salt and ground black pepper

Two 10-ounce bags frozen broccoli (see headnote)

3 medium garlic cloves, smashed and peeled

1 tablespoon white miso

¼ cup extra-virgin olive oil, plus more to serve

1 pound spaghetti OR linguine

2 ounces Parmesan OR pecorino Romano finely grated (1 cup), plus more to serve

1 tablespoon grated lemon zest, plus 2 tablespoons lemon juice

½ cup walnuts OR pine nuts, toasted

In a large pot, bring 4 quarts water to a boil. Add 1 tablespoon salt, the broccoli and garlic; return to a boil, then cook until the broccoli is fully tender, 3 to 4 minutes. Using a slotted spoon, transfer the broccoli and garlic to a blender; keep the water at a boil. Remove 2 cups of the boiling water. Add 1 cup to the blender (reserve the remainder), along with the miso and 1 teaspoon pepper. Blend until smooth, about 1 minute, then, with the blender running, stream in the oil; set aside.

Add the pasta to the boiling water and cook, stirring, until al dente. Drain and return to the pot. Add the broccoli puree, cheese and lemon zest and juice; toss, adding reserved water as needed so the pasta is lightly sauced. Taste and season with salt and pepper. Serve drizzled with additional oil and sprinkled with the nuts and additional cheese.

Optional garnish: Red pepper flakes

Fettuccine with Corn, Tomatoes and Bacon

Start to finish: 35 minutes / Servings: 4 to 6

Sweet, buttery, salty and smoky are the defining flavors of this summery pasta dish that can be made year-round thanks to frozen corn. Supermarket cherry (or grape) tomatoes are dependably good no matter the season, but briefly simmering them on the stovetop brings out their sweetness and renders them juicy and succulent. We boil the fettuccine until it's not quite al dente, then finish cooking the pasta in the sauce so it absorbs flavors.

12 ounces fettuccine **OR** pappardelle

Kosher salt and ground black pepper

4 ounces bacon, chopped

½ medium yellow onion, finely chopped

4 medium garlic cloves, minced

1½ cups frozen corn kernels, thawed

1 pint cherry **OR** grape tomatoes, halved

2 tablespoons salted butter, cut into 2 pieces

2 teaspoons balsamic vinegar, preferably white balsamic

In a large pot, bring 4 quarts water to a boil. Add the pasta and 1 tablespoon salt, then cook, stirring occasionally, until just shy of al dente. Reserve 1 cup of the cooking water, then drain; set aside.

Meanwhile, in a large Dutch oven over medium-high, cook the bacon, stirring occasionally, until brown and crisp, 3 to 5 minutes. Using a slotted spoon, transfer the bacon to a paper towel–lined plate; set aside. Pour off and discard all but 1 tablespoon of the fat in the pot.

Return the Dutch oven to medium and add the onion and garlic; cook, stirring often, until lightly browned, 5 to 8 minutes. Stir in the corn, tomatoes and ¼ teaspoon pepper. Cover and cook, stirring once or twice, until the tomatoes have softened and released their juices, about 4 minutes.

Add the pasta and ½ cup of the reserved cooking water, then cook, stirring and tossing, until the pasta is al dente and lightly sauced, 3 to 5 minutes; add more cooking water 1 tablespoon at a time as needed if the mixture looks dry. Off heat, stir in the butter, vinegar and bacon until the butter is melted. Taste and season with salt and pepper.

Optional garnish: Chopped fresh basil **OR** finely grated Parmesan cheese **OR** both

Spinach, Ham and Cheddar Strata

Start to finish: 2 hours (25 minutes active)
Servings: 6 to 8

Rich with cheese, crusty bread and an eggy custard, stratas can easily serve a crowd. These savory bread puddings are exceptionally versatile and can include a variety of vegetables and meats, such as the spinach and ham featured here. To streamline prep, we call for thawed frozen spinach; be sure to squeeze it dry so the strata won't become soggy. This is a great do-ahead dish. Assemble the strata, cover with foil and refrigerate overnight. The next day, the foil-covered strata can go directly from the refrigerator to the oven. Bake for 1 hour, then uncover and bake for about another 20 minutes.

2 tablespoons extra-virgin olive oil, divided

10-ounce box frozen chopped spinach, thawed

1 medium yellow onion, finely chopped

Kosher salt and ground black pepper

6 large eggs

4 cups whole milk

8 ounces country-style white bread, cut into 1-inch cubes (about 4 cups)

8 ounces cheddar **OR** pepper jack cheese, shredded (2 cups)

4 ounces thinly sliced deli ham, roughly chopped (1 cup)

Heat the oven to 375°F with a rack in the middle position. Brush a 9-by-13-inch baking dish with 1 tablespoon oil. Wrap the spinach in a clean kitchen towel and squeeze over the sink to remove excess moisture; set aside.

In a 10-inch skillet over medium, heat the remaining 1 tablespoon oil until shimmering. Add the onion and ½ teaspoon salt; cook, stirring occasionally, until softened, 5 to 7 minutes. Remove the pan from the heat.

In a large bowl, whisk together the eggs, milk and ¼ teaspoon each salt and pepper. Break apart the squeeze-dried spinach and add it to the egg mixture along with the bread, three-fourths of the cheese, the ham and onion; using a silicone spatula, stir until well combined.

Transfer the mixture to the prepared baking dish and distribute in an even layer. Sprinkle the remaining cheese on top. Cover with foil and bake for 25 minutes.

Carefully remove the foil, then bake until golden brown and bubbly, about another 30 minutes. Cool for at least 5 minutes. Serve warm or at room temperature.

Curried Broccoli and Cilantro Soup

Start to finish: 40 minutes / Servings: 4 to 6

Frozen broccoli makes it immensely easy to throw together this smooth, creamy, no-cream soup. It doesn't even require thawing before use, and cooking is brief so the broccoli retains its bright color. An immersion blender, if you own one, makes the recipe even simpler, as it can puree the soup directly in the pot. Either frozen broccoli florets or "cuts" (a mix of florets and stalks) will work in this recipe.

2 tablespoons salted butter

1 large yellow onion, chopped

2 tablespoons chopped fresh ginger

1 jalapeño chili, stemmed, seeded and minced

1 bunch cilantro, stems chopped, leaves roughly chopped, reserved separately

Kosher salt and ground black pepper

1 tablespoon curry powder

1 quart low-sodium chicken broth OR vegetable broth

Two 10-ounce bags frozen broccoli, unthawed (see headnote)

In a large saucepan over medium, melt the butter. Add the onion, ginger, half the jalapeño, the cilantro stems and ½ teaspoon salt. Cook, stirring occasionally, until the onion is softened and browned, 12 to 15 minutes. Add the curry powder and ½ teaspoon each salt and pepper; cook, stirring, until fragrant, about 30 seconds. Add the broth and bring to a boil over medium-high. Add the broccoli and return to a boil. Remove the pan from the heat and cool for about 5 minutes. Stir in about half of the cilantro leaves.

Using a blender and working in 2 or 3 batches to avoid overfilling the jar, puree the broccoli mixture until smooth. Return the soup to the pot and heat over medium, stirring, until hot. Taste and season with salt and pepper. Serve sprinkled with the remaining jalapeño and the remaining cilantro leaves.

Optional garnish: Plain yogurt

Rigatoni Carbonara with Peas

Start to finish: 30 minutes / Servings: 4 to 6

A favorite Roman pasta dish, carbonara comes together easily with ingredients you likely already have in the kitchen. In place of guanciale, the type of cured pork traditionally used in carbonara, we swap in smoky-sweet bacon. We also add green peas for freshness and bright color; feel free to omit them if you wish—the results still will be delicious. After draining the pasta, immediately add it to the egg and cheese mixture, then toss constantly for about a minute to coat the noodles and prevent the eggs from curdling. The pasta's residual heat will lightly cook the eggs, creating a rich, velvety coating on the noodles.

4 ounces bacon, chopped

2 medium garlic cloves, smashed and peeled

1 large egg, plus 2 large egg yolks

2 ounces Parmesan OR pecorino Romano cheese OR a combination, finely grated (1 cup), plus more to serve

Kosher salt and ground black pepper

1 pound rigatoni OR ziti

1 cup frozen peas OR petite peas, thawed

In a 10-inch skillet over medium-high, cook the bacon, stirring occasionally, until crisp, 4 to 5 minutes. Off heat, add the garlic and stir to coat with the rendered fat; set the pan aside.

In a large bowl, whisk together the whole egg and yolks, half the Parmesan and ½ teaspoon pepper; set aside.

In a large pot, bring 2 quarts water to a boil. Add the pasta and 2 teaspoons salt, then cook, stirring occasionally, until al dente. Reserve ½ cup of the cooking water, then stir the peas into the pot with the pasta and drain. Immediately pour the pasta and peas into the bowl with the egg mixture. Toss until the pasta is lightly sauced, about 1 minute; add the reserved cooking water 1 tablespoon at a time as needed if the mixture looks dry.

Set the skillet with the bacon over medium-high and cook, stirring, until the fat starts to sizzle and the bacon is heated through, 30 to 60 seconds. Off heat, remove and discard the garlic. Pour the bacon and rendered fat over the pasta, add the remaining Parmesan and toss well. Taste and season with salt and pepper. Serve sprinkled with additional cheese.

Chilean-Style Bean, Butternut and Corn Stew

Start to finish: 40 minutes / Servings: 4 to 6

Beans, corn and squash are combined in the nourishing Chilean stew called porotos granados. It traditionally is made in late summer, after these crops are harvested, but our version with frozen vegetables and canned beans is easy to throw together anytime. The recipe calls for frozen butternut squash cubes; the size of the chunks varies from brand to brand, so begin testing for doneness after 5 minutes of cooking. Larger pieces may require about 10 minutes to become tender.

Two 15½-ounce cans pinto beans OR kidney beans, drained but not rinsed

3 tablespoons extra-virgin olive oil

1 large yellow onion, chopped

2 jalapeño chilies, stemmed, seeded and minced

Kosher salt and ground black pepper

2 tablespoons sweet paprika OR 1½ tablespoons sweet paprika, plus 1½ teaspoons smoked paprika

28-ounce can whole peeled tomatoes, crushed by hand

1 quart low-sodium chicken broth OR vegetable broth

10-ounce bag frozen butternut squash cubes (about 2 cups), not thawed

1 cup frozen corn kernels, not thawed

In a medium bowl, using a potato masher, mash half of the beans until mostly smooth; set aside.

In a large pot over medium, heat the oil until shimmering. Add the onion, jalapeños and ½ teaspoon salt; cover and cook, stirring occasionally, until the onion begins to soften and brown, about 7 minutes. Add the paprika and cook, stirring, until fragrant, about 30 seconds. Add the mashed beans, tomatoes with juices, broth and 2 cups water. Bring to a simmer over medium-high, then reduce to medium and simmer, uncovered and stirring occasionally, until the onion is tender, about 15 minutes.

Add the squash, corn and remaining whole beans. Bring to a simmer over medium-high, then reduce to medium and simmer, uncovered and stirring occasionally, until the squash is tender but not falling apart, 5 to 10 minutes. Off heat, taste and season with salt and pepper.

Optional garnish: Red wine vinegar OR chopped fresh cilantro (or basil) OR both

Turmeric-Spiced Spinach and Potatoes

Start to finish: 40 minutes / Servings: 4 to 6

With chopped spinach in the freezer and potatoes in the pantry, it's easy to prepare a simplified version of the classic Indian dish known as saag aloo ("greens potatoes," literally translated). We season ours with a simple combination of spices—turmeric for its golden hue and cumin for earthy warmth. Before using the frozen spinach, thaw it and drain in a colander; if it's still very wet, pat it dry with paper towels. Basmati rice or warm flatbreads make delicious accompaniments.

3 tablespoons
salted butter

2 teaspoons cumin
seeds OR mustard seeds
OR both

1 large yellow onion,
halved and thinly sliced

2 tablespoons minced
fresh ginger

1 bunch cilantro, stems
chopped, leaves roughly
chopped, reserved
separately

Kosher salt and
ground black pepper

1½ pounds Yukon Gold
OR red potatoes, peeled
and cut into ½-inch cubes

2 teaspoons
ground turmeric

Two 10-ounce boxes
frozen chopped spinach,
thawed, drained in a
colander and patted dry
(see headnote)

In a large pot over medium, melt the butter. Add the cumin seeds and cook, stirring, until fragrant, about 30 seconds. Add the onion, ginger, cilantro stems and ½ teaspoon salt; cook, stirring occasionally, until the onion is soft and starting to brown, 13 to 15 minutes.

Add the potatoes, turmeric, ½ teaspoon each salt and pepper, and 3 cups water. Bring to a simmer over medium-high, scraping up any browned bits. Reduce to medium and cook, uncovered and stirring occasionally, until the potatoes are tender, 15 to 20 minutes. Add the spinach and cook, stirring occasionally, until heated through, 1 to 2 minutes.

Off heat, stir in the cilantro leaves, then taste and season with salt and pepper.

Optional garnish: Plain whole-milk yogurt OR chutney

Baked Butternut Squash Risotto

Start to finish: 1¼ hours (15 minutes active)
Servings: 4

In the classic Italian dish called risotto con zucca, butternut squash often takes the place of pumpkin (zucca). In this recipe, we opt for the convenience of frozen butternut squash cubes and simplify the cooking by baking the risotto, eliminating the need to add hot liquid in batches and stir the rice as it simmers. We roast half of the squash to develop a rich, caramelized sweetness and cook the other half directly in the rice to infuse the risotto with flavor and add another dimension of creaminess. Fresh butternut also works, if that's your preference. Use an equal amount and increase the risotto's time in the oven to about 55 minutes.

Two 10-ounce bags frozen butternut squash (about 4 cups total), thawed, drained and patted dry

2 tablespoons extra-virgin olive oil, plus more to serve

Kosher salt and ground black pepper

3 tablespoons salted butter, cut into 1-tablespoon pieces, divided

1 small yellow onion OR 2 medium shallots, finely chopped

1 cup Arborio rice

¾ cup dry white wine OR dry vermouth

1 quart low-sodium vegetable broth OR chicken broth

1 teaspoon dried rosemary OR 1 sprig fresh rosemary

2 ounces Parmesan OR pecorino Romano cheese, finely grated (1 cup), divided

Heat the oven to 400°F with racks in the lower-middle and lowest positions. On a rimmed baking sheet, toss half of the squash (about 2 cups) with the oil and ¼ teaspoon each salt and pepper. Roast on the lowest rack, stirring once about halfway through, until golden brown, about 20 minutes. Remove from the oven and set aside; leave the oven on.

In a large Dutch oven over medium, melt 2 tablespoons butter. Add the onion and ½ teaspoon salt; cook, stirring often, until translucent, about 5 minutes. Add the rice and cook, stirring constantly, until the grains are translucent at the edges, 1 to 2 minutes. Stir in the remaining uncooked squash and the wine; cook, stirring, until the pot is almost dry, about 2 minutes.

Stir in the broth, rosemary, 1 cup water and ½ teaspoon pepper. Cover and place in the oven on the lower-middle rack. Cook until the rice is tender but has not yet absorbed all the liquid and a skewer inserted into the squash meets no resistance, about 45 minutes.

Remove from the oven, uncover and stir in the roasted squash. Add half of the cheese and the remaining 1 tablespoon butter, then stir vigorously until the butter is melted and the risotto is creamy. Let stand uncovered for 5 minutes; the risotto will thicken as it stands.

Taste and season with salt and pepper. Serve with the remaining cheese and additional oil for drizzling.

Optional garnish: Chopped fresh chives OR thinly sliced scallions OR chopped fresh sage OR chopped toasted walnuts

Corn and Coconut Soup with Ginger and Scallions

Start to finish: 30 minutes / Servings: 4

Loosely inspired by tom kha gai, or chicken and coconut soup, this recipe features the signature flavors of Thai cooking—salty, spicy, sour and sweet—using readily available pantry ingredients, plus a couple bags of frozen corn kernels (no need to thaw the corn before use). Fish sauce lends saltiness, jalapeño brings the spice and fresh lime juice contributes tartness, while corn and coconut milk add their natural sweetness. We also toss in chunks of potatoes to create a hearty soup that's a full meal in a bowl.

2 tablespoons grapeseed or other neutral oil

1 bunch scallions, thinly sliced, white and green parts reserved separately

2 tablespoons minced fresh ginger

12 ounces russet potatoes, peeled, quartered lengthwise and sliced ¼ inch thick

Two 10-ounce bags frozen corn kernels (about 4 cups)

1 quart low-sodium chicken broth **OR** vegetable broth

14-ounce can coconut milk

2 tablespoons fish sauce

2 tablespoons lime juice, plus lime wedges to serve

In a large pot over medium, heat the oil until shimmering. Add the scallion whites and ginger; cook, stirring, until fragrant, about 30 seconds. Add the potatoes, corn, broth and coconut milk. Bring to a simmer over medium-high, then reduce to medium and simmer, uncovered and stirring occasionally, until the potatoes are tender, about 15 minutes.

Off heat, stir in the fish sauce, lime juice and scallion greens. Serve with lime wedges.

Optional garnish: Chopped fresh cilantro **OR** jalapeño chilies, stemmed and sliced **OR** Sriracha sauce **OR** a combination

Fried Rice with Peas, Corn and Bacon

Start to finish: 30 minutes / Servings: 4 to 6

This simple, freezer-friendly fried rice is studded with corn and peas that can be added in their frozen state (no need to thaw them first, though there's no harm in doing so). Bacon and oyster sauce ratchet up the flavors, adding layers of smokiness, sweetness and umami. Fried rice is always best made with cooked rice that has been fully chilled (freshly cooked rice yields a soggy, gummy texture). Regular long-grain, jasmine or Japanese-style short-grain rice are best.

4 large eggs

Kosher salt and ground black pepper

2 tablespoons grapeseed OR other neutral oil, divided

6 ounces (about 6 slices) bacon, chopped

1 medium yellow onion, finely chopped

4 cups cooked and chilled white rice

3 tablespoons oyster sauce

1 tablespoon unseasoned rice vinegar

½ cup frozen peas, not thawed

½ cup frozen corn kernels, not thawed

In a small bowl, whisk together the eggs and ¼ teaspoon salt. In a 12-inch nonstick skillet over medium-high, heat 1 tablespoon oil until barely smoking. Add the eggs and cook, stirring, until set into small curds, 1 to 2 minutes. Transfer to a plate and set aside. Wipe out the pan.

In the same skillet over medium, cook the bacon, stirring occasionally, until crisp, 4 to 5 minutes. Using a slotted spoon, transfer to the plate with the eggs. Pour off and discard all but 1 tablespoon bacon fat.

Set the skillet over medium, add the remaining 1 tablespoon oil and the onion; cook, stirring occasionally, until the onion is softened, 2 to 3 minutes. Stir in the rice, breaking up any clumps. Distribute in an even layer and cook without stirring until beginning to brown on the bottom, about 4 minutes.

Add the oyster sauce and vinegar; cook, stirring, until well combined, 1 to 2 minutes. Add the peas, corn, bacon and eggs. Stir to combine, breaking up any large clumps of egg. Distribute in an even layer and cook without stirring until the vegetables are heated through and the mixture begins to brown on the bottom, 3 to 4 minutes. Taste and season with salt and pepper.

Optional garnish: Sliced scallions **OR** chili oil **OR** lemon or lime wedges **OR** toasted sesame seeds **OR** a combination

Shrimp SUPPERS

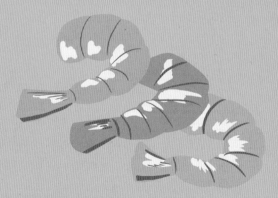

Spanish-Style Shrimp with Garlic and Olive Oil

Start to finish: 25 minutes / Servings: 4

Gambas al ajillo, or shrimp with garlic, is one of the best known Spanish tapas. Briny-sweet shrimp are gently cooked in a generous amount of olive oil infused with toasted garlic and, oftentimes, dried red chilies. The dish comes together quickly and easily, and with just a handful of ingredients, many of which you probably already have in the kitchen. In our rendition of gambas al ajillo, we add smoked paprika and pepper flakes, as well as finishing touches of parsley and lemon wedges. Feel free to use shrimp that are slightly larger or smaller, but be sure to adjust the cooking time. Serve crusty bread alongside for dipping into the flavorful oil.

1 pound large (26/30 per pound) shrimp, peeled, deveined and patted dry

Kosher salt

½ cup extra-virgin olive oil

1 teaspoon smoked paprika

½ teaspoon red pepper flakes

6 medium garlic cloves, thinly sliced

2 tablespoons finely chopped flat-leaf parsley, plus more to serve

Lemon wedges, to serve

In a medium bowl, toss the shrimp with 1 teaspoon salt. In a 12-inch skillet, combine the oil, paprika, pepper flakes and garlic. Cook over medium, stirring occasionally, until the mixture is fragrant and rust-colored and the garlic is golden brown, about 2 minutes.

Add the shrimp in an even layer and cook without stirring until pink on the bottoms, about 1 minute. Flip each shrimp and cook until opaque throughout, about 1 minute longer. Off heat, stir in the parsley. Transfer to a wide, shallow serving dish and serve with lemon wedges.

Optional garnish: Flaky sea salt

Stir-Fried Chili Shrimp

Start to finish: 30 minutes / Servings: 4

Singaporean chili crab inspired this fast, pantry-friendly shrimp stir-fry. Aside from deveining the shrimp and peeling the ginger, the only knifework needed is slicing the onion (and the scallion or cilantro, if you're using them). You can substitute shrimp that are slightly smaller or larger, but be sure to adjust the cooking time accordingly. Serve with steamed jasmine rice.

¼ cup plus
2 tablespoons ketchup

¼ cup plus 2 tablespoons
unseasoned rice vinegar

1½ tablespoons
soy sauce OR fish sauce

1½ tablespoons chili-garlic
sauce OR Sriracha

1 teaspoon white sugar

1½ pounds extra-large
shrimp (21/25 per pound),
peeled, deveined and
patted dry

Kosher salt and
ground black pepper

3 tablespoons grapeseed
or other neutral oil,
divided

½ medium red onion,
thinly sliced OR 2 large
shallots, halved and
thinly sliced

2 tablespoons finely
grated fresh ginger
OR 4 garlic cloves,
thinly sliced

In a small bowl, stir together the ketchup, vinegar, soy sauce, chili-garlic sauce and sugar; set aside. In a large bowl, toss the shrimp with ½ teaspoon salt and ¼ teaspoon pepper.

In a 12-inch nonstick skillet over medium-high, heat 1 tablespoon oil until barely smoking. Add half the shrimp in an even layer and cook without stirring until deep golden brown on the bottoms, about 2 minutes. Stir and cook until opaque on both sides, another 20 to 30 seconds. Transfer to a plate. Using 1 tablespoon of the remaining oil, cook the remaining shrimp in the same way.

To the now-empty skillet over medium-high, add the remaining 1 tablespoon oil, the onion and ginger; stir to combine. Cover and cook, stirring occasionally, until the onion begins to brown, about 1 minute. Add the ketchup mixture and cook, scraping up any browned bits, until the mixture is slightly thickened, about 30 seconds. Add ½ cup water and cook, stirring often, until a spatula drawn through the sauce leaves a trail, about 2 minutes.

Add the shrimp and accumulated juices to the skillet; stir to combine. Cover, remove from the heat and let stand until the shrimp are heated through, 1 to 2 minutes.

Optional garnish: Lime wedges OR sliced scallions OR chopped fresh cilantro OR a combination

Tuscan-Style Shrimp with White Beans

Start to finish: 25 minutes / Servings: 4

With its miles of coastline and reputation as the home of mangiafagioli—or bean eaters—it's no surprise that shrimp and white beans are a classic pairing in the cuisine of Tuscany, Italy. In this quick, easy recipe, the two are the stars, but with so few supporting ingredients, it's important to use a dry white wine that's good enough to drink on its own. Serve warm or at room temperature with a leafy salad and crusty bread to round out the meal.

3 tablespoons extra-virgin olive oil, plus more to serve

1 medium yellow onion, finely chopped

1 sprig fresh rosemary OR ½ teaspoon dried rosemary

½ teaspoon red pepper flakes

Kosher salt and ground black pepper

Two 15½-ounce cans butter beans OR cannellini beans, rinsed and drained

¾ cup dry white wine

1 pound extra-large (21/25 per pound) shrimp, peeled and deveined

1 cup lightly packed fresh flat-leaf parsley OR fresh basil, roughly chopped

In a 12-inch skillet over medium-high, heat the oil until shimmering. Add the onion, rosemary, pepper flakes and ½ teaspoon salt; cook, stirring occasionally, until the onion is translucent, 4 to 6 minutes. Stir in the beans, then add the wine and cook, uncovered and stirring occasionally, until the pan is dry, 5 to 7 minutes.

Stir in the shrimp. Cover, reduce to medium-low and cook until the shrimp are opaque throughout, 4 to 5 minutes; stir once about halfway through.

Off heat, taste and season with salt and black pepper. Remove and discard the rosemary sprig (if used). Stir in the parsley and serve drizzled with additional oil.

Veracruz-Style Rice and Shrimp

Start to finish: 1 hour (30 minutes active) / Servings: 4

A seaside classic from Veracruz, Mexico, the rice dish called arroz a la tumbada often features a medley of seafood. In our streamlined version, we opt for just shrimp to create a one-pot meal that's easy enough for a weeknight. If you seek chili heat, leave the seeds in the jalapeño that's minced and also garnish with the optional jalapeño. Serve with lime wedges for a burst of bright acidity.

1 pound extra-large (21/25 per pound) shrimp, peeled and deveined

Kosher salt and ground black pepper

3 tablespoons extra-virgin olive oil

1 medium yellow OR white onion, chopped

1 jalapeño chili, stemmed, seeded and minced, plus 1 jalapeño, stemmed and sliced into thin rounds (optional)

2 tablespoons tomato paste

1 bunch cilantro, stems finely chopped, leaves roughly chopped, reserved separately

1½ cups long-grain white rice, rinsed and drained

1 quart low-sodium chicken broth

1 teaspoon grated lime zest, plus lime wedges to serve

Season the shrimp with 1 teaspoon salt and ½ teaspoon pepper; set aside at room temperature. In a large Dutch oven over medium, combine the oil, onion and ¼ teaspoon salt; cook, stirring occasionally, until the onion starts to soften, about 5 minutes. Add the minced jalapeño, tomato paste and cilantro stems; cook, stirring occasionally, until the onion is lightly browned, 5 to 7 minutes.

Stir in the rice, broth and 1 teaspoon salt. Bring to a simmer over medium-high, then cover, reduce to low and cook without stirring until the rice is tender (it still will be slightly soupy), 15 to 18 minutes.

Uncover the pot and distribute the shrimp in an even layer over the rice. Re-cover, remove from the heat and let stand until the shrimp are opaque throughout, about 10 minutes.

Add the lime zest and, using a spatula, stir the shrimp and zest into the rice. Taste and season with salt and pepper. Serve garnished with the jalapeño rounds (if using) and the cilantro leaves, and with lime wedges on the side.

Shrimp Fra Diavolo

Start to finish: 40 minutes (25 minutes active)
Servings: 4

Most likely an Italian-American creation, the dish known as fra diavolo, or "brother devil," is indeed a spicy one. The tomato-based sauce gets a kick of heat from red pepper flakes; we call for 1¼ teaspoons, though feel free to adjust to your taste.

1½ pounds extra-large (21/25 per pound) shrimp, peeled, deveined and patted dry

Kosher salt and ground black pepper

4 tablespoons extra-virgin olive oil, divided

5 medium garlic cloves, thinly sliced

½ cup dry white wine

28-ounce can whole peeled tomatoes, crushed by hand

1¼ teaspoons red pepper flakes

½ teaspoon dried oregano

1 tablespoon unsalted butter

½ cup chopped fresh flat-leaf parsley OR basil

In a large bowl, toss the shrimp with ½ teaspoon salt. In a 12-inch skillet over medium-high, heat 3 tablespoons oil until shimmering. Add half of the shrimp in a single layer and cook without stirring until browned on the bottoms but not yet fully cooked, about 2 minutes. Using tongs or a slotted spoon, transfer to a large plate. Cook the remaining shrimp in the same way using the oil remaining in the pan. Transfer to the plate.

In the same skillet over medium, combine the remaining 1 tablespoon oil and the garlic. Cook, stirring occasionally, until the garlic is fragrant and lightly browned, about 2 minutes. Add the wine and bring to a simmer over medium-high, scraping up any browned bits. Stir in the tomatoes with juices, pepper flakes, oregano and ¾ teaspoon salt. Reduce to medium and simmer, uncovered and stirring occasionally, until the sauce thickens slightly, 15 to 20 minutes. Add the butter and stir until melted.

Add the shrimp and any accumulated juices. Cook, stirring often, until the shrimp are opaque throughout, about 2 minutes. Off heat, stir in the parsley, then taste and season with salt and black pepper.

Broiled Shrimp with Garlic, Lemon and Herbs

Start to finish: 30 minutes / Servings: 4

In this recipe, an easy puree of fresh herbs, garlic and olive oil is used two ways: Some of it coats the uncooked shrimp as a quick marinade, then a splash of lemon juice is stirred into the rest to create a bright sauce for serving. Be sure to pat the shrimp thoroughly dry so they'll brown and char nicely under the broiler. A touch of sugar in the marinade also promotes browning. We call for extra-large shrimp here; use slightly larger or smaller ones if you like, but adjust the cooking time accordingly.

1 cup lightly packed fresh flat-leaf parsley **OR** cilantro **OR** basil **OR** a combination

4 scallions, roughly chopped

2 medium garlic cloves, smashed and peeled

1½ teaspoons grated lemon zest, plus 1 tablespoon lemon juice

¼ to ½ teaspoon red pepper flakes (optional)

Kosher salt and ground black pepper

½ cup extra-virgin olive oil

1½ pounds extra-large (21/25 per pound) shrimp, peeled, deveined and patted dry (see headnote)

½ teaspoon white sugar

Line a rimmed baking sheet with foil, set a wire rack in the baking sheet and mist it with cooking spray. In a food processor, combine the parsley, scallions, garlic, lemon zest, pepper flakes (if using), ¼ teaspoon salt and ½ teaspoon black pepper. Pulse until finely chopped, about 8 pulses. Scrape the sides of the bowl, then add the oil and process until bright green and almost smooth, about 30 seconds. Transfer ¼ cup of the puree to a small bowl; set aside for serving.

In a medium bowl, toss together the shrimp, the remaining herb puree, sugar and ¼ teaspoon each salt and black pepper. Thread the shrimp onto 4 to 6 metal skewers, dividing them evenly; skewer each shrimp in a C shape, piercing through 2 points. Place on the prepared rack, slathering the top of the shrimp with any remaining puree from the bowl. Let stand at room temperature while you heat the broiler.

Heat the broiler with a rack about 4 inches from the element. Broil until the shrimp are pink with light brown spots, about 3 minutes. Remove the baking sheet from the oven, flip the skewers and continue to broil until the shrimp are just opaque and lightly charred, 2 to 4 minutes.

Transfer the skewers to a serving platter. Stir the lemon juice into the reserved herb puree and drizzle over the shrimp.

Vietnamese-Style Hot and Sour Soup with Shrimp

Start to finish: 35 minutes / Servings: 4

Vietnamese hot and sour soup with shrimp, called canh chua tôm, bursts with fresh, bright, contrasting flavors. This is our pantry-friendly version of that dish. Jalapeño chili provides the "hot" and lime juice brings the "sour." Canned, frozen or fresh pineapple works well, so use whichever is most convenient or that you happen to have. Cilantro or bean sprouts added as a garnish really enhance this soup; top bowls with one or, even better, both.

1 tablespoon grapeseed or other neutral oil

1 medium yellow onion, halved and thinly sliced

6 cups low-sodium chicken broth

2 teaspoons grated lime zest, plus 2 tablespoons lime juice, plus lime wedges to serve

1 pint cherry OR grape tomatoes, halved

1 cup drained juice-packed canned pineapple chunks OR chopped slices OR thawed frozen pineapple chunks OR chopped fresh pineapple

1 jalapeño chili, stemmed and sliced into thin rounds, plus more to serve

3 tablespoons fish sauce, plus more if needed

12 ounces extra-large (21/25 per pound) shrimp, peeled and deveined

In a large pot over medium-high, heat the oil until shimmering. Add the onion and cook, stirring occasionally, until starting to brown, about 5 minutes. Add the broth and lime zest, then bring to a boil over medium-high. Stir in the tomatoes, pineapple, jalapeño and fish sauce; cook at a vigorous simmer, uncovered and stirring occasionally, until the tomatoes begin to soften, about 5 minutes.

Add the shrimp, cover and remove from the heat. Let stand until the shrimp are opaque throughout, 4 to 5 minutes. Stir in the lime juice. Taste and stir in additional fish sauce, if needed. Serve garnished with additional jalapeño slices and lime wedges on the side.

Optional garnish: Chopped fresh cilantro OR bean sprouts OR both

Thai Stir-Fried Shrimp with Garlic and Black Pepper

Start to finish: 25 minutes / Servings: 4

In the Thai kitchen, raak phak chee kratiem prik is an aromatic mix of garlic, pepper and cilantro roots often used to season meat and seafood. We use the ingredients, minced to a paste (or pounded in a mortar with a pestle), to add bold flavor to plump stir-fried shrimp. In the U.S., bunches of cilantro usually are trimmed of the roots, so we swap in the stems. White pepper is particularly nice, but either black or white peppercorns work well. Lime juice and cilantro leaves brighten the finished dish.

1½ pounds extra-large (21/25 per pound) shrimp, peeled, deveined and patted dry

6 teaspoons fish sauce, divided

6 medium garlic cloves, chopped

2 tablespoons chopped fresh cilantro stems, plus 3 tablespoons chopped leaves, reserved separately

Kosher salt

2 teaspoons coarsely ground black OR white pepper

1 tablespoon packed light brown sugar

3 tablespoons grapeseed or other neutral oil, divided

1 medium yellow onion, halved and sliced about ½ inch thick

2 tablespoons lime juice

In a medium bowl, toss the shrimp with 1 teaspoon fish sauce. Put the garlic and cilantro stems in a mound on a cutting board. Sprinkle with a pinch of salt, then mince them together until broken down to a paste. Transfer to a small bowl and stir in the pepper. (Alternatively, use a mortar and pestle to pound the garlic, cilantro stems, salt and pepper into a paste.) In another small bowl, stir together the remaining 5 teaspoons fish sauce and sugar until the sugar dissolves; set aside.

In a 12-inch nonstick skillet over medium-high, heat 1 tablespoon oil until barely smoking. Add half of the shrimp in a single layer and cook without stirring until deep golden brown on the bottoms, about 1 minute.

Flip and cook until just opaque on both sides but not yet fully cooked, about another 30 seconds. Transfer to a plate. Cook the remaining shrimp in the same way using 1½ teaspoons of the remaining oil, then transfer to the plate.

In the same skillet over medium-high, heat the remaining 1½ tablespoons oil until shimmering. Add the onion and cook, stirring occasionally, until lightly browned, 3 to 4 minutes. Add the garlic paste and cook, stirring occasionally, until fragrant, about 30 seconds. Add the fish sauce mixture followed by the shrimp and any accumulated juices. Cook, stirring often, until the shrimp are opaque throughout, about 1 minute.

Off heat, stir in the cilantro leaves and lime juice. Taste and season with salt.

Shrimp and Cheese Tacos (Tacos Gobernador)

Start to finish: 40 minutes / Servings: 4

If you think seafood and cheese don't mix, this recipe will change your mind. Tacos gobernador, or "governor's tacos," are a modern Mexican classic said to have originated in the state of Sinaloa. A blend of shrimp and melty cheese is tucked inside tortillas that then are folded and cooked like a quesadilla. The recipe calls for medium shrimp, but since they're chopped, you can use large or extra-large—whatever is most convenient. Swap in corn tortillas for the flour if you like, though you'll need to heat them before adding the filling so they won't break when folded. Just pop them in the hot skillet for a few seconds per side until pliable.

1 pound medium (41/50 per pound) shrimp, peeled, deveined (tails removed), cut into ¾-inch pieces and patted dry (see headnote)

Kosher salt and ground black pepper

3 tablespoons grapeseed or other neutral oil, divided

1 small white OR yellow onion, halved and thinly sliced

1 green bell pepper OR poblano chili, stemmed, seeded and thinly sliced

3 medium garlic cloves, thinly sliced

8 ounces mozzarella cheese, shredded (2 cups)

½ cup chopped fresh cilantro, plus more to serve

3 tablespoons pickled jalapeños, chopped, plus 1 tablespoon brine

Eight 6-inch flour OR corn tortillas (see headnote)

Season the shrimp with ½ teaspoon each salt and pepper; set aside. In a 12-inch nonstick skillet over medium, heat 1 tablespoon oil until shimmering. Add the onion, bell pepper and ½ teaspoon salt; cook, stirring occasionally, until the vegetables begin to brown, 8 to 10 minutes. Add the garlic and shrimp, then cook, stirring occasionally, until the shrimp turn opaque, 2 to 3 minutes.

Transfer the mixture to a large bowl; wipe out and reserve the skillet. Stir the cheese, cilantro and pickled jalapeños and their brine into the shrimp mixture. Taste and season with salt and pepper. Divide the filling evenly among the tortillas (about ½ cup each) and spread it to cover half of each tortilla. Fold the unfilled sides over and press.

In the same skillet over medium-high, heat 1 tablespoon oil until shimmering. Add 4 of the tacos and cook until golden brown on the bottoms, about 2 minutes. Using a wide spatula, flip the tacos and cook, adjusting the heat as needed, until browned on the second sides, another 2 to 3 minutes. Transfer to a platter.

Cook the remaining tacos in the same way using the remaining 1 tablespoon oil. Serve sprinkled with additional cilantro.

Optional garnish: Lime wedges OR guacamole OR sour cream OR a combination

Seafood
IN A SNAP

Fish Baked with Tomatoes, Capers and White Wine

Start to finish: 50 minutes / Servings: 4

This simple fish bake delivers tons of flavor but requires minimal prep. You'll need a good amount of capers—¼ to ½ cup—along with some caper brine, which brings saltiness and tang to balance the sweetness of the vegetables. The onion and tomatoes get a head start on baking; once they're soft and jammy, the fish fillets, which have been briefly marinated, are placed on top. If your fillets are thicker or thinner than about 1 inch, adjust the baking time up or down to ensure the fish doesn't wind up dry and overcooked. Serve with warm, crusty bread or a rice or orzo pilaf.

¼ cup extra-virgin olive oil

2 medium garlic cloves, minced

2 tablespoons caper brine, plus ¼ to ½ cup drained capers

1 teaspoon dried thyme

Four 6-ounce cod OR sea bass fillets (each about 1 inch thick)

Kosher salt and ground black pepper

1 pint cherry or grape tomatoes OR 12 ounces ripe plum tomatoes, cored and cut in 1-inch chunks

1 medium red onion, halved and thinly sliced

¼ cup dry white wine

Heat the oven to 400°F with a rack in the middle position. In a small bowl, whisk together the oil, garlic, caper brine and thyme. Season the fish on both sides with salt and pepper, then place skinned (or skin) side down in a pie plate or other wide, shallow dish. Spoon 2 tablespoons of the oil mixture onto the fillets, dividing it evenly; refrigerate until ready to use.

In a 9-by-13-inch baking dish, toss together the remaining oil mixture, the capers, tomatoes, onion, wine and ½ teaspoon each salt and pepper. Bake, uncovered, until the onion has softened and the tomatoes have broken down and released their juices, 30 to 35 minutes; stir once about halfway through.

Remove the baking dish from the oven and stir the vegetables. Place the fillets on top, spacing them evenly, and bake until the fish flakes easily, 8 to 10 minutes. Using a wide metal spatula, transfer the fish to a platter or individual plates, then spoon the tomato mixture on top.

Optional garnish: Chopped fresh flat-leaf parsley OR dill

Miso-Glazed Broiled Salmon

Start to finish: 30 minutes / Servings: 4

Soy sauce, mirin, white miso and honey combine to create a sweet-savory balance in this simple recipe. Some of the glaze mixture is kept aside for serving—drizzle it over the salmon itself or onto a side of sautéed greens or broccoli.

3 tablespoons
white miso

5 teaspoons
honey, divided

1 tablespoon soy sauce

2 teaspoons mirin

1½ teaspoons toasted
sesame oil

¼ teaspoon
cayenne pepper

Four 6-ounce
center-cut salmon fillets
(each 1 to 1¼ inches
thick), patted dry

1 tablespoon sesame
seeds, toasted

In a small bowl, whisk together the miso, 4 teaspoons of honey, the soy sauce, mirin, sesame oil and cayenne. Measure out 2 tablespoons and brush onto the top and sides of the salmon fillets. Let stand at room temperature for 20 minutes.

Meanwhile, into the remaining miso mixture, whisk the remaining 1 teaspoon honey and 2 tablespoons water; set aside. Heat the broiler with a rack about 6 inches from the broiler element. Mist a wire rack with cooking spray, then set in a rimmed baking sheet.

Evenly space the fillets, skin down, on the rack. Broil until the thickest parts of the fillets reach 120°F, or are nearly opaque when cut into, 6 to 8 minutes.

Transfer to a serving platter and drizzle with about 2 tablespoons of the miso mixture, then sprinkle with sesame seeds. Serve with the remaining miso mixture.

Optional garnish: Thinly sliced scallions

Cod and Chickpeas in Tomato-Rosemary Sauce

Start to finish: 30 minutes / Servings: 4

Cod and chickpeas are a common pairing in the Spanish kitchen. We borrowed that combination for this one-pan dinner. Chickpeas simmer in a garlicky, herb-infused tomato sauce seasoned with paprika, then cod fillets are nestled in and poached until tender and flaky. This recipe requires little knifework, and with everything cooked together in a single skillet, the dish comes together quickly and easily. Hot paprika imparts a bit of heat; if you don't have any on hand, sweet paprika plus a little cayenne makes a fine substitute. Serve with thick slices of toasted crusty bread to sop up the savory sauce.

3 tablespoons
 extra-virgin olive oil

4 medium garlic cloves,
thinly sliced

1 teaspoon hot paprika OR
¾ teaspoon sweet paprika
plus ¼ teaspoon cayenne
pepper

28-ounce can whole
peeled tomatoes,
crushed by hand

Two 15½-ounce cans
chickpeas, rinsed and
drained

2 bay leaves

1 rosemary sprig OR
½ teaspoon dried
rosemary

Kosher salt and ground
black pepper

Four 6-ounce skinless cod
fillets, patted dry

2 teaspoons grated lemon
zest, plus lemon wedges
to serve

In a 12-inch skillet over medium, heat the oil and garlic, stirring often, until the garlic starts to brown, 1 to 2 minutes. Stir in the paprika, then add the tomatoes with juices, chickpeas, bay, rosemary, 1 teaspoon salt, ½ teaspoon pepper and ½ cup water. Bring to a simmer over medium-high, then reduce to medium-low and simmer, uncovered and stirring occasionally, until the tomatoes have broken down, about 10 minutes.

Nestle the cod skinned side down in the sauce, then spoon on some of the sauce. Cover and cook until the fish flakes easily, 6 to 8 minutes, adjusting the heat as needed to maintain a simmer.

Off heat, remove and discard the bay and rosemary sprig (if used). Stir in the lemon zest. Taste and season with salt and pepper. Serve with lemon wedges.

Optional garnish: Chopped fresh flat-leaf parsley

Salmon with Matbucha

Start to finish: 35 minutes / Servings: 4

Matbucha is a North African cooked "salad" made with olive oil, garlic, tomatoes, sweet peppers and spicy chilies. With a jammy, spoonable consistency, it typically is served as a dip or spread, but we think it makes a delicious sauce that complements the richness of salmon. In our matbucha, we use roasted red peppers, which are sweet and silky straight out of the jar, and we ratchet up the complexity with some harissa paste (and/or cumin) and chopped olives (and/or) capers. Serve with crusty bread or warm flatbread for dipping into the sauce.

4 tablespoons extra-virgin olive oil, divided

3 teaspoons grated lemon zest, divided, plus 2 tablespoons lemon juice

3 teaspoons sweet paprika, divided

2 teaspoons harissa paste OR ground cumin, divided OR both

Kosher salt and ground black pepper

Four 6-ounce center-cut salmon fillets (each 1 to 1¼ inches thick), patted dry

14½-ounce can whole peeled tomatoes, crushed by hand

1 cup roasted red peppers, patted dry and sliced

3 medium garlic cloves, thinly sliced

½ cup pitted black OR green olives, roughly chopped OR ¼ cup drained capers OR a combination

In a small bowl, stir together 2 tablespoons oil, 1 teaspoon lemon zest, 1 teaspoon paprika, ½ teaspoon harissa (and/or cumin, if using), ½ teaspoon salt and ¼ teaspoon pepper. Rub this mixture all over the salmon and set aside.

In a 12-inch nonstick skillet over medium-low, combine the remaining 2 tablespoons oil, the tomatoes with juices, roasted peppers, garlic, the remaining 2 teaspoons paprika and the remaining 1½ teaspoons harissa (and/or cumin, if using). Cover and cook, stirring occasionally, until the mixture is thick and jammy, 10 to 15 minutes.

Stir in the remaining 2 teaspoons lemon zest. Nestle the salmon fillets skin side up in the tomato mixture. Re-cover and cook until the thickest parts of the fillets reach 120°F or are translucent at the very center when cut into, 6 to 8 minutes.

Remove the pan from the heat. If desired, carefully peel off and discard the skin from each fillet, then transfer the fillets to individual plates, flipping them skin (or skinned) side down. Return the sauce to simmer over medium. Add the olives and lemon juice, then cook, stirring, until heated through, about 2 minutes. Taste and season with salt and pepper. Spoon the sauce over and around the salmon.

Optional garnish: Chopped fresh cilantro **OR** flat-leaf parsley **OR** thinly sliced jalapeño chili **OR** a combination

Salmon in Coconut-Curry Sauce

Start to finish: 30 minutes / Servings: 4

For this simple skillet dinner, we borrowed from "In Bibi's Kitchen" by Hawa Hassan. Instead of mackerel, we use salmon fillets and pair them with a saucy mix of vegetables simmered in coconut milk. A small measure of curry powder, a stand-in for the Somali spice blend called xawaash, flavors the dish and gives the sauce a pale golden hue. Serve with steamed rice.

Four 6-ounce center-cut salmon fillets, patted dry

Kosher salt and ground black pepper

1 tablespoon grapeseed or other neutral oil

4 scallions, thinly sliced, white and green parts reserved separately

4 medium garlic cloves, minced

1 pint cherry or grape tomatoes, halved

2 medium carrots, peeled and shredded on the large holes of a box grater

1 teaspoon curry powder

14-ounce can coconut milk

2 jalapeño chilies, stemmed, seeded and thinly sliced

1 tablespoon lime juice

Season the salmon on both sides with salt and pepper. In a 12-inch nonstick skillet over medium-high, heat the oil until shimmering. Add the salmon flesh side down, then immediately reduce to medium. Cook, undisturbed, until golden brown, 4 to 6 minutes. Using a wide, thin spatula, transfer the salmon browned-side up to a plate.

Return the skillet to medium-high and add the scallion whites and the garlic. Cook, stirring often, until lightly browned, 1 to 2 minutes. Add the tomatoes, carrots, curry powder and ½ teaspoon salt; cook, stirring, until the liquid released by the tomatoes has almost evaporated, about 5 minutes. Stir in the coconut milk, chilies and ¼ cup water, then bring to a simmer. Cover and cook over medium-low, stirring occasionally, until the carrots are softened, 6 to 9 minutes.

Stir in the lime juice and return the salmon, skin side down, to the pan. Cover, reduce to low and cook until the thickest parts of the fillets reach 120°F or are nearly opaque when cut into, 3 to 5 minutes. Off heat, taste the sauce and season with salt and pepper. Serve sprinkled with the scallion greens.

Greek-Inspired Fish Soup with Rice and Lemon

Start to finish: 45 minutes / Servings: 4

The Greek fish soup called psarosoupa traditionally is made with homemade fish broth. It typically is chunky with vegetables and sometimes rich and creamy with tempered egg, but it's always brightened up with a generous amount of lemon juice and enriched with fruity olive oil. Our much-simplified version uses store-bought chicken (or vegetable) broth as the primary liquid, but we boost the umami factor and seafood flavor with Asian fish sauce. Just before serving, drizzle individual bowlfuls with olive oil.

2 tablespoons extra-virgin olive oil, plus more to serve

3 medium celery stalks, roughly chopped

2 medium carrots, peeled and roughly chopped

Kosher salt and ground black pepper

2 tablespoons fish sauce

½ cup long-grain white rice, rinsed and drained

1 quart low-sodium chicken broth OR vegetable broth

1 teaspoon dried oregano

1 pound skinless cod fillets, cut into 2-inch pieces

¼ cup lemon juice

In a large Dutch oven over medium, heat the olive oil until shimmering. Add the celery, carrots and ¼ teaspoon each salt and pepper. Cook, stirring occasionally, until the vegetables are slightly softened, about 5 minutes. Stir in the fish sauce, followed by the rice, broth, oregano and 2 cups water. Bring to a boil over medium-high, then reduce to medium and simmer, uncovered and stirring occasionally, until the rice is tender and the broth has thickened slightly, 15 to 18 minutes.

Remove the pot from the heat. Add the fish, then quickly cover and let stand until the fish is opaque throughout and flakes easily, 6 to 8 minutes. Gently stir in the lemon juice, then taste and season with salt and pepper. Serve drizzled with additional oil.

Optional garnish: Chopped fresh flat-leaf parsley OR chopped fresh dill

Oven-Fried Fish Sticks

Start to finish: 45 minutes / Servings: 4 to 6

This recipe turns mild, firm-fleshed fillets into flavorful fish sticks, but without the hassle of stovetop frying. For a crisp, light coating, we use panko breadcrumbs, but we process them so they're a little finer and a better textural match for the flaky fish, and we mix in a couple tablespoons of cornstarch to help the crumbs adhere. Buttery Ritz crackers are a terrific alternative to panko. We skip the beaten egg typically used to bind the crumbs to the fish and opt instead for mayonnaise flavored with mustard. Serve with one of the sauces below. Or, make terrific fish tacos by tucking the fish sticks, along with shredded cabbage, cilantro and the chipotle-lime mayonnaise into warm tortillas.

2 cups panko breadcrumbs **OR** roughly crushed Ritz crackers

2 tablespoons cornstarch

2 teaspoons sweet paprika

Kosher salt and ground black pepper

⅓ cup mayonnaise

2 teaspoons yellow mustard **OR** Dijon mustard

1½ pounds boneless, skinless cod **OR** snapper fillets

Lemon wedges, to serve

Heat the oven to 475°F with a rack in the lowest position. Place a wire rack in a rimmed baking sheet and mist the rack with cooking spray.

In a food processor, combine the panko, cornstarch, paprika and ¼ teaspoon each salt and pepper. Pulse to fine crumbs, about 8 pulses. Alternatively, place the ingredients in a gallon-sized zip-close plastic bag and pound with a rolling pin until fine. Transfer to a pie plate or other wide, shallow dish.

In a small bowl, stir together the mayonnaise, mustard and ¼ teaspoon each salt and pepper.

Cut the fish into ¾- to 1-inch-thick by 2- to 3-inch long fingers. Pat dry with paper towels. Brush the fish on all sides with the mayonnaise mixture. Working a few at a time, coat the pieces on all sides with the panko mixture, pressing so the crumbs adhere. Place the fish sticks on the prepared rack. When all of the fish has been breaded, mist evenly with cooking spray.

Bake until the fish sticks are golden brown, 10 to 13 minutes; rotate the baking sheet about halfway through. Serve with lemon wedges.

Harissa Mayonnaise with Olives and Lemon
Start to finish: 5 minutes / Makes about ½ cup

In a small bowl, stir together ⅓ **cup mayonnaise, 3 tablespoons chopped pitted green or black olives, 2 teaspoons harissa paste** and **1 teaspoon grated lemon zest,** plus **1 tablespoon lemon juice.** Taste and season with **kosher salt** and **ground black pepper.**

Curried Ketchup
Start to finish: 5 minutes / Makes about ½ cup

In a small bowl, stir together ½ **cup ketchup, 1 tablespoon plus 2 teaspoons lemon juice** and **1 tablespoon curry powder.** Taste and season with **kosher salt** and **ground black pepper.**

Chipotle-Lime Mayonnaise
Start to finish: 5 minutes / Makes about ½ cup

In a small bowl, stir together ⅓ **cup mayonnaise, 1 chipotle chili in adobo sauce (minced), 2 teaspoons lime juice** and **2 tablespoons chopped fresh cilantro.** Taste and season with **kosher salt** and **ground black pepper.**

Seared Cod with Peruvian-Style Olive Sauce

Start to finish: 30 minutes / Servings: 4

Peruvian pulpo al olivo, or octopus with olive sauce, served as the inspiration for this quick but elegant dinner. The olive sauce is the standout here, and it comes together with remarkable ease. Black olives, mayonnaise and lime juice are whirred in a blender until smooth, along with a little cayenne to mimic the heat of ají amarillo, a Peruvian yellow chili paste. Cod and snapper are our first choices for this dish, but you could use salmon instead. While the fillets finish cooking with the skillet's residual heat, we throw together a simple, colorful salad to serve on the side.

½ cup mayonnaise

½ cup pitted black olives, drained, plus 1 tablespoon chopped pitted black olives

¼ teaspoon cayenne pepper

1 teaspoon grated lime zest, plus 2 tablespoons plus 1 teaspoon lime juice, divided

Four 6-ounce cod OR snapper OR salmon fillets, patted dry

Kosher salt and ground black pepper

1 tablespoon extra-virgin olive oil

6 cups lightly packed baby arugula OR baby spinach (about 4 ounces)

1 cup cherry OR grape tomatoes, halved

½ medium red onion, thinly sliced

In a blender, combine the mayonnaise, the ½ cup olives, the cayenne and the lime zest and 1 teaspoon lime juice. Blend until smooth, scraping the jar as needed, about 1 minute. Set the sauce aside.

Season the fish all over with salt and black pepper. In a 12-inch nonstick skillet over medium-high, heat the oil until shimmering. Place the fish skin or skinned side up in the pan, then immediately reduce to medium. Cook, undisturbed, until golden brown on the bottoms, 4 to 6 minutes.

Using a wide metal spatula, carefully flip the fillets, then cover the pan and remove from the heat. Let stand until the thickest parts of the fillets are opaque throughout and the flesh flakes easily, about 4 minutes for 1-inch-thick fillets or up to 7 minutes if 1¼ inches thick.

After removing the pan from the heat, in a large bowl, combine the arugula, tomatoes, onion, the remaining 2 tablespoons lime juice and the chopped olives. Toss, then taste and season with salt and black pepper.

Onto individual plates or a serving platter, spread the olive sauce. Place the fillets on top, then arrange the salad around the fish.

Sesame-Crusted Salmon with Black Pepper and Lime Sauce

Start to finish: 25 minutes / Servings: 4

For this simple salmon dish, we coat fillets with sesame seeds, which form a crisp, nutty-tasting crust as the fish cooks. A tangy, savory, pleasantly pungent Cambodian black pepper and lime sauce called tuk meric is served on the side to complement the richness of the salmon. The sauce traditionally is paired with the beef stir-fry known as loc lac, but we find it brightens up a host of other foods, including seafood. Be sure to grind the peppercorns coarsely, not finely, for the sauce using a spice mill or a mortar and pestle.

2 teaspoons coarsely ground black pepper (see headnote)

¼ cup lime juice, plus lime wedges to serve

1½ tablespoons packed light brown sugar

2 tablespoons fish sauce, divided

1 jalapeño OR Fresno chili, stemmed and sliced into thin rings (optional)

½ cup white sesame seeds OR a mix of white and black sesame seeds

Four 6-ounce center-cut salmon fillets (each 1 to 1¼ inches thick), patted dry

1 tablespoon grapeseed or other neutral oil

2 scallions, thinly sliced on the diagonal OR 2 tablespoons roughly chopped fresh cilantro

In a 12-inch nonstick skillet over medium, toast the pepper, stirring often, until fragrant and lightly smoking, about 2 minutes. Transfer to a small bowl; reserve the skillet. Into the toasted pepper, stir the lime juice, the sugar, 1 tablespoon fish sauce, the chili (if using) and 2 tablespoons water; set aside for serving.

Put the sesame seeds in a pie plate or other wide, shallow dish. Brush the tops of the salmon with the remaining 1 tablespoon fish sauce. One at a time, press the flesh side of the salmon into the sesame seeds to form an even crust; coat only the tops of the fillets.

In a 12-inch nonstick skillet over medium-high, heat the oil until shimmering. Add the salmon, seed side down, then immediately reduce to medium. Cook, undisturbed, until the sesame seeds are golden, about 6 minutes. Using a wide, thin spatula, flip the fillets, then cover the skillet and remove from the heat. Let stand until the thickest parts of the fillets reach 120°F or are nearly opaque when cut into, about 4 minutes for 1-inch-thick fillets.

Serve sprinkled with the scallions and with the sauce and lime wedges on the side.

Iraqi-Inspired Broiled Salmon with Tomatoes and Onion

Start to finish: 35 minutes / Servings: 4

This recipe was inspired by the Iraqi dish known as masgouf—fish grilled over an open fire and smothered with cooked onions and tomatoes. We cook salmon fillets under the broiler, so you don't need to fire up the grill and the dish comes together easily even on weeknights. Sliced onion and cherry tomatoes are roasted at a high temperature to caramelize them and concentrate their sweet flavors. Curry-seasoned salmon then is nestled into the sauce and quickly broiled, so make sure your baking dish is broiler-safe.

1 teaspoon curry powder

Kosher salt and ground black pepper

Four 6-ounce center-cut salmon fillets (each 1 to 1¼ inches thick), patted dry

1 medium red OR yellow onion, halved and thinly sliced

1 pint cherry OR grape tomatoes

4 tablespoons extra-virgin olive oil, divided

2 tablespoons tomato paste

2 tablespoons lemon OR orange juice, divided, plus 1 tablespoon grated lemon OR orange zest

1 teaspoon ground coriander OR ½ teaspoon ground ginger OR both

½ cup lightly packed fresh flat-leaf parsley, finely chopped

Heat the oven to 475°F with a rack in the upper-middle position. In a small bowl, stir together the curry powder, ½ teaspoon salt and ¼ teaspoon pepper. Season the salmon all over with the mixture; set aside.

In a broiler-safe 9-by-13-inch baking dish, stir together the onion, tomatoes, 2 tablespoons oil and ¼ teaspoon each salt and pepper. Distribute in an even layer and roast until the tomatoes are beginning to burst, about 15 minutes.

Meanwhile, in a small bowl, whisk together the tomato paste, 1 tablespoon lemon juice, the coriander and ½ cup water. In another small bowl, stir together the parsley, the remaining 2 tablespoons oil, remaining 1 tablespoon lemon juice, lemon zest and ¼ teaspoon pepper; set aside for serving.

Remove the baking dish from the oven and turn the oven to broil. Stir the tomato paste mixture into the onion and tomatoes. Nestle the salmon skin (or skinned) side down into the mixture, then spoon some of the onion and tomatoes over the top. Broil until both the salmon and tomato-onion mixture are spotty brown and the fish flakes easily, 4 to 6 minutes.

Cool for about 5 minutes, then spoon the parsley mixture over the top.

Optional garnish: Toasted and roughly chopped pine nuts

Salmon and Kimchi Burgers

Start to finish: 30 minutes, plus chilling / Servings: 4

In this recipe, salmon burgers get a big flavor boost from kimchi and gochujang, two Korean powerhouse ingredients that we like to keep on hand. Achieving tender, nicely textured burgers that hold together can be tricky, but we developed a technique. We process half of the salmon until smooth; this puree helps bind the remaining roughly chopped salmon and the kimchi. If you like, coat the patties with panko breadcrumbs before cooking to create an extra-crispy coating, but the results still are delicious without. Serve the burgers on toasted buns with our quick kimchi-flecked mayonnaise.

¾ cup cabbage kimchi, drained, plus 2 teaspoons kimchi juice

4 scallions, cut into 1-inch pieces OR 1 jalapeño chili, stemmed and quartered OR both

¼ cup plus 2 tablespoons mayonnaise

Kosher salt and ground black pepper

12 ounces boneless, skinless salmon fillets, pin bones removed, cut into rough 1-inch chunks

1 tablespoon gochujang

2 teaspoons toasted sesame oil

¾ cup panko breadcrumbs (optional)

3 tablespoons grapeseed or other neutral oil, divided

4 hamburger buns, toasted

In a food processor, combine the kimchi and scallions, then process until finely chopped, 30 to 60 seconds. Transfer ½ cup of the kimchi mixture to a medium bowl. Transfer the remaining mixture to a small bowl, then stir in the mayonnaise, kimchi juice and ¼ teaspoon each salt and pepper; reserve the food processor bowl and blade (no need to clean them). Cover the mayonnaise mixture and refrigerate until ready to serve.

To the food processor, add half of the salmon. Process until smooth, about 1 minute, scraping the bowl as needed. Transfer to the medium bowl with the reserved kimchi mixture and stir to combine. To the processor, add the remaining salmon and pulse until chopped, 3 to 4 pulses. Stir the chopped salmon into the kimchi-salmon mixture. Add the gochujang, sesame oil and ½ teaspoon each salt and pepper; stir until well combined.

With wet hands, divide the kimchi-salmon mixture into 4 even portions. Form each portion into a 3-inch patty and place on a large plate. Refrigerate, uncovered, to firm up the patties, about 15 minutes.

If using panko, put the panko in a pie plate or other wide, shallow dish. One at a time, coat the patties with the panko, gently pressing to adhere and reshaping the patties if needed. Return them to the plate.

In a 12-inch nonstick skillet over medium, heat the grapeseed oil until shimmering. Add the patties and cook until browned on the bottoms, 3 to 4 minutes. Using a wide spatula, flip and cook, adjusting the heat as needed, until browned on the second sides, about another 3 minutes. Transfer to a paper towel–lined plate. Serve on the buns with the kimchi mayonnaise.

Optional garnish: Lettuce leaves **OR** sliced tomatoes **OR** both

Flour
POWERED

Bread BOX

Panzanella with Roasted Tomatoes and Olives / 274

Bread and Tomato Soup with Spinach and Parmesan / 276

Kimchi Grilled Cheese with Ham / 277

White Bean Bruschette with Lemon, Parsley and Caper Relish / 278

Cheddar, Roasted Onion and Apple Tartines / 280

Frittata with Toasted Bread, Cheese and Caramelized Onions / 283

Bread, Bacon and Tomato Hash / 284

Panzanella with Roasted Tomatoes and Olives

Start to finish: 35 minutes / Servings: 4 to 6

In this spin on the classic Italian bread and tomato salad known as panzanella, we quickly broil supermarket cherry or grape tomatoes to concentrate their flavor and render them soft and succulent. But first, chunks of bread are toasted so they'll absorb the olive oil, vinegar and tomato juices without becoming soggy. During the last minute of toasting, we toss the bread with grated cheese, which forms an appealing crust. Olives lend salty, briny goodness, while arugula and fresh parsley brighten the salad.

6 ounces country-style bread, torn into 1-inch pieces (about 6 cups)

5 tablespoons extra-virgin olive oil, divided

Kosher salt and ground black pepper

1 ounce pecorino Romano OR Parmesan cheese, finely grated (½ cup), plus more to serve

1 pint cherry OR grape tomatoes

½ cup pitted black OR green olives OR a combination

½ small red OR yellow onion, thinly sliced

¼ cup red wine vinegar OR white wine vinegar OR balsamic vinegar OR lemon juice

4 cups lightly packed baby arugula OR chopped romaine OR spring mix

1 cup lightly packed fresh flat-leaf parsley OR basil OR mint, torn

Heat the oven to 450°F with a rack in the middle position. In a large bowl, toss together the bread, 1 tablespoon oil, ¼ teaspoon salt and ½ teaspoon pepper. Distribute in an even layer on a broiler-safe rimmed baking sheet; reserve the bowl. Bake until the bread is golden brown, 7 to 9 minutes, stirring once halfway through.

Remove the baking sheet from the oven; sprinkle the bread with the cheese and toss to combine. Continue to bake until the cheese starts to melt, about another 1 minute. Transfer the bread to a large plate; reserve the baking sheet. Turn the oven to broil.

On the same baking sheet, toss together the tomatoes, olives and 1 tablespoon oil. Distribute in an even layer and broil until the tomatoes have burst and are charred in spots, 7 to 8 minutes, shaking the baking sheet halfway through. Cool on the baking sheet for about 10 minutes. Meanwhile, in the reserved bowl, stir together the onion, vinegar, the remaining 3 tablespoons oil, ¼ teaspoon salt and ½ teaspoon pepper.

Add the warm tomato-olive mixture and the bread to the bowl, then toss. Let stand for about 5 minutes, tossing a few times. Add the arugula and parsley, then toss gently. Taste and season with salt and pepper. Transfer to a serving dish and sprinkle with additional cheese.

Bread and Tomato Soup with Spinach and Parmesan

Start to finish: 40 minutes / Servings: 4

The Tuscan bread soup called acquacotta, which translates from the Italian as "cooked water," makes thrifty use of day-old bread and other leftovers, transforming them into a rustic, satisfying dish. It's a cousin of the better-known pappa al pomodoro, another type of Tuscan bread and tomato soup. But whereas pappa al pomodoro simmers bread in a tomatoey broth, for acquacotta, the bread is placed in bowls, then the soup is ladled on top. Oftentimes, individual bowlfuls of acquacotta are finished with a poached egg. In our version, we skip the egg but add fresh spinach (or arugula) for color and fresh, minerally flavor.

4 ounces country-style bread, torn into ½-inch pieces (about 4 cups)

3 tablespoons extra-virgin olive oil, divided, plus more to serve

1 small yellow onion, halved and thinly sliced

1 medium carrot, peeled and chopped

1 teaspoon dried thyme OR dried rosemary

Kosher salt and ground black pepper

28-ounce can whole peeled tomatoes, crushed by hand

1 quart low-sodium vegetable broth OR chicken broth

5-ounce container baby spinach OR baby arugula

2 ounces Parmesan OR pecorino Romano cheese, finely grated (1 cup)

Heat the oven to 450°F with a rack in the middle position. On a rimmed baking sheet, toss together the bread and 1 tablespoon oil, then distribute in an even layer. Bake until the bread is light golden brown, 5 to 7 minutes, stirring once halfway through.

Meanwhile, in a large saucepan over medium, heat the remaining 2 tablespoons oil until shimmering. Add the onion, carrot, thyme and ½ teaspoon salt; cook, stirring occasionally, until the vegetables are softened and lightly browned, 6 to 7 minutes. Stir in the tomatoes with juices and ½ teaspoon each salt and pepper. Bring to a simmer over medium-high, then reduce to medium, cover partially and simmer, stirring occasionally, for 10 minutes.

Stir in the broth and bring to a simmer, uncovered, over medium-high. Reduce to medium, then stir in the spinach and cook until just wilted, about 1 minute.

Off heat, taste and season with salt and pepper. Divide the toasted bread among individual bowls and ladle in the soup. Serve sprinkled with the Parmesan and drizzled with additional oil.

Optional garnish: Chopped fresh basil

Kimchi Grilled Cheese with Ham

Start to finish: 30 minutes / Servings: 4

Spicy, garlicky kimchi ups the umami quotient of the classic grilled cheese. The pairing of cheese and kimchi actually isn't new. Budae jjigae, otherwise known as army base stew, originates with the Korean War. It's a hot pot made with American surplus foods, such as hot dogs, baked beans and instant noodles, along with kimchi and American cheese. These sandwiches aren't quite as lavish, but they're indisputably tasty.

⅓ cup mayonnaise

1 tablespoon kimchi juice, plus 1⅓ cups cabbage kimchi, drained and chopped

8 slices hearty white sandwich bread

8 slices cheddar OR pepper jack OR whole-milk mozzarella cheese

4 slices thinly sliced deli ham OR 4 slices cooked bacon

In a small bowl, stir together the mayonnaise and kimchi brine. Spread evenly over one side of each slice of bread. Flip 4 of the slices to be mayonnaise side down, then top each with 1 slice of cheese, 1 slice of ham (or 1 slice bacon, torn to fit) and a quarter of the kimchi. Top each with a slice of the remaining cheese, then with another slice of bread, mayonnaise side up. Press on the sandwiches to compact the fillings.

Heat a 12-inch nonstick or cast-iron skillet over medium until droplets of water flicked onto the surface quickly sizzle and evaporate. Add 2 of the sandwiches and cook until golden brown on the bottoms, 2 to 3 minutes. Using a wide spatula, flip the sandwiches and cook, pressing down lightly and adjusting the heat as needed, until golden brown on the second sides and the cheese is melted, 2 to 3 minutes. Transfer to a cutting board. Cook the remaining sandwiches in the same way (the second batch may cook faster). Cut each sandwich in half on the diagonal.

White Bean Bruschette with Lemon, Parsley and Caper Relish

Start to finish: 30 minutes / Servings: 4 to 6

Creamy, mild white beans seasoned with garlic, pepper flakes and lemon, then mashed to a coarse puree is a pantry-easy topping for toasted slices of baguette. The bruschette are a blank canvas for big, bold finishing touches, such as a bright relish of lemon, parsley and capers; see below for a couple variations. If your baguette is slender, slice it on a sharp diagonal to create more surface area for holding toppings. Serve these as a snack or a light main with a leafy salad alongside.

Twelve ½-inch-thick baguette slices (see headnote)

5 tablespoons extra-virgin olive oil, divided

2 medium garlic cloves, thinly sliced

¼ teaspoon red pepper flakes

15½-ounce can cannellini OR great northern beans, rinsed and drained

1 teaspoon grated lemon zest, plus 3 tablespoons lemon juice, divided

Kosher salt and ground black pepper

1 cup lightly packed flat-leaf parsley leaves, finely chopped

2 tablespoons drained capers, patted dry

Heat the oven to 400°F with a rack in the upper-middle position. Place the bread in a single layer on a rimmed baking sheet; set aside. In a 12-inch skillet over medium, heat 3 tablespoons oil and the garlic; cook, stirring occasionally, until the garlic is golden brown, 1 to 2 minutes. Remove from the heat and stir in the pepper flakes.

Brush the surface of each baguette slice with some of the oil mixture; reserve the remainder in the skillet. Toast the bread in the oven until lightly browned, 3 to 4 minutes. Remove from the oven and set aside.

To the garlic-oil mixture remaining in the skillet, add the beans, ¾ cup water and ½ teaspoon each salt and black pepper. Bring to a simmer over medium-high and cook, uncovered and stirring occasionally, until the beans are heated through and the mixture is slightly thickened, 4 to 6 minutes. Remove the pan from the heat and, using a potato masher, mash the mixture to a coarse puree. Stir in 1 tablespoon lemon juice, then taste and season with salt and black pepper.

In a small bowl, stir together the remaining 2 tablespoons oil, the remaining 2 tablespoons lemon juice plus the lemon zest, the parsley, capers and ¼ teaspoon each salt and black pepper. Divide the bean mixture among the baguette slices, spreading it to cover the surface. Top the bruschette with the parsley-caper relish, dividing it evenly.

White Bean Bruschette with Roasted Tomatoes

Heat the broiler with a rack about 6 inches from the element. On a broiler-safe rimmed baking sheet, toss **1 pint cherry OR grape tomatoes, 1 tablespoon extra-virgin olive oil and ½ teaspoon each kosher salt and ground black pepper.** Broil until the tomatoes have burst and are charred in spots, stirring a couple times, 7 to 8 minutes; set the tomatoes aside. Follow the recipe to toast the bread and make the bean mixture; omit the parsley-caper relish. Top the toasted bread with the bean mixture as directed, then spoon on the roasted tomatoes. Top each bruschetta with **shaved Parmesan cheese OR basil pesto.**

White Bean Bruschette with Lemon-Anchovy Wilted Kale

In a medium bowl, whisk together **2 tablespoons extra-virgin olive oil, 1 tablespoon lemon juice, 1 oil-packed anchovy fillet** (minced), **½ teaspoon each kosher salt and ground black pepper.** Add **4 cups stemmed and finely chopped curly OR lacinato kale** and **1 ounce finely grated Parmesan cheese (½ cup)**; toss to combine. Taste and season with **salt and pepper**; set aside. Follow the recipe to toast the bread and make the bean mixture; omit the parsley-caper relish. Top the toasted bread with the bean mixture as directed, then finish with the kale mixture.

Cheddar, Roasted Onion and Apple Tartines

Start to finish: 45 minutes (25 minutes active)
Servings: 4

Using a few basic pantry ingredients, we've transformed the classic grilled cheese into delicious open-faced savory-sweet tartines. Thinly sliced apples and onion are roasted in a hot oven to caramelize them and bring out their natural sweetness. They're layered on pieces of baguette with cheddar, Parmesan and a piquant mustard butter, then baked until toasty. Complete the meal with a tossed green salad, if you like.

2 large apples, preferably Granny Smith, peeled, cored and cut into ⅛-inch wedges

1 large red OR yellow onion, halved and thinly sliced

2 tablespoons extra-virgin olive oil

Kosher salt and ground black pepper

4 tablespoons salted butter, room temperature

2 tablespoons Dijon mustard

10- to 12-ounce baguette

2 teaspoons white wine vinegar OR red wine vinegar

6 ounces cheddar cheese, shredded (1½ cups)

1 ounce Parmesan cheese, finely grated (½ cup)

Heat the oven to 425°F with a rack in the middle position. On a rimmed baking sheet, toss together the apples, onion, oil and ½ teaspoon salt, then distribute in an even layer. Roast until the apples are tender and the onion begins to char at the edges, about 15 minutes, stirring once about halfway.

Meanwhile, in a small bowl, stir together the butter and mustard until well combined. Cut the baguette in half crosswise, then each half horizontally to create 4 pieces.

Transfer the apples and onion to a medium bowl, scraping any browned bits into the bowl; wipe off and reserve the baking sheet. Leave the oven on. Stir the vinegar into the apple-onion mixture.

Place the bread cut side up on the baking sheet. Spread the mustard butter on the bread, dividing it evenly. Sprinkle the cheddar evenly onto the bread, then top each with one-fourth of the apple-onion mixture, covering the surfaces. Sprinkle evenly with Parmesan.

Bake until the edges of the bread are toasted and the tops are lightly browned, 8 to 10 minutes. Season each tartine with black pepper.

Frittata with Toasted Bread, Cheese and Caramelized Onions

Start to finish: 40 minutes / Servings: 4 to 6

This recipe takes a handful of basic ingredients and turns them into a rich, satisfying breakfast, lunch or dinner. Each element plays an essential role. Crusty bread toasted in butter and olive oil gives the frittata substance and texture, onions cooked until sweet and caramelized add depth, cheese brings umami and gooeyness, and the eggs provide richness and tie everything together. Cooking starts on the stovetop but finishes at 425°F, so you will need a 10-inch nonstick skillet that's oven-safe. Serve a crisp green salad alongside as a counterpoint to the frittata's richness.

10 large eggs

4 ounces cheddar OR Gouda OR Gruyère cheese, shredded (1 cup)

3 tablespoons salted butter, cut into 1-tablespoon pieces, divided

2 tablespoons extra-virgin olive oil, divided

3 ounces rustic bread, cut into 1-inch cubes (about 3 cups)

2 medium yellow onions, finely chopped

Chopped fresh flat-leaf parsley OR fresh chives, to serve

Heat the oven to 425°F with a rack in the middle position. In a medium bowl, whisk the eggs with ½ teaspoon each salt and pepper, then stir in two-thirds of the cheese; set aside.

In a 10-inch nonstick oven-safe skillet over medium, heat 1 tablespoon butter and 1 tablespoon oil until the butter melts. Add the bread and cook, stirring occasionally, until golden brown, about 3 minutes. Transfer to a medium bowl; set aside.

In the same skillet over medium, heat the remaining 1 tablespoon oil until shimmering. Add the onions and ¼ teaspoon each salt and pepper. Cover and cook, stirring often and adjusting the heat as needed to prevent scorching, until the onions are lightly browned, 10 to 12 minutes. Transfer to the bowl with the bread and wipe out the skillet.

In the same skillet over medium, melt the remaining 2 tablespoons butter. Add the egg mixture, then quickly add the bread and onions; stir just to combine the ingredients and distribute them in an even layer. Cook without stirring for 5 minutes; the edges should be set. Run a silicone spatula around the edges to ensure the eggs are not sticking. Sprinkle evenly with the remaining cheese and place the skillet in the oven. Bake until the frittata is set on the surface and the cheese is lightly browned, 10 to 12 minutes.

Remove the skillet from the oven (the handle will be hot). Run the spatula around the edges of the frittata and underneath it to loosen, then carefully slide onto a cutting board. Let rest for at least 10 minutes. Serve warm or at room temperature, sprinkled with parsley and cut into wedges.

Bread, Bacon and Tomato Hash

Start to finish: 35 minutes / Servings: 4 to 6

This rustic bread hash with bacon, tomatoes and eggs "poached" right in the mix is an easy one-pan meal for breakfast, lunch or dinner. The toasted bread softens slightly as it absorbs the tomatoes' juices, yielding a satisfying crunchy-chewy texture. Sourdough bread, with its tangy flavor and aroma, works especially well here, but any loaf with a chewy, sturdy crumb does nicely.

8 ounces bacon, preferably thick-cut, chopped

3 tablespoons extra-virgin olive oil, divided

6 ounces rustic bread, preferably sourdough, cut into rough ½-inch cubes (4 cups)

1 medium yellow onion, chopped

Kosher salt and ground black pepper

2 medium garlic cloves, minced

1 pint grape tomatoes, halved

6 large eggs

Sliced scallions, to serve

Heat the oven to 450°F with a rack in the middle position. In a 12-inch oven-safe nonstick skillet over medium-high, cook the bacon, stirring occasionally, until brown and crisp, about 8 to 9 minutes. Remove the pan from the heat and, using a slotted spoon, transfer the bacon to a paper towel–lined large bowl; set aside. Pour off and discard all but 2 tablespoons fat from the skillet.

To the reserved bacon fat in the skillet, add 1 tablespoon oil and heat over medium-high until shimmering. Add the bread and cook, stirring often and reducing the heat as needed to prevent scorching, until golden brown and toasted, about 5 minutes. Transfer to the bowl with the bacon and wipe out the pan.

In the same skillet over medium, heat the remaining 2 tablespoons oil until shimmering. Add the onion and ¼ teaspoon salt; cover and cook, stirring occasionally, until the onion is softened and lightly browned, 5 to 7 minutes. Add the garlic and cook, stirring, until fragrant, about 1 minute. Add the tomatoes and ½ teaspoon salt; cover and cook, stirring occasionally, until the tomatoes begin to release their juices, about 3 minutes. Using a silicone spatula, press on the tomatoes a few times so they release more of their juices.

Return the bread and bacon to the pan. Cook, stirring, until the bread absorbs the tomatoes' juices, about 1 minute. Taste and season with salt and pepper. Use the back of a large spoon to make 6 evenly spaced indentations in the tomato-bread mixture, each about 2 inches in diameter. Crack 1 egg into each well, then sprinkle with salt and pepper. Transfer to the oven and cook until the bread is crisp and the egg whites are set but the yolks are still runny, 6 to 7 minutes. Remove the pan from the oven (the handle will be hot). Serve sprinkled with scallions.

Optional garnish: Store-bought pesto

Tortilla
TWISTS

Turkish-Inspired Beef Wraps with Tomato-Onion Salad

Start to finish: 30 minutes / Servings: 4

These sandwiches were inspired by tantuni, meat-and-vegetable wraps that originated in the coastal city of Mersin, in southern Turkey. They traditionally are made with pieces of twice-cooked lamb or beef and paired with a bright tomato-onion salad, all tucked inside lavash. To create an easy, pantry-friendly version, we've swapped flour tortillas for the lavash and ground beef (or lamb) for the filling. A simple mix of tomatoes, sliced onion and green chili (or bell pepper) is wrapped up with the meat, adding a spark of bright, fresh flavor.

2 large ripe tomatoes, cored and chopped OR 1 pint cherry OR grape tomatoes, halved

1 small red OR yellow onion, halved and thinly sliced

1 jalapeño chili OR ½ medium red bell pepper, stemmed, seeded and thinly sliced OR both

3 tablespoons extra-virgin olive oil, divided

2 tablespoons lemon juice

Kosher salt and ground black pepper

Four 10-inch flour tortillas

1 tablespoon ground cumin

1 pound ground beef OR lamb

1 cup lightly packed fresh flat-leaf parsley OR mint OR a combination, roughly chopped

In a large bowl, toss together the tomatoes, onion, half of the jalapeño, 2 tablespoons oil, the lemon juice and 1 teaspoon each salt and pepper; set aside.

In a 12-inch nonstick skillet over medium, warm the tortillas one at a time until lightly browned on both sides, 1 to 2 minutes, flipping once about halfway through. Transfer to a large plate and cover with foil to keep warm.

In the same skillet over medium, heat the remaining 1 tablespoon oil until shimmering. Add the remaining jalapeño, then cook, stirring occasionally, until beginning to soften, 3 to 4 minutes. Add the cumin and cook, stirring, until fragrant, about 30 seconds. Add the beef and cook, stirring occasionally and breaking it into small pieces, until no longer pink, 4 to 5 minutes. Off heat, taste and season with salt and pepper.

Add the parsley to the tomato mixture and toss. Lay the tortillas on a cutting board. Divide the beef evenly among the tortillas, distributing it across the center, stopping shy of the edges. Using a slotted spoon, top with the tomato mixture. One tortilla at a time, fold in the sides, then roll up the tortilla, as if making a burrito. If desired, cut each wrap in half.

Pizzadilla with Tomatoes and Olives

Start to finish: 20 minutes
Makes one 12- to 13-inch pizzadilla

Pizza meets quesadilla, yielding cross-cultural deliciousness. You'll need burrito-size flour tortillas for this, though you could make smaller pizzadillas using standard-size flour tortillas and a 10-inch skillet. Either way, be prepared to make more than one.

1 cup grape tomatoes, halved	12- to 13-inch (burrito-size) flour tortilla
½ medium red onion, thinly sliced	2 ounces mozzarella cheese, shredded (½ cup)
2 tablespoons extra-virgin olive oil, divided	2 ounces cheddar cheese, shredded (½ cup)
¼ teaspoon red pepper flakes	½ cup chopped pitted black olives
Kosher salt and ground black pepper	

Heat the oven to 450°F with a rack in the middle position. In a medium bowl, toss together the tomatoes, onion, 1 tablespoon oil, pepper flakes and a pinch each of salt and pepper.

In a 12-inch oven-safe skillet over medium, heat the remaining 1 tablespoon oil until barely smoking. Add the tortilla and, using a wide metal spatula, press it against the skillet; the edges of the tortilla will form a lip. Remove the pan from the heat. Sprinkle both cheeses onto the tortilla, then scatter on the tomato-onion mixture followed by the olives.

Place the skillet in the oven and bake until the tortilla is browned at the edges and the cheese is browned and bubbling, about 10 minutes. Remove the skillet from the oven (the handle will be hot) and slide the pizzadilla onto a cutting board. Cut into wedges.

Optional garnish: Chopped fresh basil

Chicken and Tortilla Soup

Start to finish: 40 minutes (20 minutes active)
Servings: 4 to 6

A favorite in homes and restaurants throughout Mexico and beyond, tortilla soup is a great way to use old, stale corn tortillas in your refrigerator. In this recipe, they do double duty: some are fried to create a crisp topping, while the rest are simmered into the broth, where they break down and give the soup body. The combination of chili powder, cumin and fire-roasted tomatoes lends smoky richness to the broth, and shredded chicken turns the soup into a full meal. Embellish with more garnishes if you like; see the suggestions below.

¼ cup extra-virgin olive oil	2 teaspoons ground cumin
Six 6-inch corn tortillas, cut into ½-inch strips	28-ounce can diced fire-roasted tomatoes
Kosher salt and ground black pepper	1 quart low-sodium chicken broth
1 medium red OR yellow onion, chopped, plus more to serve	Two 8-ounce boneless, skinless chicken breasts
2 tablespoons chili powder	2 tablespoons lime juice

In a large pot over medium, heat the oil until shimmering. Add half of the tortilla strips and cook, without stirring, until slightly firm, about 30 seconds. Toss with tongs, then cook, tossing often, until browned and crisp, 2 to 3 minutes. Transfer to a paper towel–lined plate and sprinkle with salt; set aside.

To the same pot over medium, add the onion and ½ teaspoon salt, then cook, stirring occasionally, until the onion begins to brown, about 5 minutes. Add the chili powder and cumin; cook, stirring, until fragrant, about 30 seconds.

Add the tomatoes with juices and the broth. Bring to a simmer over high, then add the remaining tortilla strips and the chicken breasts. Reduce to medium and simmer, uncovered and stirring occasionally, until the tortillas have broken down and the thickest part of the chicken registers 160°F, 15 to 20 minutes.

Remove the pot from the heat, then transfer the chicken to a plate. Using 2 forks, shred the meat into bite-size pieces. Stir the chicken into the pot and cook over medium, stirring, until heated through, about 1 minute.

Off heat, stir in the lime juice, then taste and season with salt and pepper. Garnish with the fried tortilla strips and additional chopped onion.

Optional garnish: Sliced radishes **OR** sliced jalapeño chilies **OR** chopped fresh cilantro **OR** chopped avocado **OR** grated cheddar cheese (or Monterey jack or crumbled cotija) **OR** sour cream (or Mexican crema) **OR** a combination

Oven-Fried Potato and Cheese Tacos Dorados

Start to finish: 55 minutes (40 minutes active)
Servings: 4

No need to stand at the stove deep-frying these tacos dorados. They crisp up beautifully in the oven using just a few tablespoons of oil—making them totally doable for weeknight meals. We fill flour tortillas with roughly mashed potatoes and cheese; pickled jalapeños and chipotle chilies in adobo lend the filling some kick. Finish the tacos with cool, crisp iceberg lettuce and fresh cilantro, then embellish with more garnishes if you like; see the suggestions below.

5 tablespoons grapeseed or other neutral oil, divided

1½ pounds Yukon Gold potatoes, peeled and cut into ¾-inch cubes

½ cup lightly packed fresh cilantro, chopped, plus cilantro leaves to serve

4 scallions, thinly sliced

1 to 2 tablespoons pickled jalapeños, chopped, plus 1 tablespoon brine

1 chipotle chili in adobo, minced, plus 1 tablespoon adobo sauce

Kosher salt and ground black pepper

Eight 6-inch flour tortillas

8 ounces cheddar **OR** Monterey jack cheese, shredded (2 cups)

Shredded iceberg lettuce, to serve

Heat the oven to 475°F with a rack in the middle position. Grease a rimmed baking sheet with 3 tablespoons oil. In a 12-inch nonstick skillet over medium-high, heat the remaining 2 tablespoons oil until shimmering. Add the potatoes, cover and cook, stirring occasionally, until well browned and fully tender, about 12 minutes.

Remove the pan from the heat and lightly mash the potatoes. Stir in the cilantro, scallions, pickled jalapeños and their brine, chipotle and adobo sauce, 1 teaspoon salt and ¼ teaspoon pepper.

Divide the potato filling evenly among the tortillas (about a scant ¼ cup each) and spread it to cover half of each tortilla, then sprinkle with the cheese, dividing it evenly. Fold the unfilled sides over. Arrange the filled tortillas on the prepared baking sheet, then flip each one so both sides are coated with oil.

Bake until the tacos begin to brown and crisp on the bottoms, about 9 minutes. Using a wide metal spatula, flip each taco. Continue to bake until browned on the second sides, about another 3 minutes. Transfer the tacos directly to a wire rack and cool for about 5 minutes. Serve topped with the lettuce and cilantro leaves.

Optional garnish: Diced avocado (or guacamole) **OR** sour cream **OR** salsa **OR** hot sauce **OR** a combination

Ham and Cheese Quesadillas with Pickled Jalapeños

Start to finish: 30 minutes / Servings: 4

In Mexico, these quesadillas are known as sincronizadas, which translates as "synchronized." For assembly, we prefer to toss together shredded cheese and chopped ham, then distribute the mixture among the tortillas. Made this way, the quesadillas hold together better than if the fillings are simply layered on. Feel free to include other add-ins if you like, such as sautéed onions or mushrooms or cooked black beans.

8 ounces cheddar OR Muenster cheese OR a combination, shredded (2 cups)

6 ounces thinly sliced deli ham, chopped

⅓ to ½ cup pickled jalapeños, minced, plus 1 tablespoon brine

2 tablespoons finely chopped fresh cilantro

2 teaspoons ground cumin

Ground black pepper

Four 10-inch flour tortillas

2 tablespoons grapeseed or other neutral oil

In a medium bowl, stir together the cheese, ham, pickled jalapeños and their brine, cilantro, cumin and ½ teaspoon pepper. Spread half the filling evenly over 1 tortilla. Lay another tortilla on top and press together firmly. Repeat with the remaining filling and tortillas.

In a 12-inch nonstick skillet over medium, heat 1 tablespoon oil until shimmering. Add 1 quesadilla and cook, moving it around a few times to ensure even cooking, until golden brown and crisp on the bottom, 2 to 3 minutes. Using a wide spatula, flip the quesadilla and cook, adjusting the heat as needed, until browned on the second side, about another 2 minutes. Transfer to a cutting board.

Toast the remaining quesadilla in the same way using the remaining 1 tablespoon oil (the second quesadilla probably will cook faster). Cut the quesadillas into wedges and serve.

Optional garnish: Salsa **OR** sour cream **OR** diced avocado **OR** guacamole **OR** hot sauce **OR** a combination

Refried Bean and Cheese Tostadas

Start to finish: 35 minutes / Servings: 4

Here's a great way to throw together a quick dinner with lots of flavor and texture using just a handful of basic ingredients. We use the oven to crisp corn tortillas into tostadas, a technique that requires less oil than pan-frying and allows you to do multiples at a time. Either canned black beans or pinto beans work for making refried beans, so use whichever you have on hand. Tostadas love garnishes, so see the list below for simple ideas, but feel free to add whatever you like, from fried bacon broken into bits to scrambled eggs.

Four 6-inch corn tortillas

3 tablespoons grapeseed or other neutral oil, divided

1 small yellow OR red onion, chopped

Kosher salt and ground black pepper

1 tablespoon chopped pickled jalapeños, plus more to serve

1 teaspoon chili powder

15½-ounce can black beans OR pinto beans, rinsed and drained

2 ounces Monterey jack OR cheddar cheese, shredded (1 cup)

Shredded iceberg lettuce OR shredded green cabbage, to serve

Sour cream, to serve

Heat the oven to 400°F with a rack in the upper-middle position. Brush the tortillas on both sides with 1 tablespoon of the oil, then place them in a single layer on a rimmed baking sheet. Bake until golden brown and crisp, 8 to 10 minutes, flipping them once about halfway through. Let the tostadas cool on the baking sheet; leave the oven on.

In a 12-inch nonstick skillet over medium, heat the remaining 2 tablespoons oil until shimmering. Add half of the onion and ½ teaspoon salt; cook, stirring occasionally, until beginning to brown, 3 to 4 minutes. Stir in the pickled jalapeños and chili powder, then add the beans and ⅓ cup water. Bring to a simmer and simmer, uncovered and stirring occasionally, until the liquid is reduced by about half, 3 to 4 minutes. Remove the pan from the heat and mash the mixture to a thick, coarse puree. Taste and season with salt and pepper.

Divide the bean mixture evenly among the tostadas, spreading it to cover. Top each with cheese, dividing it evenly, and bake until the cheese melts, 1 to 2 minutes.

Place the tostadas on individual plates. Sprinkle with the remaining chopped onion, additional pickled jalapeños and lettuce, then spoon on sour cream.

Optional garnish: Lime wedges OR chopped fresh cilantro OR chopped tomato OR sliced or diced avocado OR salsa OR hot sauce OR a combination

Enfrijoladas

Start to finish: 45 minutes / Servings: 4

To make enfrijoladas, a tortilla and bean dish from Oaxaca, Mexico, cooked black beans are pureed, then corn tortillas are dipped into the beans and folded onto the plate. But before being dipped in the bean puree, the tortillas must be cooked for a few seconds in oil so they're pliable enough to be folded, and also so they don't turn to mush when sauced. We use canned black beans for ease. Garnishes complete the dish, adding contrasting color, texture and flavor. We think chopped onion, cheese and cilantro are essential; a couple additional options are listed below.

2 tablespoons plus ⅓ cup grapeseed or other neutral oil, divided

1 large white onion, ¾ thinly sliced, ¼ finely chopped, reserved separately

2 medium garlic cloves, smashed and peeled

1 to 2 teaspoons chili powder

2 teaspoons ground cumin OR ¼ teaspoon ground allspice OR both

15½-ounce can black beans, rinsed and drained

Kosher salt and ground black pepper

Eight 6-inch corn tortillas

3 ounces cheddar OR Monterey jack cheese, shredded (¾ cup) OR cotija cheese, finely crumbled (about ½ cup)

½ cup lightly packed fresh cilantro, chopped

In a large saucepan over medium-high, heat 2 tablespoons oil until shimmering. Add the sliced onion and cook, stirring occasionally, until lightly browned, 5 to 6 minutes. Add the garlic, chili powder and cumin; cook, stirring, until fragrant, about 30 seconds. Add the beans, 2 cups water and ½ teaspoon each salt and pepper. Bring to a simmer, scraping up any browned bits, then cook, uncovered and stirring occasionally, until the water is just below the level of the beans, 10 to 12 minutes.

Meanwhile, in a 12-inch skillet over medium, heat the remaining ⅓ cup oil until just beginning to shimmer. Slip 2 tortillas into the oil and cook just until they begin to puff and brown, 20 to 30 seconds, flipping the tortillas with a spatula halfway through; do not allow the tortillas to crisp. Transfer to a baking sheet and cover with foil. Warm the remaining tortillas in the same way, reducing the heat if the oil begins to smoke; it's fine to overlap the tortillas on the baking sheet.

When the beans are done, remove the pan from the heat and cool for about 10 minutes. Using a blender and working in 2 batches to avoid overfilling the jar, puree the bean mixture until smooth, 15 to 20 seconds. Return the puree to the pan. (Alternatively, if you own an immersion blender, puree the mixture directly in the pan.) Cook uncovered over low, stirring occasionally, until heated through, 3 to 5 minutes. Taste and season with salt and pepper.

Using tongs, fold a tortilla in half and submerge it in the bean puree (still over low heat), then transfer to an individual plate. Repeat with the remaining tortillas, placing 2 on each plate. Spoon the remaining bean puree over the enfrijoladas and top with the cheese, cilantro and the chopped onion.

Optional garnish: Sliced avocado **OR** Mexican crema (or sour cream) **OR** lime wedges **OR** a combination

Sugar &
SPICE

Cupboard CONFECTIONS

Mixed Berry Crumble with Spiced Oats and Almonds

Start to finish: 1 hour (20 minutes active)
Servings: 6 to 8

Frozen mixed berries make it easy to throw together this simple fruit dessert. A mixture of oats, spices and sugar does double duty here. We add a small amount to the berries to sweeten and thicken the filling; into the remainder we add almonds and softened butter to make a crumble topping that bakes up toasty and crisp, a delicious flavor and textural contrast to the soft, juicy berries. Quick-cooking oats are best here; old-fashioned oats remain too firm and chewy. Serve warm or at room temperature, ideally with vanilla ice cream.

1 cup quick-cooking OR instant oats

½ cup packed light OR dark brown sugar

½ teaspoon ground cardamom

½ teaspoon ground coriander

1-pound bag frozen mixed berries (about 4 cups), not thawed

1½ cups sliced almonds OR 1 cup slivered almonds

¼ teaspoon table salt

8 tablespoons (1 stick) salted butter, cut into ½-inch cubes, room temperature

Heat the oven to 350°F with a rack in the middle position. In a medium bowl, stir together the oats, sugar, cardamom and coriander, breaking up any lumps of sugar with your fingers.

Place the berries in a 9-inch pie plate. Add ¼ cup of the oat mixture and toss until well combined; break up any large clumps of frozen berries.

Into the remaining oat mixture, stir the almonds and salt. Add the butter and, using a silicone spatula, work it in until well combined. Using your hands, form the mixture into rough bits and clumps no larger than about the size of an olive and scatter them evenly over the berries.

Bake until the edges are bubbling and the crumble is golden brown, 40 to 45 minutes. Serve warm or at room temperature.

Streusel-Topped Jam Tart

**Start to finish: 1 hour (20 minutes active), plus cooling
Makes one 9-inch tart**

This rustic tart is a breeze to prepare with a few pantry staples. The dough, which comes together quickly in a food processor, is dual purpose. Pressed into a tart pan, it forms the bottom crust and, pinched into small bits and scattered onto the filling, bakes into a buttery streusel topping. A little cornmeal in the dough adds textural interest and subtly sweet, corn flavor. Just about any type of fruit jam or preserves works well. We particularly like cherry preserves and seedless raspberry jam; marmalade is a great option, too. A little black pepper mixed into the preserves offers just a hint of savoriness that balances the sweetness.

⅓ cup white sugar

3 teaspoons grated lemon zest, divided, plus 1 tablespoon lemon juice

1¾ cups all-purpose flour

⅓ cup fine yellow cornmeal

¼ teaspoon table salt

10 tablespoons (1¼ sticks) cold salted butter, cut into ½-inch cubes

1 large egg, plus 1 large egg yolk, lightly beaten

1¼ cups fruit jam or preserves **OR** marmalade (see headnote)

½ teaspoon ground black pepper

Heat the oven to 375°F with a rack in the lowest position. Mist a 9-inch tart pan with a removable bottom with cooking spray.

In a food processor, combine the sugar and 1½ teaspoons lemon zest. Process until fragrant and the sugar is moistened, about 15 seconds. Add the flour, cornmeal and salt; process until combined, about 5 seconds. Scatter the butter over the dry ingredients and pulse until the mixture resembles coarse sand, 10 to 12 pulses. Add the egg and egg yolk, then process until the mixture is evenly moistened and begins to clump together, 20 to 30 seconds.

Transfer about 1 cup of the dough mixture to a small bowl; set aside for the topping. Transfer the remainder to the prepared pan, scattering it across the bottom. Using your hands, press the dough into an even layer into the bottom of the pan and up the sides.

In a small bowl, stir together the jam, the remaining 1½ teaspoons lemon zest, the lemon juice and pepper. Spread the jam mixture in an even layer in the dough-lined pan. Form the reserved dough into rough, pebbly pieces by squeezing bits between your fingers, then scatter them evenly over the filling; it's fine if they are not uniform. Bake until the crust is golden brown and the filling is bubbling in spots, 40 to 45 minutes.

Cool in the pan on a wire rack for 45 minutes. Remove the outer ring from the tart pan. Serve warm or at room temperature.

Optional garnish: Powdered sugar

Coconut Bars with Almonds and Chocolate

Start to finish: 40 minutes (20 minutes active), plus cooling and chilling / Makes 16 bars

These treats are an adaptation of a recipe from "Golden" by Itamar Srulovich and Sarit Packer of London's Honey & Co. The bars are akin to coconut macaroons, but studded with nuts and dried fruit and cut into squares. For the chocolate bottom, chips are convenient—they can be used straight from the bag—but 9 ounces of bar chocolate works, too. Be sure to chop it finely so it melts readily. Store leftovers in an airtight container in the refrigerator for up to five days.

1½ cups dark chocolate OR semi-sweet OR milk chocolate chips

½ cup dried cherries OR dried cranberries OR raisins, roughly chopped

2½ cups unsweetened shredded coconut

½ cup salted roasted almonds OR cashews OR pistachios, chopped

5 tablespoons salted butter, melted and slightly cooled

2 large eggs

2 teaspoons vanilla extract

¼ teaspoon table salt

Heat the oven to 350°F with the rack in the middle position. Mist an 8-inch square baking pan with cooking spray. Line the pan with a 14-inch length foil, folded widthwise so it fits neatly in the bottom of the pan; allow the excess to overhang the sides.

Distribute the chocolate chips in an even layer in the prepared pan. Put the pan in the oven and warm until the chocolate is softened, 3 to 5 minutes. Remove the pan from the oven and, using a silicone spatula, spread the chocolate in an even layer; set aside.

In a small microwave-safe bowl, combine the cherries and 1 tablespoon water. Microwave, uncovered, on high for 1 minute, stirring once halfway through. Stir again, then let cool slightly.

In a large bowl, stir together the coconut, nuts, butter and cherries. In the same bowl used to microwave the cherries, whisk together the eggs, vanilla and salt. Add the egg mixture to the coconut mixture and stir until the ingredients are well combined. Transfer to the prepared pan and, using a spatula, lightly compact into an even layer. Bake until the surface is light golden brown, 15 to 18 minutes.

Cool in the pan on a wire rack until barely warm, about 45 minutes. Refrigerate uncovered until completely chilled and set, about 2 hours.

Remove the bars from the pan using the foil overhang as handles and set on a cutting board. Using a chef's knife, cut into 16 squares, wiping the knife blade after each cut for the cleanest slices. Serve chilled or at room temperature.

Meringue Cookies with Salted Peanuts and Chocolate

Start to finish: 2½ hours (35 minutes active), plus cooling / Makes 12 small or 6 large meringues

These light, crisp, cloud-like meringue cookies are the perfect way to use a pileup of egg whites, along with small amounts of nuts and chocolate chips. If you prefer to use chocolate in bar form, you'll need about 2 ounces, chopped. The meringues can be made into a dozen 3-inch cookies or six oversized 6-inch puffs. Serve them alone or split them open and fill them with whipped cream and scattered with fresh berries. The cookies will keep in an airtight container for up to five days.

¼ cup salted roasted peanuts OR almonds OR cashews OR pistachios, chopped

⅓ cup dark chocolate OR semi-sweet OR milk chocolate chips, chopped

6 large egg whites

½ teaspoon cream of tartar

¼ teaspoon table salt

1 cup white sugar

1 teaspoon vanilla extract

1 teaspoon grated orange zest

Heat the oven to 250°F with a rack in the middle position. Line a rimmed baking sheet with kitchen parchment. In a small bowl, toss together the nuts and chocolate.

In a stand mixer fitted with the whisk attachment or in a large bowl with a hand mixer, whip the egg whites, cream of tartar and salt on medium until frothy and opaque, 1 to 2 minutes. With the mixer running, gradually add the sugar. Add the vanilla, then increase to high and beat for 5 minutes (no less, or the meringues may fall slightly during baking); the whites will be thick, shiny and hold stiff peaks. Remove the bowl from the mixer. Using a silicone spatula, fold in the orange zest and half of the nut-chocolate mixture.

Scoop the meringue into mounds onto the prepared baking sheet, dividing it into 12 portions of about ½ cup each or 6 portions of about 1 cup each; space the mounds evenly apart. Slightly smooth the tops and sprinkle with the remaining nut-chocolate mixture.

Bake for 1¼ hours for small meringues or 1½ hours for large meringues; they will be very pale golden brown and have expanded slightly. Turn off the oven, prop open the door with the handle of a wooden spoon and allow the meringues to fully dry and crisp, about 45 minutes.

Remove from the oven and transfer the meringues from the baking sheet to a wire rack. Cool to room temperature.

Meringue Cookies with Cashews, Coconut and Lime

Follow the recipe, using **salted roasted cashews,** replacing the chocolate chips with ¼ cup **dried unsweetened wide-flake coconut** and substituting an equal amount of **lime zest** for the orange zest.

Golden Meringue Cookies with Pistachios and Candied Ginger

Follow the recipe, using **salted roasted pistachios,** replacing the chocolate chips with ¼ **cup chopped candied ginger** and adding **1 teaspoon ground turmeric** and ½ **teaspoon ground cinnamon** to the egg whites along with the cream of tartar and salt.

Yogurt Cake with Citrus and Spice

Start to finish: 1 hour (15 minutes active), plus cooling
Makes one 8½-inch loaf cake

In France, gâteau au yaourt is a cake that comes together so easily it's often the first recipe children are taught. It has a fine, moist crumb similar to a pound cake, but isn't nearly as rich. We boost the flavor by adding grated citrus zest and fragrant spice to the batter. Citrus juice whisked with powdered sugar makes a quick finishing glaze, though the cake is equally good unadorned. Feel free to use whatever kind of citrus you have on hand—lemon, lime, orange or even grapefruit. The cake will keep for up to three days, tightly wrapped and stored at room temperature.

1¾ cups all-purpose flour, plus more for the pan

2 teaspoons baking powder

1 teaspoon ground cinnamon OR ground allspice OR ground ginger

¼ teaspoon plus ⅛ teaspoon table salt, divided

3 large eggs

1 cup white sugar

2 tablespoons grated citrus zest, plus 2 tablespoons citrus juice, plus more if needed (see headnote)

½ cup plain whole-milk yogurt OR ½ cup plain whole-milk Greek yogurt thinned with 3 tablespoons water

½ cup grapeseed or other neutral oil

1 cup powdered sugar

Heat the oven to 350°F with a rack in the middle position. Mist an 8½-by-4½-inch loaf pan with cooking spray, dust evenly with flour, then tap out the excess.

In a medium bowl, whisk together the flour, baking powder, cinnamon and ¼ teaspoon salt; set aside.

In a large bowl, whisk the eggs, white sugar and zest until well combined and lightened in color, about 1 minute. Add the yogurt, then whisk until well combined. Add the oil and whisk until homogeneous. Add the flour mixture and whisk just until no streaks remain. The batter will be very fluid.

Pour the batter into the prepared pan. Bake until a toothpick inserted at the center of the cake comes out with a few crumbs attached, about 45 minutes.

Let the cake cool in the pan on a wire rack for 10 minutes. Invert the cake onto the rack, lift off the pan and turn the loaf upright. Cool completely, about 1½ hours, before glazing.

In a small bowl, whisk together the powdered sugar and the remaining ⅛ teaspoon salt, then gradually whisk in the juice; the glaze should be smooth, with the consistency of regular yogurt. If it is too thick, whisk in additional juice ½ teaspoon at a time to achieve the proper consistency.

Set the wire rack with the cake on a rimmed baking sheet. Using a spoon, drizzle the glaze over the top of the cake, letting some drip down the sides. Let the glaze set for about 30 minutes before slicing and serving.

Tahini and Browned Butter Cookies

Start to finish: 45 minutes, plus cooling
Makes 18 cookies

Tahini isn't just for hummus and sauces. Here, it gives rich, chewy cookies a nutty flavor and pleasant bitterness that plays off the sweetness of the sugar. Browned butter is butter that is cooked until the milk solids caramelize, which infuses the fat with a flavor reminiscent of toasted nuts. The browned butter in these cookies accentuates the sesame notes of the tahini. The cookies will keep in an airtight container at room temperature for up to five days.

2 cups all-purpose flour	**½ cup tahini**
1 teaspoon baking soda	**1½ cups packed light**
½ teaspoon table salt	**OR dark brown sugar**
10 tablespoons (1¼ sticks) salted butter	**¼ cup white sugar**
	2 large eggs

Heat the oven to 350°F with racks in the upper- and lower-middle positions. Line 2 rimmed baking sheets with kitchen parchment. In a medium bowl, whisk together the flour, baking soda and salt; set aside.

In a 10-inch skillet over medium-high, melt the butter. Cook, swirling the pan frequently, until the milk solids at the bottom are golden brown and the butter has a nutty aroma, 1 to 3 minutes. Pour into a large heatproof bowl, being sure to scrape in the browned bits. Whisk in the tahini. Cool, stirring occasionally, until just warm to the touch.

Whisk in both sugars and the eggs until homogeneous. Add the flour mixture and stir with a wooden spoon until no streaks remain.

Scoop the dough into 18 even portions (a generous 2 tablespoons each), placing 9 on each prepared baking sheet, spaced evenly apart. Using the palm of your hand, flatten each portion into a round about ½ inch thick. Bake until the cookies are light golden brown at the edges, 16 to 18 minutes, switching and rotating the baking sheets halfway through.

Let the cookies cool on the baking sheets for about 5 minutes. Using a wide metal spatula, transfer to wire racks and cool completely, about 30 minutes.

Chocolate-Dipped Tahini and Browned Butter Cookies

Once the cookies are fully cooled, in a medium saucepan over medium, bring about 1 inch of water to a bare simmer. Put **1 cup semi-sweet OR dark chocolate chips OR 6 ounces semi-sweet OR bittersweet chocolate** (chopped) in a heatproof medium bowl and set the bowl on top of the saucepan; be sure the bottom does not touch the water. Stir occasionally until the chocolate is completely melted. Remove the bowl from the pan. Dip half of the surface of each cookie in the chocolate and return dipped side up to the wire rack. If desired, sprinkle the chocolate-coated areas with **sesame seeds** (toasted). Let stand until the chocolate sets, about 1 hour.

Banana-Cashew Hand Pies

Start to finish: 40 minutes, plus cooling
Makes 8 hand pies

For these fun, easy-to-make fruit-filled hand pies, we use store-bought refrigerated pie crusts (the type sold rolled or flat, not those fitted into a disposable pie plate); they're typically sold two to a box. The baking temperature varies by brand, so check the packaging and set your oven to the temperature indicated in the directions. The hand pies are great warm or at room temperature.

1 large egg

3 tablespoons coconut milk OR half-and-half, divided

1 cup roughly mashed ripe banana (from 1 large or 2 medium bananas)

2 tablespoons packed light OR dark brown sugar

1 teaspoon vanilla extract OR 1 tablespoon dark rum

½ teaspoon ground cinnamon

Pinch of table salt

Box of two 9-inch refrigerated pie crusts (see headnote)

3 tablespoons finely chopped cashews OR peanuts (see headnote)

Heat the oven to the temperature indicated on the pie crust packaging, with a rack in the middle position. Line a rimmed baking sheet with kitchen parchment.

In a small bowl, whisk together the egg and 1 tablespoon coconut milk; set aside. In a medium bowl, stir together the remaining 2 tablespoons coconut milk, the banana, sugar, vanilla, cinnamon and the salt.

Lay 1 pie crust on the counter; keep the second in the packaging to prevent it from drying. Using a metal bench scraper or pizza wheel, cut the crust into quadrants, forming 4 triangles. Brush each piece with egg mixture. Spoon 1½ tablespoons of the banana mixture onto the center of each triangle, then enclose the filling by folding the triangle in half along its center line; align the corners. Using the tines of a fork, seal and crimp the two non-folded edges. Place the pies on the prepared baking sheet.

Repeat the process with the remaining pie crust and the remaining filling; place the pies on the baking sheet with the first batch, spacing them evenly apart.

Brush the tops of the pies with egg mixture. Using the fork, poke 3 sets of holes, 1 inch apart, in the top crust of each. Sprinkle with the nuts, evenly dividing them. Bake until the pies are golden brown, 15 to 18 minutes, rotating the baking sheet about halfway through.

Cool on the baking sheet on a wire rack for about 5 minutes, then transfer the pies directly to the rack. Serve warm or at room temperature.

Pineapple and Cream Cheese Hand Pies

Heat the oven to the temperature indicated on the packaging of **two 9-inch refrigerated pie crusts,** with a rack in the middle position. Line a rimmed baking sheet with kitchen parchment. In a small bowl, whisk together **1 large egg** and **1 tablespoon water.** In a medium bowl, mix together **¾ cup (6 ounces) cream cheese** (room temperature), **½ cup white sugar, 2 teaspoons grated lime zest, 1 teaspoon vanilla extract, ¼ teaspoon cayenne pepper** and a **pinch of table salt** until homogeneous; add water 1 teaspoon at a time as needed so the mixture is smooth. Stir in **1 cup drained canned juice-packed pineapple tidbits OR finely chopped fresh or thawed frozen pineapple.** Follow the recipe to form the hand pies, using cream cheese–pineapple mixture as the filling and the beaten egg in place of the egg–coconut milk mixture. Poke holes in each pie as directed. Sprinkle with additional grated lime zest, additional cayenne and **turbinado sugar** (optional). Bake and cool as directed.

Chocolate Pudding with Brown Sugar and Miso

Start to finish: 35 minutes, plus chilling
Servings: 4 to 6

Made with butter, brown sugar, a combination of cocoa and chocolate, plus umami-packed white miso to add layers of depth and complexity, this chocolate pudding is a standout. Dutch-processed cocoa is best because it gives the pudding a darker hue and a smoother, richer flavor, but natural cocoa will work, if that's what you have on hand. Serve chilled and topped with whipped cream, if you like.

3 large egg yolks

3 tablespoons cornstarch

3 tablespoons Dutch-processed cocoa powder (see headnote)

2 cups whole milk

½ cup boiling water

4 teaspoons white miso

3 ounces semi-sweet OR bittersweet chocolate, finely chopped OR ½ cup semi-sweet OR dark chocolate chips

1 cup packed light OR dark brown sugar

6 tablespoons salted butter, cut into 6 pieces

In a medium bowl, whisk together the egg yolks, cornstarch, cocoa and about ¼ cup milk, then whisk in the remaining milk; set aside. In a small bowl, combine the boiling water and miso; whisk until the miso dissolves.

Put the chocolate in another medium bowl and place a fine-mesh sieve across the top; set aside. In a medium saucepan over medium, combine the sugar and butter. Cook, stirring occasionally, until the mixture is bubbling vigorously and thickens, 5 to 7 minutes. Remove the pan from the heat and whisk in the miso mixture; the sugar mixture will sizzle and seize up. Continue whisking until smooth.

Return the pan to medium. Whisk the yolk-milk mixture to recombine, then gradually whisk it into the sugar-butter mixture in the saucepan. Bring to a simmer, stirring constantly; once simmering, cook, stirring vigorously, for another 30 seconds. Pour the pudding into the prepared sieve; push it through with a silicone spatula and scrape the bottom of the strainer to collect all of the pudding. Whisk until smooth, incorporating the chocolate.

If desired, divide the pudding among serving dishes. Cover and refrigerate until chilled, at least 2 hours or up to 3 days.

Italian Almond Crumb Cookie (Fregolotta)

Start to finish: 50 minutes (25 minutes active), plus cooling / Servings: 4 to 6

Fregolotta, a Venetian cookie akin to buttery streusel topping, takes its name from "fregola," the Italian word for "crumb." The unbaked mixture has a pebbly, crumby appearance and the cookie is broken into rustic shards or coarse crumbs for serving.

1¼ cups whole almonds

3 large egg yolks

2 tablespoons whole milk

1 cup all-purpose flour

1 cup white sugar

¼ teaspoon table salt

6 tablespoons cold salted butter, cut into ½-inch cubes

Heat the oven to 350°F with a rack in the lower-middle position. Place the almonds in a 9-by-13-inch metal baking pan and toast in the oven until lightly browned, 5 to 7 minutes, stirring once. Transfer the almonds to a cutting board and cool; reserve the pan and leave the oven on. Meanwhile, in a small bowl, whisk together the egg yolks and milk.

When the almonds are cooled, roughly chop them and add them to a large bowl along with the flour, sugar and salt; stir to combine. Scatter the butter over the top and, using your fingers, rub the butter into the dry ingredients until the mixture resembles coarse crumbs. Drizzle on the yolk-milk mixture and stir with a silicone spatula until the mixture resembles a combination of pebbles and sand; it should not form a cohesive dough.

Mist the bottom and sides of the reserved baking pan with cooking spray. Transfer the mixture to the reserved pan and distribute it in an even layer but do not compress or compact it.

Bake until light golden brown, 25 to 30 minutes. Cool in the pan on a wire rack for about 10 minutes. Using a metal spatula, carefully pry the fregolotta out of the pan and transfer directly to the rack; it's fine if it breaks during removal. Cool to room temperature. To serve, break the fregolotta into pieces of the desired size.

Index

312

hash, bread, bacon, and tomato, 284

hoisin sauce, xxiv
  broccoli and noodles with, 146
  chicken and peppers with, 194
  noodles with ginger and, 52
hummus, quick creamy, 18

J

jalapeños, xxvi
  quesadillas with, 293
  red stew with, 193
  rice and shrimp with, 243
  soups with, 99, 248
  tacos with, 251, 292
jam, streusel-topped tart with, 301

K

kale
  beans with, 159, 212
  Greek-style braised, 153
  melt with cheddar and, 148
  pesto with, 150
  soups with, 11, 129, 155
  two-cheese farro with, 73
  white bean bruschette with, 278
kebabs, tandoori chicken, 203
ketchup, curried, 262
kibbeh, baked, 115
kimchi, xxv
  burgers with salmon and, 269
  grilled cheese with, 277
  soups with, 106, 175

L

lahmajoun, weeknight, 210
lemon
  breadcrumbs with, 57
  broiled shrimp with, 246
  bulgur and squash pilaf with, 125

chicken and potatoes with, 199
dressing with tahini and, 151
fried white beans with, 15
hummus with, 18
jam tart with, 301
mayonnaise with, 262
parsley-caper relish with, 93
pesto with, 65
pinto beans with, 17
risotto with peas and, 225
smashed chickpeas with, 14
soups with, 109, 132, 261
spaghetti with, 226
tuna tostadas with, 46
white bean bruschette with, 278
lentils
  dal (stew) with coconut and, 90
  rice and, 88
  salad with, 89
  sausages and, 93
  Spanish-style stew with, 92
  Umbrian-style soup with, 94
lettuce, iceberg
  tacos dorados with, 292
  tostadas with, 294
lime
  black bean-pepper salad with, 5
  mayonnaise with, 262
  meringue cookies with, 304
  Peruvian-style sauce with, 264
  rice and shrimp with, 243
  sesame-crusted salmon with, 266
  soups with, 8, 25, 102, 236, 248

M

matbucha (sauce), salmon with, 258
mayonnaise
  burgers with, 75, 269
  egg salads with, 166

fish sticks with, 262
kimchi grilled cheese with, 277
sauces with, 262, 264
tuna tartines with, 45
migas, cheesy Tex-Mex, 163
milk
  bread strata with, 229
  chocolate pudding with, 310
mirin, xxv
  salmon glazed with, 256
  tofu and kimchi soup with, 175
miso, xxv
  chocolate pudding with, 310
  salmon glazed with, 256
  slashed chicken with, 201
  soups with, 106, 155
  spaghetti with, 226
mushrooms
  curry with, 30
  soup with shiitake, 106
  spaghetti with, 42
mustard
  agrodolce squash with, 123
  butter-browned potatoes with, 137
  fish sticks with, 262
  kale and cheddar melts with, 148
  tartines with, 280
  vinaigrette with, 78

N

noodles
  with cabbage, bacon, and sour cream, 62
  garlicky peanut, 59
  hoisin-ginger, 52
  Mexican soup with, 99
  pork and oyster sauce, 213
  stir-fried broccoli and, 146
  tuna gochujang, 43
  See also pasta

Acknowledgments

Writing a cookbook is an endeavor that is endless, and one of the great creative projects, especially when a book is the work of a team of people. This requires bringing together disparate talents to achieve one well-conceived concept, from recipe conception and development through to photography, editing and design. In particular, I want to acknowledge J.M. Hirsch, our tireless editorial director; Michelle Locke, our relentlessly organized books editor; our exacting food editors Dawn Yanagihara and Bianca Borges; Matthew Card, creative director of recipes; and Shaula Clark, managing editor, for leading the charge on conceiving, developing, writing and editing all of this.

Also, Jennifer Baldino Cox, our art director, and the entire design team who captured the essence of what Milk Street stands for. Special thanks to Connie Miller, photographer, Christine Tobin, stylist, Gary Tooth, book designer, and Ali Zeigler, who art directed photography for the book.

Our talented kitchen crew, including our kitchen director Wes Martin; Diane Unger, recipe development director; and our recipe developers and kitchen team, including Courtney Hill, Rose Hattabaugh, Elizabeth Mindreau, Malcolm Jackson, Kevin Clark, Calvin Cox and Hector Taborda. Deborah Broide, Milk Street director of media relations, has done a spectacular job of sharing with the world all we do at Milk Street.

We also have a couple of folks to thank who work outside of 177 Milk Street. Michael Szczerban, editor, and everyone at Little, Brown and Company have been superb and inspired partners in this project. And my long-standing book agent, David Black, has been instrumental in bringing this project to life both with his knowledge of publishing and his friendship and support. Thank you, David!

And, last but not least, to all of you who have supported the Milk Street project. Each and every one of you has a seat at the Milk Street table.

Christopher Kimball

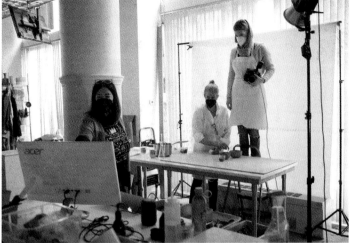

About the Author

Christopher Kimball is founder of Christopher Kimball's Milk Street, a food media company dedicated to learning and sharing bold, easy cooking from around the world. It produces the bimonthly *Christopher Kimball's Milk Street Magazine*, as well as *Christopher Kimball's Milk Street Radio*, a weekly public radio show and podcast heard on more than 220 stations nationwide, and the public television show *Christopher Kimball's Milk Street*. He founded *Cook's Magazine* in 1980 and served as publisher and editorial director through 1989. He re-launched it as *Cook's Illustrated* in 1993. Through 2016, Kimball was host and executive producer of *America's Test Kitchen* and *Cook's Country*. He also hosted *America's Test Kitchen* radio show on public radio. Kimball is the author of several books, including *Fannie's Last Supper*.

Christopher Kimball's Milk Street is changing how we cook by traveling the world to learn bold, simple recipes and techniques. Adapted and tested for home cooks everywhere, these lessons are the backbone of what we call the new home cooking. We are located at 177 Milk Street in downtown Boston, site of our editorial offices and cooking school. It also is where we record *Christopher Kimball's Milk Street* television and radio shows and is home to our online store, which curates craft food and cookware products from around the world. Visit 177milkstreet.com to shop and for more information.